A Postcolonial Leadership

A Postcolonial Leadership

Asian Immigrant Christian Leadership and Its Challenges

Choi Hee An

Published by State University of New York Press, Albany

© 2020 State University of New York

All rights reserved

No part of this book may be used or reproduced in any manner whatsoever without written permission. No part of this book may be stored in a retrieval system or transmitted in any form or by any means including electronic, electrostatic, magnetic tape, mechanical, photocopying, recording, or otherwise without the prior permission in writing of the publisher.

For information, contact State University of New York Press, Albany, NY
www.sunypress.edu

Library of Congress Cataloging-in-Publication Data

Names: Choi, Hee An, author.
Title: A postcolonial leadership : Asian immigrant Christian leadership and its challenges / Choi Hee An.
Description: Albany : State University of New York Press, 2020. | Includes bibliographical references and index.
Identifiers: LCCN 2019036503 | ISBN 9781438477497 (hardcover) | ISBN 9781438477480 (paperback) | ISBN 9781438477503 (ebook)
Subjects: LCSH: Church work with immigrants. | Christian leadership. | Leadership—Religious aspects—Christianity. | Asian Americans—Religion. | Postcolonial theology. | Leadership—United States. | Asian Americans. | Postcolonialism.
Classification: LCC BV639.I4 C46 2020 | DDC 253.089/95073—dc23
LC record available at https://lccn.loc.gov/2019036503

10 9 8 7 6 5 4 3 2 1

For My Mother
(*Reverend Choi Yang Ja,* 최양자 목사님)

For My Father
(*Elder Choi Jong Kil,* 최종길 장로님)

Contents

Acknowledgments — ix

Introduction — xi

Part I. Understandings of Leadership

Chapter 1. Leadership in a Secular Context — 3

Chapter 2. Leadership in Christianity — 25

Part II. Leadership and Its Challenges in US Culture

Chapter 3. Leadership in US Culture — 53

Chapter 4. Challenges of Asian Immigrant Leadership — 107

Part III. Postcolonial Leadership in an Asian Immigrant Christian Context

Chapter 5. Asian Immigrant Christian Leadership — 139

Chapter 6. Critical Features of a Postcolonial Leadership — 181

Conclusion — 217

Notes	221
Selected Bibliography	255
Index	269

Acknowledgments

When I think about leadership, I think about my mother, Reverend Choi Yang Ja and my father Elder Choi Jong Kil. They are two of the greatest communal leaders who worked continuously and tirelessly their entire lives for and with the oppressed, the marginalized, the orphans, the prisoners, the sick, the poor, the old, and people with disabilities. They have taught me how to breathe with and in others and walk with others. They have shown me how to love and care for others and community in their daily lives. Throughout my whole life, I have witnessed their resistant, resilient, collaborative, communal leadership that they have embodied in their faith. Without their model of leadership, I would not be able to write this book.

I want to thank my two younger sisters, Choi Jae Yeon and Choi Kyong Hwa, who hold me in their prayers and support me spiritually and psychologically. As they also have worked for and with the powerless, the poor, the children, and the youth who suffer from violence, poverty, and marginalization, they have taught me how to love and be with others with humility and joy.

I want to thank my beloved friend the late Dr. Dale P. Andrews, who showed me how to love and lead others equally with amazing friendship and mentoring. Even though he is in heaven right now, his leadership continuously inspires my scholarship and teaching. I am and will always be grateful for his friendship forever. I also want to thank Rev. Dr. HiRho Park, who always supports me and shows me how to be a powerful, resistant, and resilient leader through her national leadership role without losing her sincere heart. I want to thank Rev. Dr. Cristian De La Rosa, who cried for me and with me in our academic sisterhood with her warmest heart. I am grateful for Dr. Amy Limpitlaw who works hard to cross over cultural differences and who nurtures our friendship with generosity and care. I am also grateful for Dr. Steven Sandage whose attentiveness and willingness to engage in genuine dialogue have been a deep source of empowerment to me. I especially want to thank Sharon Hunter-Smith, who provided me with good critical comments on this book project. Her continuous friendship made me not feel like a stranger in the United States. I want to thank my mentors, Dr. Lee H. Butler Jr., Dr. Andrew Sung Park, Dr. Eunjoo Mary Kim, and Dr. Peter Phan, who support and encourage me to teach with love and write with integrity and persistence through their mentoring. I also want to thank the Anna Howard Shaw Center Staff, Hazel Monae Johnson Uchenna Joan Awa, and Sadiqa Seona Delaney and all the Anna Howard Shaw Board members who support me and work with me in collaborative leadership. I am grateful for Mary Elizabeth Moore, dean of the School of Theology, and Bishop Susan W. Hassinger, who have exemplified collaborative leadership particularly in developing multicultural competency and in the struggle against white privileges. I also want to thank all BU School of Theology colleagues, who work with me in different capacities of leadership with grace.

I thank the State University of New York Press and my editor, Christopher Ahn, who believed in the value of this book and gave me critical comments with great enthusiasm. I also want to thank my copyeditor, Dana Foote, who read my work line by line with detailed comments.

My deepest gratitude goes to my beloved husband, Rev. Dr. So Kee Boem, who demonstrates powerful collaborative communal leadership in his ministry with lay leaders and community leaders. From this leadership and thoughtful knowledge of theology, he always challenges me with keen insights and wonderful inspiration. With his love, I have been able to continue this walk for the last five years and finally finish this book. I am very grateful for this entire journey walking with my beloveds.

Introduction

"The late Filipino immigrant labor leader Philip Vera Cruz once wrote: "Leadership, I feel, is only incidental to the movement. The movement should be the most important thing. If the leader becomes the most important part of the movement, then you won't have a movement after the leader is gone. The movement must go beyond its leaders. It must be something that is continuous, with goals and ideals that the leadership can build upon."

Philip Vera Cruz's vision of leadership is rooted in the concept of Shared Leadership that has long characterized the movements of Asian immigrant workers. Historically and today, one of the greatest contributions of immigrant workers to our community is to expand thinking about leadership. Vera Cruz's vision of leadership stands in contrast to the prevailing concept of leadership in society that emphasizes command and management functions, charisma, and personality qualities relating to individual advancement such as assertiveness. Thus, in the minds of most Americans, a leader is like a general in the military, a CEO in a corporation, or the US president. From the prevailing framework, Asian immigrant workers are not leaders."

—Glenn Omatsu, "Mobilizing Students to Respond to Community Needs: Organizing a Class around a Community Project"

When I teach a leadership class, I often ask the question, "What are some positive and negative images of leaders?" Many students answer with various images of leaders and definitions of leadership. However, when I ask the question, "What are some images of Asian immigrant leaders, especially Asian immigrant women?" there is a long pause. A few images, such as Asians as quiet and submissive, are hesitantly offered. However, these images are discussed in the context of followers rather than leaders. They are either negative or vague images. In fact, some students add that there are almost no famous Asian immigrant leaders or Asian immigrant religious leaders in the US public square.

Leadership is a difficult subject to talk about. Asian immigrant leadership is not only a difficult subject to talk about, but it also is strange to think about because it challenges so many aspects of leadership and images of leadership that currently exist in the US context. As Glenn Omatsu notes, many Asian immigrant workers are never seen as leaders in the US public square.

Even though the challenges of immigrant life produce immigrant leaders with entirely different skill sets and strengths than those recognized as ideal by the US standards, the prevailing concepts of leadership and the ideal images of leaders do not include that of Asian immigrant workers. Rather, Asian immigrants in this society are perceived as followers, students, and permanent guests. Asian immigrant women, in particular, are seen as followers both by this society as well as their own ethnic communities. Even though they demonstrate great leadership through shared, collaborative, communal leadership, their leadership is intentionally trivialized and characterized as followership.

Why? There are many complicated answers to this question. Furthermore, before this question can be answered, there are many more questions to ask. Who are leaders? How do people characterize leaders? What is leadership? Is Asian immigrant leadership different from leadership as it is currently defined and performed? How do people define Asian immigrant leadership? Is Asian immigrant leadership different from leadership other ethnic groups perform? How different? What are the common perceptions of Asian immigrant leadership? What prejudices and discrimination do Asian immigrants experience? What are the necessary concepts of leadership that Asian immigrant leaders need to know and perform?

Leadership in various ethnic groups, including African Americans, Latinx, and Asian immigrants, is frequently performed through religious organizations. Regardless of ethnicity, most immigrant communities work with and through religious organizations. For Asian immigrants, religious organizations, including the Christian church, are the foundation for forming and performing leadership. Asian immigrant leadership is deeply involved in and evolving with Asian immigrant religious leadership. Because Asian immigrant religious leadership, especially Christian leadership, is always engaged with sociopolitical, cultural, and historical movements, it is never recognized as simple spiritual leadership, which distances itself from any secular sociopolitical issues. Asian immigrant religious leadership is inseparable from issues of social justice and human/immigrant rights. Communal concerns and goals are foremost, within and beyond religious propaganda.

However, both Asian immigrant leadership and Asian immigrant Christian leadership are seldom discussed as the subject of leadership studies. In Christian religious discourse, the field of leadership itself has not been seriously investigated and studied as an area of practical theology until recent years, even though some evangelical churches and many pastors often discuss leadership as the subject of ministry. Asian immigrant leadership in religious discourse is particularly scarce. Therefore, it is imperative to bring Asian immigrant leadership and Asian immigrant Christian leadership simultaneously to the table of leadership studies within and beyond theological studies, because Asian immigrant Christian leadership cannot be discussed without an understanding of Asian immigrant leadership. The task of this book is to understand Asian immigrant leadership and Asian immigrant Christian leadership as an interwoven relationship. This book demonstrates how Asian immigrant leadership has been presented in a US context and what challenges Asian immigrant leaders face. As this volume analyzes the current landscape of US leadership and its challenges, it explores how Asian immigrant leaders, including Christian leaders, exercise leadership and create the possibility of a new Asian immigrant leadership in dialogue with several current leadership theories such as trait theory and transformational leadership theory. Examining multilayered dynamics of the Asian immigrant community and Christian congregations in a postcolonial context that analyzes the power and influence of colonial paradigm and offers a new liberative interpretation of the colonized history and culture, this study proposes a postcolonial leadership as a new form of leadership model for Asian immigrant leaders.

Before I introduce in the detail the three parts of this book, I want to explain the scope of Asian immigrants in this book. Who are Asian immigrants in this book? Asian immigrants are not one fixed group. They are not exactly identified as Asian Americans only. They include Asian Americans, but go beyond Asian American groups. In fact, US society creates various categories to define Asian immigrants such as immigrant generations, sociopolitical status, nationalities, and other characteristics. In terms of immigrant generations, Asian immigrants can be the people who both migrated from Asian countries and are born in the United States. First-generation immigrants are defined as people who migrate to this country when they are adults. Second-generation immigrants are people who are born in this country with Asian ancestry. 1.5 generation immigrants are the people who migrate to this country before adulthood. In terms of visa status and citizenship, Asian immigrants can include people who permanently live in the United States and people who temporarily stay in the United States with the intention to go back to their mother countries such as students and temporary workers. In terms of nationality, they can be both Asians from Asia and US Asian Americans who stay in the US. It includes transnational Asian groups. In terms of Asian ancestry, Asian immigrants can include both Asians from non-interracial marriages and Asians from interracial marriages. In terms of legal status, Asian immigrants can include both documented and undocumented populations of Asians and people with Asian ancestry. Even though these binary distinctions exist in the US social system, in reality, Asian immigrants do not hold fixed statuses or clear boundaries. Especially, in terms of economic status, they are all over in the spectrum from the upper class to the lower class. Most of them do not or cannot stay in fixed positions. Rather, their social, political and economic positions are always in flux. The boundaries are not static but are permeable and open. Therefore, in this book, Asian immigrants can be defined as the people who belong to these various categories and go beyond and in-between colonial and postcolonial immigrant spaces simultaneously. It means that when I talk about Asian immigrant leadership, it includes leadership of both Asians and Asian Americans who live in these interstitial spaces. Furthermore, because this book is primarily focused on Asian immigrant Christian leadership, the main population of this leadership is described in the intersectional spaces of immigrant Christian church in the US context that have more dialogues with Buddhist and Confucian traditions along with Taoist tradition in the forms of embedded culture, but less with Hindu and Islamic traditions.

This book has three parts. The first part provides a brief sketch of leadership studies in both secular and Christian contexts, and it examines the field from postcolonial and feminist perspectives. The second part delineates current understandings and challenges of leadership, explores various images of leadership among ethnic groups, and introduces the challenges of Asian immigrant leadership. With a focus on Asian Christian leadership, the third part proposes that postcolonial leadership is a new type of leadership, practices by Asian immigrant leaders, especially women clergy and lay leaders, and is characterized by four different features: hybridity, authenticity, communality, and individuality.

The first part introduces various definitions of leadership and leadership theories, explores similarities and dissimilarities between secular leadership and Christian religious leadership, and it demonstrates how these leadership practices have served the goal of each context and influenced the current structure of society. Three leadership theories—namely, trait theory, transformational theory, and feminist theory—are selected in order to compare these similarities and dissimilarities and to understand the essential concepts of current leadership in both secular and religious contexts. Acknowledging the fact that traditional leadership has long been the domain of privileged white males in both secular and religious contexts, this part describes the powerful impact of the feminist movement in a secular context and women's ordination in Christian contexts; how female secular leaders and clergy challenge current male leadership; and what difficulties they confront in both contexts.

Chapter 3 in the second part focuses on three different leadership contexts: white leadership in a socioeconomic context, African American leadership in a socioreligious context, and Latinx leadership in an immigrant context. There are two reasons to introduce white, African American leadership, and Latinx leadership in relation to Asian immigrant leadership. First, it is important to demonstrate the existence of different styles of leadership in the current US context. Even though the privileged white leadership predominates and greatly influences the current leadership practices, African American leadership and Latinx leadership have challenged this white leadership from the beginning of US history. It is important to explore the historical and cultural environment within which they struggle and how they develop different leadership styles and strategies in this struggle in relation to each other. Second, the purpose of introducing these three groups of leadership is not to compare differences and similarities of their leadership with Asian immigrant leadership, but to understand Asian immigrant leadership more deeply by reflecting on these groups of leadership development historically and socioculturally. Asian immigrant leadership is not developed in isolation. It is a product of interaction between other groups and their leadership dynamics and of influences under sociopolitical, religious, and cultural dynamics of the US immigrant postcolonial history. By looking into white, African American, and Latinx leadership, especially in relation to racial struggles, understanding the formation of Asian immigrant leadership becomes clearer and richer.

Traditional images of ideal leaders are modeled on "great" white men. Many traits of leaders are influenced by what these great white men did and how they exercised power. These images and the leadership formation process are described, and the discourses of sexism and racism are deeply engaged. This part explores how, through the civil rights and social justice movements, African American leaders dismantle this discourse, challenge a predominantly white leadership, and create a new leadership. Through an exploration of the leadership in the civil rights movement and the women's movement in the black church, this study illustrates how African American leaders struggle to achieve liberation. Understanding African American leadership within these movements, Latinx immigrant leadership is explored in a similar manner. The stories of Latinx immigrant leaders and their immigrant movements presented here reveal how these immigrant leaders exercise leadership and exhibit characteristics of leadership in the complex context of the immigration process.

In chapter 4, concepts of Asian leadership are closely examined. These concepts of leadership are described in relation to Asian cultural religious values and how they differ from their US cultural counterparts is explained. The chapter explores critical Asian images of leadership and leadership practices and illustrates prominent concepts and practices of Asian leadership, especially in pluralistic Asian religious contexts. Asian leadership emphasizes communal harmony, while Western leadership emphasizes individual excellence. Both types of leadership function in their respective contexts. However, when Asian immigrants exist in both cultures simultaneously, Asian leadership is seen as problematic from a US perspective. Therefore, this chapter explores why Asian immigrant leadership becomes problematic in a US context and how it actually functions in an Asian immigrant context. Comparing differences and conflicts between Asian leadership and US leadership, this chapter analyzes complex challenges of Asian immigrant leadership.

The third part proposes a postcolonial leadership as a new way to understand Asian immigrant leadership. Asian immigrant Christian leadership and its actual practices are examined and the dynamics of postcolonial interactions within a US Asian immigrant context are analyzed, and how Asian immigrant scholars and church leaders understand leadership and develop it in their own ways is explored. Through this examination and analysis, part III demonstrates how a postcolonial leadership has been formed and exercised both consciously and subconsciously by Asian immigrant leaders. Exploring the necessity of coexistence between hybridity and authenticity and between the concepts of communality and individuality, chapter 6 exposes critical features of postcolonial leadership.

The introduction of a postcolonial leadership as an example, it may extend current understandings of Asian immigrant leadership studies and possibly deepen the critical analysis of historical and contemporary leadership studies and practices in various immigrant and transnational leadership developments.

PART I

UNDERSTANDINGS OF LEADERSHIP

Even though Christian leadership has created its own definition of leadership and its practices throughout Christian history, Christian leadership studies has not been recognized as an area of academic study within leadership studies. However, in recent years, it has become one of the most significant topics in the area of theological studies. It is deeply influenced by and actively interacts with business, management, and social psychology theories pertaining to leadership and its formation by analyzing who leaders are, what characteristics/behaviors they demonstrate, and how these characteristics function in organizations and in relation to others. Therefore, it is important to briefly explore prominent leadership theories in a secular context and how these theories understand, interpret, and evaluate leadership before exploring what Christian leadership is and how it is exercised in and beyond the Christian church.

Chapter 1

Leadership in a Secular Context

The word *leadership* appeared for the first time in Webster's *An American Dictionary of the English Language* (1818). It was defined as "the state or condition of a leader."[1] However, this word was often either absent or defined in a very simplistic manner in nineteenth-century dictionaries. Almost no definition existed. At the turn of twentieth century, all four dictionaries, *The Century Dictionary* (1889–1911), *Universal Dictionary of the English Language* (1898), *Chambers's Twentieth Century Dictionary* (1904), and Murray's *A New English Dictionary on Historical Principles* (1908), defined *leadership* in a standardized manner, as an office or a position that intimates guidance or control.[2] After 1965, many dictionaries defined leadership in variations that encompassed two themes: 1) "the office or position of a leader" and 2) "the ability to lead."[3] Even though these dictionaries began to reflect different views of defining leadership, such as the social psychologist's and behaviorist's views, they did not illustrate the complexities of the concept of leadership. Definitions of leadership in dictionaries remained simplistic and instructive. However, these definitions influenced leadership studies and its assumptions in the early stage of the discipline.

Over the course of leadership studies' development as an academic discipline, there have been overwhelming numbers of definitions of leadership created. In fact, Joseph C. Rost counted 221 definitions of leadership from 1900 to 1990[4] and 110 definitions of leadership in 1980s literature alone.[5] As leadership studies develop, there are several prominent groups or approaches that represent common definitions of leadership. Some scholars emphasize leaders' traits, skills, or styles and others emphasize context, situation, or interpersonal relationship. For example, Jean Lau Chin classifies leadership in three distinct ways: by "leadership characteristics," "contextual leadership," and "interpersonal process of leadership,"[6] whereas other scholars, such as Victor Dulewicz and Malcolm Higgs, categorize these theories into six schools: "the trait school," "the behavioral or style school," "the contingency school," "the visionary or charismatic school," "the emotional intelligence school," and "the competency school."[7] Still others, such as Rost, categorize these definitions in different frameworks, such as "leadership as do the leader's wishes," "leadership as achieving group or organizational goals," "leadership as management," "leadership as influence," "leadership as traits," "leadership as transformation."[8]

Peter G. Northouse defines leadership as "a process whereby an individual influences a group of individuals to achieve a common goal," while he conceptualizes this definition based on four components: "1) Leadership is a process, 2) leadership involves influence, 3) leadership occurs in groups, and 4) leadership involves common goals."[9] Grounded on his own definition, he considers leadership through the lens of several approaches and theories, such as trait approach, skills approach, style approach, situational approach, contingency theory, path-goal theory, leader-member exchange theory, transformational leadership, servant leadership, authentic leadership, team leadership, psychodynamic approach, women and leadership, culture and leadership, and leadership ethics.[10]

The definition of leadership changes widely based on the perspectives of theorists. Joanne B. Ciulla sees these definitions as the key to explaining the same thing despite disagreement among scholars, and she claims these definitions have one purpose: "leadership is about one person getting other people to do something. Where the definitions differ is in how leaders motivate their followers and who has a say in the goals of the group or organization."[11] John Antonakis, Anne T. Cianciolo, and Robert J. Sternberg interpret these definitions as "the nature of the influencing process that occurs between a leader and followers, and how this influencing process is explained by the leader's dispositional characteristics and behaviors, follower perceptions, and attributions of the leader, and the context in which the influencing process occurs."[12]

Even though there is no single definition of leadership upon which all scholars agree, it is quite possible to agree about two assumptions. First, as Ciulla, Antonakis, Cianciolo, and Sternberg indicate, most of the current leadership theories are within the paradigm of one leader and multiple followers. These theories assume that only one person is a leader in any organization or situation. Others are exclusively treated as followers. Second, these theories assume a clear power difference between leaders and followers and designate different roles for them. A leader is not just a leader. The position of the leader is understood to occupy the top of the power hierarchy. Each school or group has its own assumptions, but these two assumptions are commonly embraced by most leadership theories. These assumptions are explored in more detail along with three theories in the next sections. Instead of exploring all different leadership groups, let's consider three prominent theories that deeply engage Christian leadership: trait leadership theory, transformational leadership theory, and feminist leadership theory.

These three theories are the most influential in shaping how leadership, including that of countless Christian leaders, is practiced. As trait theory has been continuously studied from the premodern period to the modern period, common characteristics and features of leaders are collected and examined. Based on this research, the fundamental framework of leadership studies has been formed. Trait theory still strongly influences the formation of images of current leaders. Unlike trait theory, transformational leadership and feminist leadership theories have been intensely developed in recent years. However, because these theories challenge and reconceptualize traditional leadership, the meaning of leadership is continuously reconstructed. They greatly impact the development of a new concept of modern leadership. Therefore, it is important to explore these theories historically and culturally to understand how Christian leadership interacts with them throughout Christian history.

Trait Leadership Theory

Early classic leadership studies focused on the leader's innate personality characteristics. The common statement of this theory is: "He is born to be a leader."[13] It is the so-called great men theory. It claims that great leaders, great men, have biologically inherited certain qualities that make them uniquely fit for leadership. In 1869, Sir Francis Galton was among the first to make this statement. Studying the hereditary background of great men, he asserted that some individuals were natural leaders.[14] Several early theorists, such as Frederick Adams Woods and Albert Edward Wiggam, studied kings and the aristocratic class and postulated biological class differences between superior leaders and followers. Their studies reinforced the concept of leaders as great men who were born to be leaders. Jerome Dowd claimed that "there is no such thing as leadership by the masses.

The individuals in every society possess different degrees of intelligence, energy, and moral force, and in whatever direction the masses may be influenced to go, they are always led by the superior few."[15] The assumption of these early great men theorists is that leaders have distinctive inherited qualities of character and ability, implying, furthermore, that leaders are chosen by God or by natural selection. This assumption is the primordial foundation of modern trait theories of leadership, which have influenced many psychologists and social scientists.

Dimensionalizing Personality into Human Traits

In the twentieth century, Gordon Allport was one of the first scholars who initiated this discussion of the biological inheritance of human traits. Based on the contrasted notions of "nomothetic disciplines vis-à-vis idiographic ones," he believed that humanity "possesses a unique configuration and assortment of polymorphic traits found 'in any age or land' and, in an individual, 'personal dispositions.'"[16] He classified these as "cardinal, central, and secondary traits."[17] Cardinal traits pertain to an individual's prevalent personality and are deeply interrelated with emotions, cognitions, self-esteem, and certain behaviors, both private and public. Central traits are the same as cardinal traits, but several central traits can be exhibited simultaneously in the same individual whereas secondary traits are shown only in certain situations. Allport's understanding of these traits helped other theoreticians develop correlational approaches to trait formulation that impacted further development in this theory.

One of the most influential scholars in this theory is Raymond B. Cattell, who combined the mathematical skills of a statistician and the great skills of a clinician. As a nomotheticist, he developed this theory more analytically and structurally than others. Reducing forty-five hundred personality descriptors to under two hundred, he analyzed data and presented sixteen source traits. He generated sixteen primary factor descriptions (warmth, reasoning, emotional stability, dominance, liveliness, rule-consciousness, social boldness, sensitivity, vigilance, abstractedness, privateness, apprehension, openness to change, self-reliance, perfectionism, and tension) and five global-factor scale descriptors (extraversion, anxiety, tough-mindedness, independence, and self-control) along with constitutional traits and environmental-mold traits.[18] His profuse data and analysis became the critical resource of the five-factor model (the Big Five), one of the best-known current trait theories.

Like Cattell, Hans J. Eysenck is another scholar who devoted his work to dimensionalizing personality and developing measures for assessing those dimensions. He formulated personality in two dimensions, *introversion* and *extraversion*. He characterized extraversion as "quiet plausibility, spontaneity, expressiveness, impulsivity, optimism, gregariousness, assertiveness, and dominance," and he understood the characteristics of introversion as "shyness, pessimism, unobtrusive social behavior, a tendency to solitude and quietude, and inhibitedness."[19] Later, he added a third dimension, *psychoticism*, that "ranges from extreme emotional liability, moodiness and chronic anxiety, and depressed affect at the one pole to high levels of self-esteem, self-confidence, emotional stability, and calm, reasoned approaches to problem-solving at the other."[20] These three traits are often called the "three-factor model." His understanding of personality development is situated in both environmental and biological genetic factors but heavily relies on the emphasis of "genetic contribution to individual biological bases of temperament," especially to intelligence.[21] He set up the preliminary foundation of the modern work of personality theory.

Along with the three-factor model, one of the most influential trait theories is the Five-Factor Model theory (the Big Five) that has been widely accepted and used until now. Based on Cattell's data and his analysis, many scholars, such as Ernest Tupes, Raymond Christal, Donald Fiske, John M. Digman, Robert McCrae, Paul Costa, Lewis Goldberg, and others, intensely examined and formed this theory. Even though some scholars chose other terms, McCrae and Costa labeled neuroticism, extraversion, openness to experience, agreeableness, and conscientiousness as the five higher-order factors:

> 1) Neuroticism is a factor to assess adjustment versus emotional instability in characteristics from worrying, nervous, emotional, and insecure to calm, relaxed, secure, and self-satisfied. 2) Extraversion is a factor to measure quality and intensity of interpersonal interaction and activity level from sociable, active, talkative, and person-oriented at the one pole to reserved, sober, and task-oriented at the other. 3) Openness to experience is a factor to assess proactive seeking and appreciation of experience for exploring the unfamiliar. The characteristics of the high scorer are curious, broad interests, creative, imaginative, and untraditional and that of the low scorer are conventional, narrow interests, and unanalytical.

4) Characterizing agreeableness from soft-hearted, good-natured, trusting, forgiving and straightforwardness, at one pole to cynical, rude, suspicious, uncooperative, and manipulative at the other, agreeableness is a factor to understand the quality of one's interpersonal orientation from compassion to antagonism in thoughts, feelings, and actions. 5) Conscientiousness is a factor to assess the individual's degree of organization, persistence, and motivation in goal-directed behavior. The characteristics of the high scorer are described in organized, reliable, hard-working, self-disciplined, punctual, ambitious and persevering and that of the low scorer are aimless, unreliable, lazy, careless, negligent, and weak-willed.[22]

McCrae and Costa developed widely accepted questionnaires for testing these factors and nurtured broader concepts of human dispositions and traits. Each factor was understood as an important characteristic that leaders should develop. Extraversion was considered the most significant trait for interpersonal relationships.

Reducing countless descriptors of human personality into certain traits, trait theories/personality theories try to identify the commonalities of personality descriptors. They wrestled with understanding human characteristics. However, these theories started from questions such as "why some persons are better able than others to exercise leadership."[23] They assumed that some people are better than others in terms of character and abilities, including the physical, psychological, intellectual, emotional, and spiritual dimensions of character and abilities. The assumptions of this study are based on hierarchal relationships between a leader who is better than others and the rest, who are less than the leader, even though the goal of these theories is to find commonalities in the human character. Individual differences are not treated as differences but as a source of dominance/submission. In other words, even though these theories provide the evidence to show in general how different and similar people are, they are used to prove that effective leaders share common traits that are innate.

Leadership Traits from the 1900s to the 1990s

According to Ralph M. Stogdill, leadership traits in 1904–1947 are different from those in 1948–1970. In 1904–1947, there were several surveys that concluded that leaders demonstrated better traits than others when challenged in various situations. Fifteen or more surveys homogenously selected five traits ("intelligence, scholarship, dependability in exercising responsibilities, activity and social participation, socioeconomic status") in which leaders exhibited better traits than the average members of the group, and ten or more studies confirmed ten traits ("sociability, initiative, persistence, knowing how to get things done, self-confidence, alertness to and insight into situations, cooperativeness, popularity, adaptability, and verbal facility") as traits of leaders.[24] These surveys also illustrated what the highest overall correlation with leaderships is, such as "originality, popularity, sociability, judgment, aggressiveness, desire to excel, humor, cooperativeness, liveliness, and athletic ability, in approximate order of magnitude of average correlation coefficient."[25] These studies were based on biographical and historical data analysis along with direct observation about leaders, whereas the studies in 1948–1970 showed the awareness of situational approaches and different cultural expectations. Comparing to the studies in 1904–1947, the studies in 1948–1970 showed that physical characteristics such as physical body images and age showed little impact, whereas social status certainly provides an advantage to leaders in a higher political position. In the case of personality, studies both in 1904–1947 and in 1948–1970 listed alertness, originality, personal integrity, and self-confidence as positive characteristics.[26]

Looking at leaders and observing organizations, various trait theories try to find how leaders practice leadership. This methodology continued in the 1990s. In 1990, John Gardner published *On Leadership* and listed fourteen leadership attributes: "1) Physical vitality and stamina, 2) Intelligence and Judgment-in-Action, 3) Willingness (Eagerness) to accept responsibilities, 4) Task competence, 5) Understanding of followers/constituents and their needs, 6) Skill in dealing with people, 7) Need for achieve, 8) Capacity to motivate, 9) Courage, resolution, Steadiness, 10) Capacity to win and hold trust, 11) Capacity to manage, decide, set priorities, 12) Confidence, 13) Ascendance, Dominance, Assertiveness, 14) Adaptability, flexibility of approach."[27] These attributes are selected as the necessity for leaders to accomplish tasks. Intelligence and self-confidence are continuously selected as the best and most popular traits of leaders since the early stages of leadership studies.

In the 1990s, there was another trait theory that was popular and practiced by many practitioners—that is, emotional intelligence (EI). Referring to "an individual's capacity to process emotional information in order to enhance cognitive activities and facilitate social functioning," emotional intelligence is defined "as the perception, use, understanding, and management of one's own and others' emotional states to solve problems and regulate behavior."[28] It includes the ability to understand one's own emotion as well as that of others and to express emotion effectively and appropriately in relation to others and the situation. Instead of emphasizing intelligence based on cognitive knowledge, this theory claims that emotional intelligence is a significant trait that a successful leader demonstrates in social relationships. However, there is one significant problem—that is, how to measure EI. Various scholars propose numerous methodologies to measure emotional intelligence—but the Mayer-Salovey-Caruso Emotional Intelligence Test (MSCEIT) is the best-known test to measure EI.[29] Both cognitive and emotional intelligence along with social intelligence are recognized as the most important traits for leaders in the twentieth and twenty-first centuries.[30]

Studying many organizations and interviewing hundreds of leaders, many trait theorists such as Gardner, Warren Bennis, James M. Kouzes, and Barry Z. Posner affirmed trait theories as a good way to understand leaders and leadership. Trait theories were popular in early leadership studies, and they continue to be useful in the twentieth and the twenty-first centuries. Based on the assumptions of differentiating leaders from followers, they characterize who leaders are, their personalities and temperaments, and how they work.

Strengths and Weaknesses

Trait theories have many strengths and criticisms. Behavioral theories and situational theories offer different perspectives. Instead of focusing on personality, behavioral theories focus on leader behaviors. Looking at the behaviors of effective leaders and ineffective supervisors and managers, researchers such as Rensis Likert, Robert Blake, Jane Mouton, and others, analyze leaders and define leadership styles. They carefully look at how effective leadership functions and ineffective leadership fails in similar circumstances.

Situational theories are similar to behavior theories. From three angles, that of "the leader, the follower, and the situation," situational theories examine one behavioral aspect of leadership.[31] The path-goal theory is a popular situational theory. The assumption of this theory is that leaders can change their styles of leadership depending on the situation and the group. The oppositional position of the path-goal theory is the LPC (Least Preferred Coworker) theory. LPC theory postulates that leaders hold certain behaviors and do not change general behaviors easily. This theory studies broad orientations of leader behaviors rather than behaviors that are changed by situations. Cognitive resources theory is in between behavior theories and traits theories. It observes leader behaviors in interaction with cognitive traits. In a similar manner, multiple linkage theory tests the interaction between "managerial" behaviors and situational factors" in the same way that the Life Cycle model theory seeks the correlations between "collaborators' job experience and emotional maturity."[32] There are also other theories, such as the Leader-Member Exchange (LMX) model, that try to explain leadership in the dynamics between in-groups and out-groups along with characteristics of leaders.

Despite severe criticism, trait theories are considered classic but still very influential in current leadership studies. They have been adopted and used as an ideology to understand Christian leadership, which is explained later in this chapter. The study of leadership has transitioned from trait theories to situational and behavior theories or contingency theories. All these theories focus on an individual leader; they concern a single leader with mass followers. Trait theories depend heavily on leaders and their characteristics, behaviors, situations, and so forth. They do not give much attention to followers and their growth under the guidance of leadership. However, these trends are now challenged by another set of leadership theories, such as expectancy theories of motivation, transactional leadership, and transformational leadership that have great interest in followers and how they grow in their potential for leadership.

Transformational Leadership Theory

Transformational leadership theory is one of the most dominant modern leadership theories that has been developed and used by both management/business and the Christian church. It shows higher satisfaction and motivation from the followers, better job performance, and greater leader effectiveness.[33] It is also referred to as transactional leadership, charismatic leadership, inspirational leadership, and others. Some scholars use these names as synonyms for transformational leadership theory, whereas many others, such as James MacGregor Burns, Bernard M. Bass, Jane M. Howell, and Bruce J. Avolio, distinguish these names from transformational leadership theory. Transactional leadership theory is often compared to transformational leadership theory in several distinct points. Therefore, before exploring transformational leadership theory, it is helpful to understand what transactional leadership is and how it is different from transformational leadership theory in practice.

Transactional Leadership

According to Burns, transactional leaders "approach followers with an eye to exchanging one thing for another: jobs for votes, or subsidies for campaign contributions. Such transactions comprise the bulk of the relationships among leaders and followers, especially in groups, legislatures, and parties."[34] He defined a transactional leader who meets the needs of followers with an exchange for followers' services. While Burns understood a transactional leader in terms of exchange, Bass described a transactional leader in relation to followers: "1) Recognizes what it is we want to get from our work and tries to see that we get what we want if our performance warrants it. 2) Exchanges rewards and promise of reward for our effort. 3) Is responsive to our immediate self-interests if they can be met by our getting the work done."[35] He equates one's effort with the results of that effort. In his understanding, transactional leaders clarify the role of the followers and require them to finish the task on the level of desired outcome by recognizing what they need and want. It means that transactional leaders need to know their followers' needs and set goals for them without questioning the goals of their organizations and focusing on control and management.

All these scholars explain transactional leadership as an exchange of the needs of followers with expected outcomes. It stresses benefits for the followers and makes them satisfy organizational expectations. Transactional leadership emphasizes both the followers' and organization's needs. It does not challenge organizational goals and needs, but rather follows and supports them. The aim of this leadership is sustaining the current structure of the organization based on current employees' performance. Therefore, the role of the transactional leader is neither inspiring nor stimulating but controlling and managing within the existing structure and culture. These leaders control human resources and manage the tasks and outcomes rather than earning trust and respect. In this perspective, they are managers and monitors.

As transactional leaders manage followers, they practice two skills: contingent reward and management-by-exception. Contingent reward is a part of the structure or program that many organizations have created and transactional leaders have performed. When organizations determine the designated goal, transactional leaders offer contingent reward depending on the followers' satisfactory performance.[36] Common practices of contingent reward are promotion, raises, special bonuses, among others. By offering these rewards, transactional leaders set high standards and facilitate goal achievement for followers.[37]

Management-by-exception is another practice that transactional leaders exercise. If contingent reward is a positive practice to facilitate the followers' higher achievement, management-by-exception is a negative practice to modify followers' performance.[38] When the expected outcome is not delivered, transactional leaders examine the problem, reprimand performance and deliver a penalty. They diagnose followers' performance and provide negative feedback. Their advice usually concerns what went wrong and how to fix it by punishment and "contingent aversive reinforcement."[39] They teach followers how to control problems and emphasize consistency and predictability. It means that a new challenge is not easily welcomed. As long as desired outcomes are delivered, these leaders do not seek to exceed current organizational expectations.

If transactional leadership is about meeting the existing needs of both followers and the organization in return for desired outcomes, transformational leadership is about motivating followers beyond given expectations and raising them to meet a higher level of needs and expectations. The focus of transactional leadership is an exchange between desired outcomes for the organization and the needs of followers, whereas the emphasis of transformational leadership is to expand followers' ability and performance by inspiration and stimulation from leaders. Transactional leaders tend to work within or follow organizational culture, and transformational leaders tend to not to work within organizational culture but to transform the culture itself. Transactional leaders set up the goal based on followers' current confidence, whereas transformational leaders create a vision based on the rise of followers' confidence.

Transformational Leadership

Many transformational leadership scholars, such as Bass, Howell, Avolio, and others, conducted factor studies and proposed four components of transformational leadership that differ from transactional leadership: "1) Charismatic leadership (or idealized influence), 2) Inspirational motivation, 3) Individual stimulation, and 4) Individualized consideration."[40]

Leadership is charismatic such that the follower seeks to identify with the leaders and emulate them. The leadership inspires the follower with challenge and persuasion providing a meaning and understanding. The leadership is intellectually stimulating, expanding the follower's use of their abilities. Finally, the leadership is individually considerate, providing the follower with support, mentoring, and coaching.[41]

Transformational leadership expects to work for transformation. Bass elaborates the achievement of transformation by developing and nurturing followers' level of awareness, transcending their interests and passion to organizational goal, and increasing their needs.[42] For Bass, these interrelated ways are the core of transformational leadership because he recognizes the possibility of transformation in the consciousness or awareness of *followers* and in the process of transcending *follower's* individual interests and passion for the organizational goals. Unlike Burns, Bass gives more attention to followers and their consciousness rather than leaders and their consciousness. He emphasizes how to transform followers by leaders' abilities. However, it does not mean that Bass equalizes followers and leaders. For Bass, there is a clear boundary between leaders and followers, whereas there is no distinguishable boundary between leaders and followers for Burns. Bass requires more qualifications for leaders. He emphasizes the flawless ethical integrity and higher standard of trustworthiness of transformational leaders. Bass does not clarify whether followers can be leaders in his theory. However, for Burns, leaders do not have fixed positions. By training, mentoring, couching, and by inspiration from leaders, followers can be leaders and leaders can be followers. Both leaders and followers can challenge each other and raise one another. They transform together. Burns allows the possibility of exchange between leaders and followers.[43]

In order to transform, leaders are required to obtain certain qualifications or attributes. As Bass described above, first, Charisma is one of the most popular images or components of transformational leaders created by sociopolitical psychoanalytic scholars and various scholars. It is used to describe characteristics of war heroes, religious leaders, political leaders such as presidents, and civil rights leaders. Today, people look for this charismatic character in CEOs of multinational corporations and heroes in literature and movies who appear in actual or fictional times of great distress. Martin Luther King Jr., Abraham Lincoln, John F. Kennedy, Franklin D. Roosevelt, Thomas J. Watson (IBM), Andrew

Carnegie, and other male religious and political leaders are identified as charismatic leaders. Many of these leaders demonstrate the ability to understand the needs of people, to give their lives meaning and to provide hope for the future. A common attribute of these leaders is that all of them appear in times of stress and transition. The main traits of these transformational leaders are "self-confidence," "self-determination," "abilities required to be transformational," "resolution of internal conflict," among others.[44] However, certain personal flaws such as too ambitious, being too idealistic, too adventurous, inconsistency, unpredictability, and failure to assign or build a team are the pitfalls that transformational leaders often fall into.[45]

Robert J. House offered the charismatic leadership model in the context of complex organization with seven propositions:

> 1) Charismatic leaders are more dominant and self-confident; 2) Followers model these leaders' values, expectations, emotional responses, and attitudes toward work; 3) Charismatic leaders are more likely to engage in behaviors that give the impression of competence and success; 4) They are more articulate about ideological goals; 5) They engage with followers to increase goal achievement and to challenging performance standards; 6) They engage in behaviors that arouse motives related to the accomplishment of the mission; 7) They provide definable roles that appeal to followers.[46]

He pointed out these propositions as personality traits that charismatic leaders demonstrate for followers to model. Charismatic leaders should be respected and trusted. They are expected to be role models. A higher level of ethical and moral conduct is essential for charismatic transformational leaders.

Second, inspirational leadership is another component of transformational leadership, but it exists within charismatic leadership. Inspirational leaders use inspirational speech and emotional pleas to motivate followers to turn their own interests into a communal goal for the specific group. They use their charisma to evoke enthusiasm to build confidence among followers to deliver strong performances and achieve a higher level of group goals. In a ROTC and Air Force officer study, Gary A. Yukl and David D. Van Fleet reported that instilling confidence is the first and most important element for inspirational leaders.[47] Without this element, it is impossible for followers to believe in a greater cause and be willing to work toward it. Essential concepts of inspirational leadership are found in the words of Dwight D. Eisenhower and Harry Truman. Eisenhower defined leadership as "the ability to decide what is to be done, and then to get others to want to do it."[48] Similarly, Truman understood leadership as performed by "a man who has the ability to get other people to do what they don't want to do, and like it."[49] The purpose of this type of leadership is not only letting followers do more work than expected but also making them work with more enthusiasm, willingness, and confidence. Using power and authority, politicians such as Eisenhower and Truman manipulate the masses for more productivity and dedication to their own goals. By eloquently cultivating a vision or creating a goal, inspirational transformational leaders increase the fundamental values of goal achievement. They motivate followers to work beyond expectations. The original goal is discounted, and, as leaders raise the confidence of followers, the goal needs to be reset and reevaluated by the followers themselves.

Third, intellectual stimulation is the other component that transformational leaders provide. The meaning of intellectual stimulation is explained by various scholars. Robert E. Quinn and Richard H. Hall classify intellectual stimulation in four ways: rationality, existentialism, empiricism, and idealism.[50] Bass illustrates the importance of emotional stimulation along with intellectual stimulation turning "into consciousness-raising, thought reform, and brainwashing."[51] As many transformational scholars define these leaders as teachers who are better in terms of intelligence and emotional maturity, the role of transformational leaders is to educate followers to grow intellectually and emotionally. In fact, intellectual stimulation has not only been recognized as an important component of transformational leadership, but it is also already treated as one of the most significant characteristics of leaders in trait theory.

The last component of transformational leadership is that the leader be "individually considerate," providing followers with support, mentoring, and coaching. Transformational leaders must care for followers and support them to transform. They need to create new values and desired outcomes for followers. The designated outcomes move to the desired outcomes that the followers wish to create. The vision or goal that these leaders develop becomes the vision or goal of each follower personally with the leader's support and mentoring. As each follower shares this vision personally, this vision becomes the vision of the group. Thus, group identity is formed and nurtured. Reinforcing more commitment, involvement, loyalty, and performance, transformational leaders invite followers to move beyond rational calculations.[52] Despite contingencies, leaders need to coach followers how to deal with problems in the existing order and to transform these problems and environments beyond the existing order.

Challenges of Transformational Leadership

Conveying the meaning of organizational goals and raising the follower's potential abilities to a higher level, transformational leaders need to demonstrate extraordinary ability, to inspire others, to exhibit skills to solve problems in an innovative way, and to care for others by nurturing and mentoring. Unlike transactional leaders who provide contingent reward in the exchange of desired outcomes and monitor the follower's errors and mistakes (managing-by-exception), transformative leaders need to model these outstanding individual abilities, behaviors, skills, knowledge, morality, and even hearts. Moreover, transformational leadership transforms not only followers and leaders but also values and environments.[53] Considering sociopolitical cultural values, time of distress and change, and organizational characteristics and environment, transformational leaders need to change or adjust their leadership. For example, if these leaders deal with a mechanistic inflexible organization that appears to function with strict bureaucratic control, they need to know that a reward system and management-by-exceptions will be more effective and change will be hard. If they deal with an organic organization that exhibits a more interdependent relational culture, they expect more variations, diversities, experimentation, imagination, and greater risk-taking.[54] Therefore, along with their extraordinary abilities and skills, transformational leaders need to know or learn how to understand the organization, how to read the times, and how to see sociopolitical cultural values.

Some scholars emphasize the importance of charisma in transformational leadership, others emphasize the leader's capacity for inspiration, stimulation, and individual caring. Transformational leadership transforms people, values, and environments. Its emphasis is to increase productivity beyond expectations. By providing charisma, inspiration, stimulation, mentoring, coaching, empowerment, and more, transformational leadership stresses the enhancement of communal organizational goals. Transformational leaders are expected to have superior power to lead followers on all levels and in all directions. They are expected to control the situation, change it, and challenge it by being a visionary, prophet, inspirer, supporter, mediator, facilitator, encourager, and savior of the institution and individuals at the same time. It is not clear whether transformational leaders can be trained to have these abilities. However, it is clear that transformational leaders must have these abilities and characteristics as described earlier.

Feminist Leadership/Collaborative Leadership Theory

Deconstructing Male Leadership and Reconstructing Women's Experience

The focus of most leadership theories has been exclusively on male leaders. Studying political male leaders, male CEOs, and male religious leaders, these theories are focused on the traits, behaviors, and leadership styles of men. Female leadership theorists have begun to develop women's leadership based on the deconstructions of male leadership and the reconstruction of female experience. For example, trait theories are primarily male-dominated leadership theories. As trait theorists recognize men born to be leaders and examine leadership only from male leaders, the traits and characteristics of leadership become male-centric. Observing only male heroes and political leaders, trait theorists misread irreconcilable images of male leaders as "the" image of leaders. Another example can be found in transactional leadership theory. Feminist theorists point out that this theory sees a clear hierarchy between leaders (who happen to be men in most cases) and followers (who happen to be women in most cases) in power by setting rewards and punishments. As long as male leaders have power to dispense rewards and punishments and create the rules themselves, the relationship between male leaders and female followers is always fraught with hierarchical power dynamics. This theory reinforces the current patriarchal structure when it reinforces the roles of transactional leaders. Many feminist theorists criticize these prominent male-centered leadership theories and analyze the problems of inequality of patriarchal power.

Most leadership theories treat women as only subordinates or followers in organizations. Until the twentieth century, women's work was categorized as the "feminization" of clerical work and women's roles were limited to secretaries and wives of management men.[55] Women leaders were rarely seen. Gender roles and stereotypical images influenced the effect of leadership against women. By introducing the "Damned if she does, damned if she doesn't" dilemma, Beth J. Haslett, Florence L. Geis, and Mae R. Carter show how these gender roles and stereotypes negatively influenced women's performance and leadership.[56] By analyzing the problems of masculine and feminine traits and recognizing the importance of female authority role models, they conclude that as women gain more experience in leadership, they gain more confidence and become better leaders. Many feminist leadership theories begin to analyze problems of gender roles and leadership effectiveness. They disclose the problems of various leadership theories and a lack of gender analysis.

Feminist leadership theory is not one specific theory, unlike transformational leadership theory and trait leadership theories. However, there is one theory that many feminist leadership theorists accept as a feminist approach. Jean Lau Chin, Margaret E. Madden, Marceline M. Lazzari, Lisa Colarossi, Kathryn S. Collins, and many other feminist theorists, whether they are social workers or psychologists, claim collaborative leadership as a way of defining feminist leadership. Even though collaborative leadership is a recent development in leadership theories, many feminist theorists consider this theory as feminist because it decenters the process of hierarchal decision-making and challenges a top-down power structure.

What is collaborative leadership? Traditional leadership assumes one person, usually a man, as a leader. Especially in large complex institutions or governments, organizational hierarchy is still considered the critical structure for leadership, and one single man is most often found at the top of this hierarchy. However, in recent decades, the feminist movement and postmodernism have challenged the exercise of authority and power. Feminist leadership theorists question the possibility of deconstructing the power structure between leaders and followers. One of the attempts to deconstruct this hierarchal structure is found in a reluctance to use the word "leader" by some female leaders. The research of Karen L. Suyemoto and Mary B. Ballou indicates that several feminist leaders hesitate to see themselves as leaders because of the connotations the word carries. With a keen awareness of the power of language, these female leaders resist the hidden supposition within the word leader that "differentiates" leaders and followers.[57] Many feminist leadership theorists contest the positionality of power between leaders and followers. They refuse to accept the hierarchal positioning of "a leader" and followers. They recognize the singularity of the leader and the anonymity of masses of followers. The language of leadership itself perpetuates male bias in the discipline. As feminists seek plural forms of leadership and dismiss the hierarchal positionality between a leader and followers, collaborative leadership comes into play. In fact, collaborative leadership is currently one of the most influential leadership styles. Even in the public domain, instead of hierarchal government styles of leadership, a collaborative process of leadership is expected.

When traditional governments and organizations exhibited hierarchal characteristics such as emphasizing authority, orders, and rules, a strongly top-down hierarchal leadership was encouraged. However, with the recent arrival of global networks characterized by the need for reciprocity, agreements, interdependence, mutual trust, and partnership, the hierarchal leadership is challenged. Different rules of the game are applied. The new rule is "leading together." As a hierarchical relationship between leaders and followers is refused, the passive position of followers is dismissed. Therefore, the language of followers is replaced by the language of participants. Particularly when many groups or various organizations work together, collaborative leadership is required and the language of participants becomes the language of co-leaders. Ensuring egalitarian participation in collaborative leadership is the foundation of feminist leadership.

Collaborative Leadership

The supposition of collaborative leadership is based on strong participation, which is the core of collaborative leadership. However, strong participation does not occur easily. When many groups or various organizations work together, it is especially difficult. These groups are easily led by the strong and equal participation is resisted. Therefore, the role of collaborative leaders is making sure to bring all participants to the table with equal access and encouraging them to actively engage with each other. Collaborative leaders must allow participants to recognize the importance of interdependence as they work together in respect. The role of collaborative leaders is empowering participants to take responsibility for outcomes in a process of mutual engagement. Creating a common ground, these leaders negotiate, set, and guide rules of engagement together with participants and build trust with each other. Some scholars, such as Roz D. Lasker and Elisa S. Weiss, for instance, illustrate collaborative leaders as those who "have the skills to 1) promote broad and active participation, 2) ensure broad-based influence and control, 3) facilitate group dynamics, and 4) extend the scope of the process."[58] David D. Chrislip and Carl E. Larson describe these leaders as stewards of the process, and Chris

Ansell and Alison Gash understand them as facilitators or mediators instead of using the word leaders.[59] In fact, many female leaders identify themselves not as leaders but as facilitators, "influencers, collaborators, or contributors."[60] Collaborative leaders have to guard the process and facilitate the dialogue. Their role is helping participants commit to a collaborative process.

The methods of collaboration vary depending on the contexts. However, many collaborative leadership scholars, such as David D. Chrislip, Carl E. Larson, Stephen Goldsmith, William D. Eggers, Robert Agranoff, Chris Ansell, Alison Gash, Rosemary O'Leary, Lisa Blomgren-Bingham, Russell M. Linden, David Archer, and Alex Cameron, reach consensus about the nature and dynamics of the collaborative process.[61] Some of these scholars identify this process as several stages, steps, or phases. Lawrence Susskind and Jeffery Cruikshank identify a process with three stages: "a prenegotiation phase, a negotiation phase, and an implementation phase,"[62] whereas Barbara Gray identifies a three-step collaborative process: "1) problem setting, 2) direction setting, and 3) implementation."[63] They understand the collaborative process as a developmental process. It starts with recognizing problems and ends with finding solutions and implementing them.

Others, such as Ansell and Gash, understand this process as a cycle. Ansell and Gash start the process with

> face-to-face dialogue (good faith negotiation) and then trust-building, commitment to process (mutual recognition of interdependence, shared ownership of process, openness to exploring mutual gains), shared understanding (clear mission, common problem definition, identification of common values), intermediate outcomes (small wins, strategic plans, joint fact-finding), and back to face-to-face dialogue.[64]

They explain that the collaborative process is not linear. It is a cycle that shows the nonlinear character of interaction. It is not a developmental stage, but an evolved and revised process in a cycle. As the cycle of the collaborative process repeats, group identity is interwoven and becomes clear.

Paul 't Hart brings this collaborative process into the public domain. Working with several groups, parties, and institutions across various organizational cultural boundaries is often very complicated. It involves four distinctive "chunks" of collaborative leadership: "framing work (defining issues and identifying stakeholders), seduction work (enlisting parties to a joint problem-solving process), process work (orchestrating and sustaining dialogues), and consolidation work (institutionalizing momentum)."[65] This public leadership working with multiple groups and organizations necessitates collaborative leadership. Leading with others is not a choice, but a requirement. Then, the collaborative process becomes obligatory. The collaborative process in collaborative leadership is similar to the process of transforming participants and environments in transformational leadership. Because of this similarity, scholars such as Chin understand collaborative leadership as a part of transformational leadership.

Adopting a consensus concerning the nature and dynamics of the collaborative process, many feminist leadership scholars apply this process to transform sex/gender inequality. Feminist leadership theories are intentionally focused on analyzing the problems and challenges of gender dynamics in the context of hierarchal organizations. Marceline M. Lazzari, Lisa Colarossi, and Kathryn S. Collins define feminist leadership as "a dynamic, interactive, process among individuals in groups for which the objective is to lead one another to the achievement of group or organizational goals or both. This influence process often involves peer, or lateral, influence and at other times involves upward or downward hierarchical influence."[66] Chin also observed "a collaborative style and process as essential to a feminist leadership style" and interpreted this process as "leveling the playing field between leader and follower, and to create more egalitarian environment."[67] Many feminist theorists adopt collaborative leadership, shared leadership, relational-cultural theory, and participatory and democratic leadership as feminist leadership approaches, emphasizing gender equality and equalizing power dynamics. The purpose of feminist leadership is to challenge the hierarchal top-down structure.

To challenge this hierarchal structure, there are two practices that many feminist leaders exercise: empowering others and sharing power. Empowering others is the most common practice, one not only exercised by many women leaders but also expected of many men leaders in recent years. It is also used by many transformational leaders as their leadership practice as was described earlier in this chapter. However, it has a slightly different purpose in feminist leadership. Chin notes that

for women leaders and feminist leaders, the objectives of leadership include empowering others through (a) one's stewardship of an organization's resources; (b) creating the vision; (c) social advocacy and change;

(d) promoting feminist policy and a feminist agenda (e.g., a family-oriented work environment, wage gap between men and women); and (e) changing organizational cultures to create gender-equitable environments. For many women, an effective leadership style is transformational.[68] Through sharing resources, creating a vision, supporting and promoting social equality, and changing environments, feminist leaders and women leaders empower others. As mentors, role models, and coleaders, they empower others to challenge the hierarchy. The goal of this practice is deconstructing patriarchal gender inequality and its social transformation.

If empowering others is a transformative leadership practice shared with feminist leadership practices, sharing power is a unique practice that feminist leadership intentionally emphasizes. It is the most crucial step to creating gender-equitable environments. Similar to collaborative leadership, which pursues "leading with others,"[69] feminist leadership aims for leading with others by sharing power. As collaborative leadership emphasizes strong participation from others, feminist leadership practices strong participation by sharing power. Many women leaders have shown their collaborative leadership by sharing power. However, sharing power is the most difficult practice, one that many leaders fail to exercise, including feminist leaders, because gender is not the only factor to challenge the hierarchy. Without an intentional approach and care, this leadership practice is not possible.

However, feminist scholars such as Judy B. Rosener argue that sharing power and empowerment for others are not choices that women make but a survival skill that they learn from society. They explain that because women were never given the authority to exercise leadership on the top, they had to develop other strategies to be leaders. Sharing power and collaborative behaviors have been seen as socially acceptable behaviors. As women leaders exercise them, they experience success. If they do not share power, they fail the mission and are criticized by others. Therefore, for women to be successful leaders, they must share power. When they share power, they improve outcomes from participants and increase their success. Sharing power is a survival strategy by which women leaders maximize employees' contributions and use their labor at maximum capacity for the organization.

> They now have formal authority and control over vast resources, but still they see sharing power and information as an asset rather than a liability. They believe that although pay and promotion are necessary tools of management, what people

> really want is to feel that they are contributing to a higher purpose and that they have the opportunity as individuals to learn and grow. The women believe that employees and peers perform better when they feel they are part of an organization and can share in its success. Allowing them to get involved and to work to their potential is a way of maximizing their contributions and using human resources most efficiently.[70]

Whether understood as a tool to dismantle patriarchal power, the goal of sharing power is not the sharing itself, but transforming active participation from participants into producing satisfied outcomes for common goals. By promoting gender equality and creating a common vision in multidimensions of diverse experiences, feminist leadership in business or other organizations intends to transform patriarchal organizational cultures into gender-equitable cultures and exercise intentional inclusivity and diversity. However, the goal of feminist leadership is not this transformation itself. By eliminating a toxic patriarchy, this leadership aims to create better environments for women, so that this better, gender-equitable environment can help all participants to produce better outcomes beyond expectations. In the end, a better outcome is the ultimate goal of feminist leadership in a socioeconomic context.

The goal of leadership including feminist leadership is obtaining desired outcomes or exceeding outcomes beyond expectations. It is cultivated by influencing, motivating, inspiring, organizing, managing, monitoring, nurturing, empowering, and transforming people to achieve certain organizational goals. The purpose of exercising leadership in a secular context is to achieve organizational goals, not to help people. To attain organizational goals, the role of leaders is clear: maximize people's capacity to have better outcomes by any means.

Chapter 2

Leadership in Christianity

Leadership in a Christian Historical Context

Leadership from Biblical Context

Leadership in Christianity is commonly discussed from the characters of biblical leaders such as Jesus, Moses, Miriam, David, Esther, Paul, Peter and so forth. The model of Jesus's leadership is the most popular leadership model in Christian church and history. This model is intensely discussed in chapter 5. The model of Moses's leadership is another popular example of Christian leadership that many priests and pastors consider. However, Moses's leadership is not just considered as a good model of leadership in the Christian church and ministry but in the circle of management and organizational leadership studies. As Moses is considered as the Great Man and a transformative leader,[1] his leadership is commonly approached by the Great Man theory, trait theory, and charismatic transformative leadership theory.[2] Because of Moses' personal characteristics such as visionary, charisma, humility, empathy, integrity, tenacity, and self-confidence known by both God (Numbers 12:7–8) and his community (Numbers 12:3), his leadership can be easily named as individual heroic charismatic leadership.[3]

However, in recent leadership studies, Moses is recognized as more than just an individualistic transformative charismatic leader. Observing his collaborative work with Aaron, Miriam, Joshua, Caleb, and other officers, several scholars such as Hal M. Lewis, Evangeline Anderson, and Arthur J. Wolak suggest shared leadership as Moses's leadership model. Moses formed collaborative leadership from the beginning of his ministry. As he received his calling from God, he asked God to work together with his older brother, Aaron, in Exodus 4 and his sister, Miriam, in Exodus 15. As he was aware of his disability of speech, he chose to work with Aaron as a co-leader to effectively communicate with his community as well as his enemies. As Aaron covered Moses' disability and became a mediator between Moses and the others, Moses trusted Aaron's ability and shared authority with Aaron. Unlike Aaron, it is not written in the Bible how Miriam becomes a co-leader with Moses and Aaron. However, the Bible reveals her leadership skill even in her young age when she saved Moses, led him to Pharaoh's daughter, and connected Pharaoh's daughter with her mother.[4] She was a risk-taker, negotiator, and mediator. She became a co-leader with Moses and Aaron with shared authority and respect. Even when she was punished by God and confined outside the camp for seven days, all of Israel showed her respect and trust. They did not move but waited for her to be brought back to the community (Numbers 12:15). Evangeline Anderson claims that Miriam was "not just a leader of the women's wing of Israel but of the *whole people*."[5] As Aaron and Miriam shared authority with Moses, they often debated and challenged Moses even in front of God (Numbers 12:4). As Moses, Aaron and Miriam were recognized as co-leaders in their community (Numbers 12:15 and 20:29), their collaborative leadership was continuously and successfully performed until their deaths. Furthermore, their collaborative leadership was extended with Joshua, Caleb and other leaders in the community. When Jethro visited Moses, he advised Moses to work with other officials over thousands, hundreds, fifties, and tens (Exodus 18:19–26). Moses took the advice from Jethro and shared the leadership with other leaders. He transformed the community to take responsibility to share leadership together. He was an efficient organizer, effective manager, and collaborative, transformative open-minded leader. His leadership model has been proposed as the model of collaborative transformative team ministry in many Christian churches.

Like Moses, Esther is another leader that demonstrates heroic charismatic and collaborative leadership. She was chosen to be a queen because of her obedience to King Ahasuerus,[6] but her obedience to God led her into disobedience to the existing law and tradition. Her disobedience can be interpreted as individual heroic rebellious action. She put her life for her people of Israel. She was ready to sacrifice herself even if she might be killed (Esther 4:16). Instead of choosing her personal safety and comfort, she chose her community. She puts "people as a priority," not her individual priority.⁷ Despite the fact that she is a charismatic, rebellious leader, her leadership is not just performed as individual heroic charismatic leadership. She collaboratively worked with Mordecai and communicated with the community to work with her. As she put her life for the community, she made a request for the community to fast for the event with her (Esther 4:16). Communal fasting is an important act because of two reasons. First, requesting communal fasting leads her into revealing her Jewish identity or her connection with the Jewish community. Her reluctance to reveal her Jewish identity or the family connection with the Jewish community can be interpreted as an action to protect her identity in secret[8], but requesting the communal action for fasting could be understood that Esther was ready to reveal her personal secret of identity.[9] Through fasting, she wanted to reconnect with her Jewish community and God.[10] Working with her Jewish community, Esther wanted to confirm her Jewish identity over her social role as a queen of Persia. As a leader, she gave up her secret and privilege for her community. Second, communal fasting leads the community into reconnection with Jewish identity.[11] By requesting the whole community's participation in fasting, members of the community had to participate in Jewish rituals. This action would lead the community to make a distinction from the Persian populace and rediscover their communal identity in a diasporic context.[12] She encouraged the community to reform their Jewish identity and remember who they were in God. As she collaboratively worked with her community, she transformed the community including herself from fear to faith. In the action of collaboration between Esther, Mordecai, and the community, the survival of the Jewish community was achieved.

As these analyses are shown, many biblical figures such as Moses, Esther, Joseph, Miriam, Peter, Mary, Paul and others are easily selected and presented as the models of Christian leadership. However, even though models of leadership from biblical figures are common practices to understand leadership in Christianity, many leadership scholars in both business and theology agree that leadership studies did not appear until the nineteenth century. As the leadership analysis of both Moses and Esther are shown, the analysis of leadership from biblical figures and historical Christian leaders are products of the current leadership studies. In fact, theological leadership study has vibrantly formed its concepts and theories of Christian leadership in the twentieth century. As many theologians and pastors recognize the importance of leadership and try to define the meaning of leadership, they seek concepts of leadership from the Bible, the Early Church, the priesthood in church offices, and current church ministry.

The Meaning of Leadership in an Early Christian Context

The early Christian concept of leadership was not formed from scripture and the Early Church model of leadership alone. As Christianity itself was formed under the great influences of Greek and Roman cultures, the concept of leadership naturally developed within those influences.

As trait theories demonstrate, leadership in Greek culture is exemplified by the characteristics of warriors. Lifting up the warrior's nobility and excellence, Greek culture understands leader as harmonizers and teachers.[13] Plato advanced the concept of leaders in a philosophical sense of justice, politics, and ethics in dialogue with Socrates, who seriously struggled with the concept of justice. Reflecting on Socrates, in the *Republic*, Plato constructed the ideal city and categorized people in three classes: "philosopher-rulers, auxiliaries (soldiers), and workers (moneymakers)."[14] Understanding human nature to be self-interested and assuming the human desire to exercise "power over others," Plato claimed the concept of rational philosopher-kings as ideal leaders who seek for truth, protect it, and attain wisdom, and "knowledge of the Good."[15] He pointed out three notions of leadership:

> The first is the general notion that the best educated people, who are able to distinguish knowledge and truth from mere opinion and belief, should have the principal leadership positions and principal positions of responsibility. . . . The second is the notion that leaders should have a broader moral horizon than followers; leaders are to look beyond immediate desires and concerns and see a larger picture, and to take action on behalf of a broader public good. . . . (The third is) that the character of leaders makes a large difference in whether they are able to rule effectively on behalf of the community.[16]

Plato believed that leaders should be the best-educated people and have certain intellectual philosophical qualities, emphasizing the importance of proper education for leaders. Because he understood the ideal city as aristocratic, there was a clear boundary between leaders and followers in terms of class, education, and character. He selected elites as leaders, those who possessed reason and wisdom to see the city as a whole and to cultivate better relationships with other states so that they could transform knowledge of the Good into good practices, such as just laws and effective education programs for all people in the city.[17] He strongly argued that leaders should work for the benefit of everyone and on behalf of the community. Plato's concepts of leadership and ideas concerning leaders were among the most powerful influencing Christian leadership.

Thomas Aquinas in the thirteenth century developed the concept of Christian leadership, integrating the Plato's concepts of leadership with that of Aristotle. He set up the divine model as a model for leaders. God or Jesus was always on the top of this leadership model. In his understanding, a king was a leader who needed to teach virtue to his subjects and take care of their needs. The goal of this leadership was to make the king's subjects as fully human as possible and give them the happiness of the world.[18] For Aquinas, the ideal leader is a teacher, and morally, ethically, spiritually superior person who emulates Jesus. Many church fathers, such as Saints Augustine, Clement, Anselm, Aquinas, and others, followed the life of Jesus and demonstrated his leadership practices in their lives. The model of Jesus's leadership has been the subject of church ministry from the early Christian fathers to current theological educators and pastors. It is frequently discussed in most theological leadership studies.

Christian Clergy Leadership in Catholic and Protestant Contexts

One of the most prominent leadership studies in Christianity is the study of church officers and their leadership styles, from the pope, bishops, and priests in Catholic traditions to ordained pastors in Protestant traditions. In fact, Christian leadership study has been exclusively focused on male clergy leadership. By studying male clergy leadership, Christian leadership is formed and presented to the public.

Clergy leadership is commonly claimed to originate in a divine calling. Representing Jesus and following Jesus's leadership, these clergy believe that they are chosen to follow Jesus. The rationales of clergy leadership establishment are found in 1 Corinthians 15:7. Jesus commanded everyone to serve but chose twelve to be the apostolate in his resurrection. It is interpreted that the meaning of Jesus's "eschatological revelation of salvation" was revealed in this divine calling.[19] The Early Church government in Acts was led by the twelve apostles under the leadership of Peter. By selecting additional officers in Acts 1:5–26 and

6:1–6, the apostles agreed to have more church representatives. The Early Church recognized the position of the apostles as leaders of entire church communities beyond Jerusalem.

Even though Paul was not one of the twelve apostles, he greatly influenced church government. He established the concepts of order and subordination.[20] In 1 Corinthians 12:28, his writing implies that there is an order or even rank of church officers: "God has appointed in the church first apostles, second prophets, third teachers, then deeds of power, then gifts of healing, forms of assistance, forms of leadership, various kinds of tongues."[21] This verse is often interpreted as indicating that this order is a hierarchical order approved by God. Emphasizing order and submission as "expression of service," Paul understood the purpose of these leadership roles as service that is "acting out of faith" for demonstrating love for others.[22] For him, the goal of these positions is to provide help for other people.

The word "bishop" originated in the Greek word *episkopos* and implied "overseer," "often illustrated in the Old Testament through comparisons with the duties of a shepherd (Jer. 23:2; Ezek. 34:6; Zech. 10:3, 11:16)."[23] Even though elders and bishops were the same or similar positions in the first century, in I Timothy 3:2, 4–5, and Titus 1:9, the role of bishop became distinguished by teaching and supervision, and this distinction led to "the formation of the *monarchical episcopate*" in the beginning of the second century.[24] Comparing the images of Jesus as a shepherd and his leadership with monarchical episcopacy, the office of bishops claimed legitimate succession and authority. Ignatius was one of the Early Church Fathers who supported this hierarchical arrangement. He identified the office of bishops with the church and equated "bishop, presbyter, and deacon" with "God, the Apostles, and Christ."[25] He understood the office of bishops as a necessary and important hierarchical organization.

By the debates and discussions of many Early Church Fathers, this succession and its doctrine were successfully established in the fourth and fifth centuries, establishing an institutionalized official ordination process to produce specific ordained clergy and church administrators. As the episcopal office developed, a hierarchal distinction between the roles of bishop, presbyter, and deacon existed. The bishop was regarded as the protector of the apostolic tradition and the minister of ordination with oversight of several congregations in particular vicinities, whereas presbyters became representatives of the bishop and performed word and sacrament in local churches only.[26] The bishop occupied the top of this hierarchy. This institutionalized process strongly affirms the Catholic conception of the apostolate and its continuation through papacy, bishops of the diocese of Rome, and the ordained priesthood.

> Under Constantine the Great the bishops as the highest ecclesiastical dignitaries were also publicly and legally granted their full power to teach, to consecrate, and to exercise jurisdiction (within their dioceses). . . . The public tasks of the Church grew immeasurably through the complete Christianization of the empire. . . . It certainly remained true that belonging to the Church depended legally and dogmatically on the connection with the bishop, that "only where the bishop is, there is the Church," and the Church understood itself to be an episcopal Church.[27]

Both the church and the office of bishops were completely integrated in the constitution of the empire. They performed not only as spiritual religious leaders but also as political leaders. They commonly exercised their spiritual authority as political power, such as by leading religious rituals as a way of influencing political decisions. As they developed imperial ecclesiastical systems through the church and later beyond the church, they became essential parts of the empire as leaders. The duties of the office of bishop served not only the church but also the states, even after the collapse of the Roman Empire. Kings performed as the protectors of this office. However, when the Frankish-Ottonian-Salian imperial ecclesiastical system broke down, disintegration between empire and papacy appeared. As Western Christian history was reflected in many different countries, with many complicated historical, sociopolitical, and cultural clashes and conflicts, the office of bishops repeatedly exercised its power over an independent ecclesiastical territorial system, but received strong resistance from the elites to the masses, and then, finally reestablished its power and influence within the church.

In the century of the Reformation, legitimation of the office of bishops was seriously questioned and criticized. The office of bishops lost its expanded, exceeded power. "In the end the concentration of the work of the Church in the pastoral office was that which helped most Reformation Churches to abandon the episcopal office,"[28] even though the proletariat priests provided great leadership models in many Catholic countries. Based on the new understanding of the Gospel, Martin Luther denounced the divine right of the papacy to rule in the church. He repudiated the thought that "the pope alone possessed the prerogative of the exposition of the Scriptures" and positioned himself above the council.[29] When Luther claimed that Christ was the only the Head of the church and all Christians could be members of ecclesiastical offices, he declared the universal priesthood of all believers. Because he saw roles of bishop and pastor were equal and same, he rejected the authority of the bishop's office to appoint pastors or preachers.[30] Witnessing the Peasants' Revolt and different situations in various congregations, Luther and his reformers were urged to restructure the church and clarify legal relationships for pastors and religious institutions. They challenged the office of leadership in the Catholic Church and formed a new leadership in the churches of the Reformation that "promoted the cause of the Gospel personally and governmentally over against the emperor, the empire, and the pope."[31]

Even though the Catholic Church continued to maintain the high status of clergy in its hierarchy, Protestant clergy proclaimed their status outside the Catholic Church. Denouncing the problems of the Catholic Church and its restrictive and hierarchal rules of clergy selection under the influence of the Reformation and the Enlightenment, Protestant clergy groups formed their own denominations and exercised the same rights and services that they could provide for the church such as preaching, communion, church law and disciplines, among others.

However, leadership in the church did not expand beyond clergy leadership, even in the Protestant church. The characteristics of Protestant clergy and their leadership positions have been understood as the characteristics of leaders in the church. Instead of the office of bishops (pope and bishops), the pastoral office (pastors) occupied leadership positions. Leadership in the church was equated with power and the authority of ordained clergy only in Protestant churches. Even though the Protestant church criticized the office of the pope and bishops in the Catholic Church for its exclusive leadership, the pastoral office in the Protestant church held similar privileges and rights over individual congregations in terms of leadership. Declaring their spiritual authority as a power given by God, pastors often exercise their spiritual gifts over parishioners in the name of service. The role of leadership in both the Catholic and Protestant churches is performed exclusively by ordained clergy, whether they are appointed by the office of bishops or called by individual congregations. They are expected to be leaders in the church. In other words, whether in the Catholic or Protestant church, Christian leadership is still greatly concentrated in the clergy. Members of the church remain followers. They are seen as helpless sheep that need to be led by the Shepherd.

Servant Leadership

It is the common assumption of both Protestant and Catholic clergy that they be recognized as leaders. Even though they gain privilege and power in the church through their positions, both claim that the goal of leadership is service only to others, not for themselves. Many Christian leadership scholars in fact agree with this claim as the predominant concept of Christian leadership. Based on the model of Jesus's leadership, Christian leadership is service that imitates Jesus.

Servant leadership is a popular Christian leadership theory that exemplifies "serving others to follow Jesus." This leadership was a very popular theory that many theologians and pastors discussed. However, the theory of this leadership was not created by Christian theologians or pastors. Even though many theologians and pastors referred to Jesus's leadership as servant leadership, it was Robert K. Greenleaf, a researcher in the field of management, who initiated this concept of leadership. In his 1977 book *Servant Leadership*, he conceptualized leadership as servant leadership in business, education, foundations, the church, bureaucratic society, and the world. He recognized institutions and trustees as servants to all people. Inspired by the protagonist, Leo, in Hermann Hesse's *Journey to the East*, Greenleaf understood a servant as a person capable of hearing the prophetic voice and seeing the disparity between society and the institutions that serve society. He believed that a servant would know where resources were and how to use them. A servant would relate to people not in a coercive way but in a supportive way. Greenleaf viewed churches as "the institutionalization of humankind's religious concern" and saw a Christian leader as a servant who would learn to "know experimentally" with superior wisdom.[32]

To practice this leadership, he suggested four elements of a general strategy: 1) goals-concept, 2) leadership, 3) structure, 4) trustees[33] and defined "a concept of a distinguished serving institution" as the institution that should consider all people to meet "nobler stature and greater effectiveness than they are likely to achieve on their own."[34] In this definition, this serving institution needs to understand both leadership and followership because everyone in this institution is both a leader and a follower. The challenge of this leadership is then how to handle power and authority. He suggested trustees as a solution to this challenge.[35] Forming trustees and their collaborative work and service are integral to the process of this leadership.

The focus of servant leadership is not making a profit but serving people. Leaders provide service by leading. They give more power to followers and the community. While they cultivate interdependence, respect, and trust, they commit themselves to communal and individual growth. There are some characteristics of leaders that define this leadership. However, the characteristics of this leadership are in fact not developed by Greenleaf himself. It is Larry C. Spears who identifies Greenleaf's servant leadership in ten characteristics: "1) listening, 2) empathy, 3) healing, 4) awareness, 5) persuasion, 6) conceptualization, 7) foresight, 8) stewardship, 9) commitment to the growth of people, and 10) building community."[36]

Many transformational leadership scholars in a business context classify servant leadership as a part of transformational leadership. In fact, servant leadership and transformational leadership have similar concepts of leadership in a business context. Both leadership theories emphasize appreciation for all group members, listening, valuing, mentoring, encouraging, and empowering. The common elements of both leaderships are "influence, vision, trust, respect/credibility, risk-sharing/delegation, integrity and modeling."[37] Both theories demonstrate great concern for followers. However, there are many differences, too. Servant leadership accentuates higher trust for followers and requires more service from leaders. Even though it stresses the importance of influence, the way that servant leaders relate to people is quite different from how transformational leaders relate to them.

There is yet a more distinctive difference to be noticed. That is the focus of leadership. The focus of servant leadership is service to followers, but the focus of transformational leadership is transforming followers and the institutional environment.[38] In other words, the focus of transformational leadership is transformation, whereas the focus of servant leadership is service. While servant leaders attend to understanding followers and serving them as people who constitute organizations, transformational leaders attend to the institution to which followers belong. By providing more service, servant leaders influence and motivate others to find the meaning of work, whereas transformational leaders influence and motivate others to produce better results by demonstrating their individual charisma and inspiration.[39]

As servant leadership analyzes some similarities and differences with transformational theory, scholars such as Margaret Benefiel, Jerry Biberman, Louis W. Fry, A.L. Jue, Robert A. Giacalone, and Carole. L. Jurkiewicz classified this leadership as part of a "spiritual," "spirit-centered," or "valued-based leadership" that is often treated also as a part of transformational leadership. Whereas traditional leadership theories are based on the organizational benefits in terms of a modern business setting, spiritual leadership and/or servant leadership theories emphasize "vision, altruistic love, faith/hope" based on the needs of others.[40] The focus of servant leadership theories is "mutual trust and empowering others" by enhancing followers' autonomous intrinsic and extrinsic motivational behaviors.[41] However, the goal of spiritual leadership differs from the focus of spiritual leadership. Fry claims that "spiritual leadership is necessary for the transformation to and continued success of a learning organization. Spiritual leadership taps into the fundamental needs of both leader and follower for spiritual survival so they become more organizationally committed and productive."[42] Even though the immediate focus in spiritual leadership is taking care of spiritual survival, the ultimate goal of this leadership is the same as transformational leadership that produces better results. In a similar manner, even though servant leadership is focused on service to others, the goal of servant leadership in a business setting is not about service itself but about better productivity through better service. Servant leadership is frequently used in a consumerist context and the concept of the servant is strongly beneficial to consumerism.[43] Providing better service, it anticipates greater profit for organizations. The way that servant leadership is used in a consumerist society is similar to the way transformational leadership functions in that society.

In a modern business setting, spiritual leadership, servant leadership, and transformational leadership have a common goal: making followers perform better and produce more. These three leadership styles have similar approaches to this goal and share similar characteristics of leadership styles. However, Chin-Yi Chen, Chun-Hsi Vivian Chen, Chun-l Li, Don Page, and Paul T.P. Wong, among others, claim that servant leadership has its own extensive set of characteristics, therefore requiring its own measurement. Chen, Chen, and Li characterize the servant leadership style as "caring for others," viewing their work as a "calling, ethical decisions, integrity, modeling, authenticity, vision/mission, empowering others/supporting personal decisions, emphasizing the development and accomplishment of employees, and emphasizing the nature of service, humility, self-sacrifice, and altruism."[44] These characteristics emphasize the qualities of servant leaders ethically, morally, intellectually, psychologically, spiritually, and even physically. They are expected to encompass all dimensions of leaders' lives. To deliver better quality of service to others, servant leaders are expected to demonstrate these unrealistic characteristics.

Because of this unrealistic higher expectation, assessment of servant leaders is often unquantifiable. Since many religious leaders are recognized as servant leaders, it is often believed that servant leaders are not made, but chosen by God, especially in a Christian context. Their religious leadership is led by God or the Spirit. This implies that servant leadership is not measurable. However, in a business setting, many leadership scholars attempt to measure qualifications or characteristics of servant leaders. Don Page and Paul T.P. Wong created a twelve-dimension scale, including "integrity, humility, servanthood, caring for others, empowering others, developing others, visioning, goal-setting, leading, modeling, team-building, and shared decision-making."[45] Unlike servant leadership in a Christian context, servant leadership in a business context operates under the assumption that servant leadership is not just for the select few. Servant leadership is measurable. It is learnable like other types of leadership. "Leadership isn't a position; it's a process. It's an observable, understandable, learnable set of skills and practices available to everyone anywhere in the organization."[46] As the name "servant leadership" indicates, anyone can be a servant if he or she wants. Few can be masters or owners, despite their wishes, but anyone can be a servant. Servant leadership is a choice for everyone.

However, the path forward for Christian servant leaders is not clear based on this assumption. On the one hand, servant leaders are chosen by God: as reflected by the history of the office of bishops or ordination history in both the Catholic and Protestant churches, Christian leaders, especially clergy, are considered people who are called by God. The logic is that Jesus calls everyone, but only a few people are chosen to be leaders, such as the twelve apostles. On the surface, more authority rests with God, but beneath, more authority is invested in privileged selected clergy. Servant leadership is given. On the other hand, God calls everyone to be servant leaders. Whoever answers the call can be servant leaders. Servant leadership is not given but open to anyone. It is not chosen, but made. It is learnable and followable. It is not a position of privilege, but a service to others.

Servant leadership in a Christian context is based on what Jesus said and did. Many theologians and pastors try to find characteristics of servant leadership from Jesus. Based on several biblical foundations, many theologians and pastors claim Jesus's leadership as servant leadership.

> So Jesus called them and said to them, "You know that among the Gentiles those whom they recognize as their rulers lord it over them, and their great ones are tyrants over them. But it is not so among you; but whoever wishes to become great among you must be your servant, and whoever wishes to be first among you must be slave of all. For the Son of Man came not to be served but to serve, and to give his life a ransom for many." (Mark 10:42–45, NRSV)

For who is greater, the one who is at the table or the one who served? Is it not the one at the table? But I am among you as one who serves. (Luke 22:27, NRSV)

After he had washed their feet, had put on his robe, and had returned to the table, he said to them, "Do you know what I have done to you? You call me Teacher and Lord-and you are right, for that is what I am. So if I, your Lord and Teacher, have washed your feet, you also ought to wash one another's feet. For I have set you an example, that you also should do as I have done to you." (John 13:12–15)

Whereas the goal of servant leadership in a business context is producing better results for institutional goals in the end, Christian leadership scholars and pastors claim that the goal of servant leadership in a Christian context is service to others. Both the focus and the goal of servant leadership in a Christian context are people, not products. The process of caring for people itself is the object to be achieved of Christian servant leadership. When Jesus demonstrated his service of foot washing (John 13:1–20), he said that he set an example of how to serve others. Jesus acted as a servant to his followers. Even though he was Teacher and Lord who needed to be served, he was the one who served others. He used his higher social status and intellectual power not to be served, but to serve. Based on these biblical foundations, many theologians and pastors claim that Christians who want to follow Jesus should be servants to others as Jesus did because they are chosen to be leaders.

Diakonia as Christian Leadership

Christian theologians and pastors seek the meaning of service from the Greek word *diakonia*, understood as service. The meaning of this word is interpreted as "to serve as a slave, with a stress on subjection," to have "the special quality of indicating very personally the service rendered to another," and to show "a stronger approximation to the concept of a service of love."[31] It is service to all people, both neighbors and strangers, the local and world communities. *Diakonia* is one of the most important virtues and disciplines that many Christian churches cherish, regardless of denominations. It is one of the actions that many Christian traditions emphasized. John W. Stewart interprets it as "service," "service at the table," "waiting at tables, serving food, pouring wine," and, in a more expansive sense, "caring for the physical needs of others" and a service connecting "available resources to crippling human needs."[47] In the context of the Christian church, service is the main function that Christians are expected to perform not only within the church but beyond the church. In fact, its importance is greater "beyond the Church." Service to others was never meant to be performed inside the church and to church members only. It must be on earth as it is in heaven.

In traditional teaching, many Christians believe that Jesus came to this world to serve people and died to save them from their sins. It was a "service" that Jesus delivered from heaven to earth. Stewart interprets Jesus's crucifixion as the ultimate and fundamental signifier of *diakonia*.[48] Service is a way to invest the *kin-dom* of God on the earth. It should be provided in the public square. Creating a space of *diakonia* is an important task for Christian theologians and pastors. To create this space, they propose different practices of *diakonia*. For example, Stewart proposes a gospel-derived, Spirit-empowered *diakonia* with three programmatic efforts: "1) creative acts of compassion in a congregation's surrounding community, 2) cooperative efforts to redress and change local social and cultural systems that perpetuate injustices, and 3) missional efforts across cultural boundaries."[49] Using church as a base, he creates different ways to serve both the people and their community. There is another example. To emphasize the importance of service (*diakonia*), James Martin imagines the celebration of foot washing every Sunday in addition to the Eucharist.[50] By interpreting the meaning of foot washing, he urged people to think about what Jesus asked us to do: service in action. Jesus's service was not by word, but by deed, such as foot washing, healing the sick, feeding the hungry, and comforting those in despair.

Many Christian scholars and pastors repeatedly confirm that church is the place to perform these services for others. Working quietly at the local level, most members of mainline congregations practice *diakonia* "by doing volunteer work in their communities, attending lectures about social issues, and supporting congregational activities such as soup kitchen and day-care centers."[51] However, most North American mainline churches invest their time and resources in the spiritual well-being of members before service.[52] Standing in relatively privileged places, they assign social issues and public services to certain members. Service is an obligation of the church, but not an obligation to individual church members in the church, because church members are "free agents."[53] As long as service is carried out by certain members, the church fulfills its mission, service. Therefore, service becomes certain individuals' responsibility.

As capitalism and consumerism become the norm of modern society, the church becomes "simply one more organization that is marketing goods and services."[54] The meaning of the church is challenged and the function of the church is questioned. As a consequence, the concept of servant leadership in the Christian church is understood under the heavy influence of consumerist behaviors. It is not understood as Jesus showed, but rather as a process that makes consumers satisfied. In other words, church leadership is often evaluated by rating the quality of music and worship service for church members. The expectation is to make church members satisfied as an audience by the worship service and as a consumer of fellowship after worship service. Excellence of service is not intended to serve the poor, the hungry, and the powerless, but to serve people who are members and visitors of church in worship.

Struggling with this consumerist mentality, some mega churches demonstrate a CEO-style of leadership. However, observing this influence and responding to multicultural challenges in a church context, various Christian scholars and pastors exhibit different practices of leadership. Especially after the approval of women's ordination, which is intensely discussed in the next section, many churches emphasized a collaborative leadership and partner leadership, even though many other churches still operate under patriarchal hierarchal leadership.

Creating a space for *diakonia* requires various leadership approaches. Depending on different cultural, social, and racial contexts, each church or each denomination adopts different leadership approaches. Some churches, such as the Roman Catholic Church, United Methodist Church, Episcopal Church, and others, constitute a strong hierarchical leadership, whereas other churches, such as the Congregational Church, United Church of Christ, Presbyterian Church (USA), some Baptist churches, Holiness Church, and others, assert horizontal relational leadership in terms of church relations. Besides these traditional mainline churches, there are many new small, multicultural, immigrant independent churches that practice a new type of leadership. Many Christian churches encounter a new complicated, multi-intercultural era locally and globally. Considering multi-intercultural churches, many practical theologians and pastors try to develop or suggest a new Christian leadership approach. Mark Lau Branson's model is one example. He suggests a new approach of Christian leadership with three steps: interpretive leadership, relational leadership, and implemental leadership.

> Interpretive leadership is about meaning: it provides the resources and guidance needed to shape a community of leaders that pays attention to and interprets both texts and contexts. Relational leadership shapes all of the human connections (internal and external) and attends to the health and synergism of those relationships. Implemental leadership guides and initiates activities and structures so that a church embodies gospel meanings and relationships. Even though this description notes separate spheres, they overlap and they must remain vitally connected. If they lose their cohesion, then organizational dysfunction results.[55]

Guiding people to understand the current situation systematically, culturally, and sociopolitically, Branson believes that interpretive leadership is the first step that churches should take. After the analysis of these three steps, he suggests that church leaders should examine existing connections, build new connections and nourish them together for new and better action. When consistency is reached between these two processes, he proposes that churches should reform current structures and implant new activities. Like Branson, many Christian scholars and pastors have developed different approaches of leadership reflecting their own contexts. They observe complex situations, challenge the systems, and start new practices of leadership. Struggling with racism, sexism, classism, capitalism, consumerism, postmodernism, colonialism/postcolonialism, immigration, globalization, multiculturalism, and many other ideologies, they seek a new leadership. They try to create new goals of Christian modern leadership engaged in multidimensional layers of these struggles and work to redefine the meanings of leadership in the twenty-first century.

Women's Ordination and Leadership in a Church Context

One of the most powerful leadership shifts in the Christian church came with women's ordination. Under the pressure of the feminist movement, women's ordination brought the most critical paradigm shift in Christian leadership. As reflected by Christian history, Christian leadership was exclusively and solely occupied by male clergy. From the beginning of Christian history, women's leadership was ignored and dismissed. Even in the Bible, women's leadership was performed and evaluated within a patriarchal paradigm. Establishing and legitimating male clergy ordination, the Christian church recognized women's leadership as illegitimate and abnormal. Women leaders were imagined as treacherous and malicious figures. The suspicion of witchcraft was one example of that. Women's leadership was demonized and disdained. Women's ordination was the mission of impossible possibility in Christian history. However, as feminist movements challenged every aspect of sociopolitical cultural belief and its infrastructure, issues of women's ordination were rigorously raised and severely challenged. After long, relentless challenges, many Protestant churches and denominations approved women's ordination, even though the Roman Catholic Church and some Protestant denominations still do not approve women's ordination even today.

The Issue of Women's Ordination

The issue of women's ordination had been interpreted as a non-biblical act until the last two decades of the twentieth century. Even though there were various theological debates to reject women's ordination in different denominations, the most influential debate played out in the *Declaration on the Question of Admission of Women to the Ministerial Priesthood*, published by the Vatican on October 15, 1976, at the Sacred Congregation for the Doctrine of the Faith, the feast of Saint Teresa of Avila.[56] In this document, the Roman Catholic Church illustrated six points against women's ordination. First, "the church's constant tradition."[57] The Catholic Church stands on its constant tradition that, "by calling only men to the priestly Order and ministry in its true sense, the Church intends to remain faithful to the type of ordained ministry willed by the Lord Jesus Christ and carefully maintained by the Apostles."[58] Second, "the attitude of Christ."[59] "Jesus did not call any women to become part of the Twelve."[60] Third, "the practice of the Apostles."[61] "On the day of Pentecost, the Holy Spirit filled them all, men and women (Acts 2:1, 1:14), yet the proclamation of the fulfillment of the prophecies in Jesus was made only by 'Peter and the Eleven' (Acts 2:14)."[62] Fourth, "permanent value of the attitudes of Jesus and the Apostles."[63] Fifth, "the ministerial priesthood in the light of the mystery of Christ."[64] "When Christ's role in the Eucharist is to be expressed sacramentally, there would not be this 'natural resemblance' which must exist between Christ and his minister if the role of Christ were not taken by a man: in such a case it would be difficult to see in the minister the image of Christ. For Christ himself was and remains a man."[65] Sixth, "the ministerial priesthood illustrated by the mystery of the church."[66] These six points emphasize the maleness of Christ and the calling of the Twelve "males." Priesthood was prescribed and limited to only males. Gender difference was the reason to reject women's ordination and denied their leadership in the church.

After this document, there are two more documents, *Mulieris Dignitatem* (Apostolic Letter on the Dignity and Vocation of Women, 1988)[67] and a *Letter to the Bishops of the Catholic Church on the Collaboration of Men and Women in the Church and in the World* (by Cardinal Joseph Ratzinger, 2004)[68] that develop the argument against women's ordination in the Roman Catholic Church. As *Mulieris Dignitatem* defined women strictly in terms of motherhood and women's role of bearing children, it dismissed the existence of single women and childless women.[69] Since women were defined as mothers only, they were valued only as the body to carry the child. This argument was affirmed again in the *Letter to the Bishops of the Catholic Church on the Collaboration of Men and Women in the Church and in the World*. Women's work and value were defined only in relation to the family, and their main *normative* identity was recognized only in motherhood. In this document, women's role was seen to be the helpmate and their values were fundamentally connected with women's capacity for caring for others. Emphasizing women's contribution as the nourishment and protection of others, this document limited women's call into service without ordination. In the final chapter, it concluded, "In this perspective, one understands how the reservation of priestly ordination solely to men does not hamper in any way women's access to the heart of Christian life. Women are called to be unique examples and witnesses for all Christians of how the Bride is to respond in love to the love of the Bridegroom."[70] Manipulating the meaning of women's service as women's unique call from God, this document designated women's roles in a submissive position in the church and dismissed women's ordination as unnecessary effort.

These documents were widely used not only in the Roman Catholic Church but also in various Protestant churches beyond a Western context. These were globally accepted and circulated, regardless of denominations of the Protestant and Catholic churches. Emphasizing the maleness of the Apostles as the legitimated authority of leaders in the church and images of Jesus as a male, the Roman Catholic Church and Protestant churches have rejected women's ordination on these grounds.

Rejection of women's ordination is not only the subject of biblical and theological debates; it is also the product of cultural and social prejudices. Cultural and social prejudices against women inherently relate to women's sexuality. "As in all the monotheistic religions, the negative images associated with priesthood of women are often derived from pagan rites (idolatry is thus adultery and prostitution)."[71] As images of male priests were imagined as the only legitimated leaders of the church, images of priestesses were intentionally manufactured as prostitutes. As the body of the male priest represents Jesus, the body of the priestesses represents an idolater. Characteristics of female leaders in religious rites were often described as lascivious, lustful, manipulative, treacherous, wicked, devious, and so forth. As women's bodies were labeled unclean and unsacred, men's bodies were labeled as holy and sacred. For women to be accepted in religious circles, they had to remain as submissive, those who needed help and needed to be saved. Man became a savior to woman. Consequently, the roles of submissive "servants" are assigned to women—not as leaders but as followers. Even though Christian servant leadership is frequently practiced by women, their leadership is trivialized and recognized not as leadership but as followership only. Christian leadership is not service to others, but dominance over women when the Christian church fortifies the authority of the priesthood with the image of Jesus as male.

Feminist Debates on Women's Leadership

Many feminist scholars critically analyzed these debates and fought for women's ordination. They understood the approval of women's ordination as approval of women's leadership in the church and beyond. From a sociopolitical perspective, it was a task for women to have equal power and accessibility to privileges of clergy positions in religious institutions. It was a restoration of women's human rights to obtain leadership positions in the church and to be granted equal benefits as clergy. It was a sociopolitical struggle for Christian women to be institutionally legitimated leaders in the church. From a religious perspective, it was a spiritual movement to restore women's equal participation in God's work as leaders. It was a restoration of divine calling for not only women but all humanity. The impact of the approval of women's ordination was felt, in fact, beyond the church. Women's ordination became the foundation for a restoration of justice and equality for all people, regardless of sex and gender, race, and religion. It was a consecrated religious fight, and it remains a resilient sociopolitical fight beyond mere Christian religious boundaries.

Tracing women's leadership roles from the Bible and the Early Church, and reinterpreting the images of maleness of God, many feminist scholars engage in this fight and challenge male clergy leadership in various ways. For example, some feminist theologians, such as Karen Jo Torjesen, debate the roles of women leaders in the Early Church, as others, such as Ruth Edwards and Elisabeth Behr-Sigel, try to argue the problems of biblical interpretation and theological hermeneutics for women's ordination. Torjesen starts her argument by critically reviewing the usages of *diakonos, apostolos, presbyteros, episcopos*, prophet, and teacher in the Early Church period and claims that women held these positions in the Early Church.[72] As she analyzes the social context of the Early Church, she points out that women's leadership in the private sphere was certainly stronger. Before women leaders moved to the public domains of empire and city, they were core leaders in the Early Church. When women householders supported Early Church communities, women's leadership in the church took the form of prophets and deacons.[73] Torjesen believes that when the Early Church shifted from house church to basilica in the fourth century, women's leadership became invisible because women's presence in public was scandalous at that time. The social context did not allow women to be seen as leaders in public.[74] She insists that women need to reclaim their equal and rightful place to be leaders in the current society, remembering Jesus's message and practice for radical egalitarianism. Her argument draws a connection between women's leadership as it existed in the Early Church and the need for its restoration today.

Looking into the New Testament, cultural traditions and modern debates, Ruth Edwards argues for women's ordination from the perspective of an Anglican. Examining the assumption that only a man can represent God and comparing the male images of God with female images of God, she claims that women and men are created as equals. She understands women's ordination as a new way to meet the needs of the church in current society under the continuous guidance of the Spirit.[75] Edwards introduces seven principles to support women's ordination: "1) the real equality of the sexes, 2) the complementarity of the sexes, 3) Christian ministry as service rather than the exercise of domination, 4) priesthood and ministry as belonging to the whole people of God, 5) women and men as equally "representing" humanity, 6) women and men as equally "representing" God, and 7) all ministry as by God's grace, not by right."[76] Reflecting on scripture, tradition, reason, and experience, she underlines the equality of women and men as the foundation of women's ordination. She points out that ordination functioned not as service to others, but as domination over others. She claims that Christian leadership should start from equality of women and men.

To prove a precedence of women's leadership in the Christian tradition, Elisabeth Behr-Sigel uses the Early Church Fathers' notion of egalitarianism, such as that of Gregory of Nazianzus, who proclaimed "the same creator for man and for woman, for both the same clay, the same image, the same death, the same resurrection."[77] From an Orthodox perspective, she believes that both men and women are derived from the same images of God, just as their priesthood derives from Jesus who is the only high priest on earth. Therefore, both women and men can fully participate in the royal priesthood.

> All through the centuries, Christian women have been baptized, chrismated and invested with the fullness of the royal priesthood; they have confessed their faith in Christ, endured martyrdom, evangelised, prophesied, and attained the heights of holiness in the life of consecrated virginity as well as in married life.[78]

Behr-Sigel lifts up the fullness of women's participation in images of God and in the royal priesthood. To show the fullness of women's royal priesthood, she focuses on Mary and her role as a priest. She indicates that Mary's life has been used as an idealized symbol of womanhood. In Christian history, it is assumed that she is a role model for all women. Mary represents all women, and all women are encouraged to follow her and her submission. Her submission to God becomes women's submission to others. However, the virgin mother is an impossible concept that ordinary women cannot follow. Even though women are encouraged to follow Mary, Mary is not the woman whom women can identify and follow. Again, women remain unredeemable. The more Mary is described as the model of all women, the more Mary is apart from all women. Her leadership is untouchable and unfollowable. Mary's obedience is used to escalate the oppression of women. It has been used to fortify all women's obedience and submission to others. However, as Behr-Sigel analyzes this vicious circle, she uses this logic and changes it with a different interpretation. She sees Mary as "a symbol of the mystery of women," "the new Eve," "the new beginning of the dignity of woman, of all women, of every woman."[79] As Mary becomes an archetype of all women, she becomes a symbol of the perfect woman for every woman. Mary represents all women who can be perfect. Behr-Sigel describes Mary as birth-giver of God, and inseparable from Christ. "Mary is the image and personification of the spirit-bearing church, the womb of the new humanity."[80] Now she represents not only women but men, the whole of humanity and is in solidarity with all humanity. Behr-Sigel finds the validity of women's ordination in the notion that Mary was "God's first coworker"[81] who has a woman's face and body. As the office of bishops traces the apostolic tradition and the Early Church as the root of their ordination, Behr-Sigel traces Mary and her priestly ministry in the church as the foundation of women's ordination.

The issue of women's ordination has still not been completely resolved in various churches, even though there are many churches that ordain women. Many feminist/womanist/Asian women/Latina theologians have developed numerous approaches to support women's ordination. There are two prominent approaches for this issue. First, as the maleness of Jesus and the maleness of God are revealed as the focal point of this issue, countless women theologians, such as Elizabeth A. Johnson, Susan Thistlethwaite, Rita Nakashima Brock, Sallie McFague, Merlin Stone, Carol P. Christ, Jacquelyn Grant, Mary Daly, Rosemary Radford Ruether, and others, see the problems of patriarchy originating in the maleness of God, reconstruct images of God, and redefine the meaning of these images. The concepts of trinity are also redefined and reconceptualized by these women theologians. Second, as the church legitimates the authority of male leadership from the apostolic tradition, many female biblical scholars, such as Katheryn Pfisterer Darr, Elisabeth Schüssler Fiorenza, Delores S. Williams, Phyllis Trible, and others, rediscover the existence of women leaders and their activities in the church from the Bible and the Early Church. They reclaim the leadership of biblical female prophets in the Hebrew Bible and female leaders of the Early Church. Through a critical rabbinical and feminist perspective, Darr reconstructs the stories of Ruth, Sarah, Hagar, and Esther and redefines the meaning of their leadership.[82] Critically analyzing the story of Hagar, Williams uncovers significant problems of a cross section between race, gender, and class focused on white and black relations from the perspective of an African American woman, especially in relation to the experience of slavery.[83] Reconstructing Christian origins, Fiorenza claims "women's history as the history of the discipleship of equals" and "women as paradigms of true discipleship."[84] As all of these biblical scholars reconstruct the stories of female leaders and prophets, they try to show equality of women and men from the beginning of Christian history and validate women's leadership in the church from its origins.

Establishing gender equality in the Bible, the Early Church, and the early Christian history is the main starting point for women's ordination. To uncover this equality, many female scholars choose different strategies. From reimagining images of God to reconstructing biblical, theological, social, political, anthropological, economic, and cultural contexts and texts, they develop various approaches to advocate women's ordination. Women's ordination is a task to restore human rights and divine calling for all people. The legitimation of women's leadership supports the legitimacy of all people's leadership. Because of this implication, it becomes one of the most critical paradigm shifts of leadership in Christian history. As women's ordination has been approved, the landscape of Christian leadership has been greatly changed.

Women's Leadership in a Church Context

The first woman formally ordained in an established denomination was Antoinette Brown, who was educated at Oberlin College and "called to a small Congregational church in South Butler, New York, in 1853."[85] By the end of that century, Disciples, Unitarians, Congregationalists, Universalists, and Northern Baptists started to ordain women, whereas

Presbyterians, several Holiness denominations and Methodists had just opened this issue.[86] Most mainline Protestant denominations approved women's ordination around the middle of the twentieth century. The Presbyterian Church (USA) ordained its first female minister in 1956. Presbyterians celebrated 60-years-of women teaching elders as they celebrated "110 years of women deacons and 85 years of women ruling elders" in 2015–2016.[87] "The UMC and its forerunner has ordained women for five decades; the ELCA (Evangelical Lutheran Church in America) and its predecessor has for almost 40 years, and the Episcopal Church has ordained women since 1976."[88] Feminist movements have brought dramatic changes for women's equality and social positions, and they have had great influence on women's ordination.

However, women in general are still underrepresented in leadership positions, especially in the church. Though many churches approve women's ordination, female clergy and their leadership are not widely appreciated. Regardless of the church or denomination, female clergy commonly experience discrepancies in salary in comparison with male clergy, difficulty in finding positions, and limited choices that lead them to work for small congregations. They often receive harsh treatment from church members because of their gender. In general, female clergy are rarely called by congregations as senior pastors in many mainline denominations.

> From the early 1990s through 1999 just 5% of the Senior Pastors of Protestant churches were female. Since that time the proportion has slowly but steadily risen, doubling to 10% in 2009. . . . Women in the pulpit are generally more highly educated than are their male counterparts. . . . Despite their higher educational attainment, though, female pastors typically have smaller compensation levels than do male pastors. The average package for female pastors in 2009 is $45,300. The median compensation for male pastors is $48,600. As striking as the gap may be, it has diminished somewhat over the last ten years. The Barna study noted that while male pastors have experienced a substantial increase in compensation packages since 1999—up 21%—female pastors received an even greater jump, growing by 30%. In other words, the difference in compensation has been cut by more than half, from $6,900 per year to about $3,300 annually. One of the reasons for the discrepancy in pay rates between male and female pas-

tors is the size of the congregations they lead. Male pastors lead congregations that average 103 adults in attendance on a typical weekend compared to 81 adults at churches led by female pastors.[89]

Whereas denominations such as the United Methodist Church and Episcopal Church led by the office of bishops must assign women as senior pastors, several Protestant denominations, such as the Presbyterian Church (USA) and the Congregational Church, that have a calling system do not have to assign women as senior pastors or to any pastor position in the church. For this reason, women in the Presbyterian Church (USA) and Congregational Church have a harder time getting a call from the church. As previously mentioned, only 10 percent of senior pastors were female in Protestant churches in general. Even in denominations such as the United Methodist Church, a few women are assigned as senior pastors in larger congregations. HiRho Park conducted research through the Lead Women Pastors Project with Susan Willhauck in 2009 and found critical discrepancies between women and men pastors of one thousand or more membership churches in United Methodist Church. Among these 1,154 mega churches, only sixty-four churches had women pastors.[90] Moreover, in comparison with mainline churches, women in non-mainline churches have fewer opportunities to have pastorate positions.[91] In the case of ethnic minority female pastors, there are almost no cases reported because traditional ethnic churches such as African American congregations and immigrant congregations only call ethnic male pastors as senior pastors. Many ethnic minority female pastors must confront their own ethnic cultural and patriarchal barriers and Western Christian patriarchal walls simultaneously.

Eunjoo Mary Kim and Deborah Beth Creamer in *Women, Church, and Leadership: New Paradigms* point out that "a change in gender roles within the church" is the first element of challenges to the current church leadership.[92] In fact, the presence of female pastors itself becomes a change in gender roles in the landscape of church leadership and its practices. Though female pastors have fewer opportunities to be pastors, especially senior pastors, in the church, growing numbers of female pastors and lay leaders demonstrate nontraditional but outstanding styles of leadership and challenge the configuration of church leadership.

As described in the previous chapter in the section on feminist/collaborative leadership theory, many women, including female clergy and lay leaders, practice collaborative leadership in their churches. Instead of using an authoritarian approach, they lead the collaborative process and share power together. "Leading with others" equally,[93] many female clergy and lay leaders try to decenter top-down hierarchal leadership structures and encourage collaboration between laity and clergy. The emphasis on a horizontal relationship with others in leadership is one of the most distinctive features of women's leadership in the church. Susan Willhauck and Jacqulyn Thorpe call this leadership "web leadership,"[94] while Eunjoo Mary Kim calls it "shared leadership," meaning "a collaborative ministry between leaders of the church and its members."[95] Kim understands the original model of the Christian ministry is the shared ministry between traveling apostles and local church leaders before the institutionalization of the church. Grounded on the shared leadership in the Trinitarian structure of God, she invites all people to the pulpit and encourages them to share their experiences of witnessing God's redemptive power.[96]

Just as Kim, Willhauck, and Thorpe describe, many feminist theologians and pastors intentionally invite church members to the pulpit and want to share leadership together. Their leadership is often described as a "flexible," inclusive, "ever-changing," "loosely construed," decentered, sensitive to the needs of others, collaborative, "not either, but both" type of leadership.[97] Many female pastors and lay leaders see themselves as leaders who are not higher than laity. They recognize themselves as moderators, mediators, supporters, facilitators, conductors, gardeners, "influencers, collaborators, or contributors."[98] They practice inclusivity and nurture hospitality as a new model of leadership. Because of their different styles of leadership, they have challenged not only traditional church leadership but also the traditional church structure itself.

PART II

LEADERSHIP AND ITS CHALLENGES IN US CULTURE

Chapter 3

Leadership in US Culture

Leadership positions in US culture have been occupied by an elite upper-class white Anglo-European heterosexual male group without disabilities (the privileged white group) throughout US history. Whether in a secular context or a religious context, most leadership positions are occupied by this group. In the complexities of race, sex/gender, class, and colonial/postcolonial dynamics, this group has formed the power to maintain and fortify white identity as the core image of leadership in the United States. Because of this sociopolitical cultural reality, subjects of leadership studies in the past fifty years are predominantly conducted by and from this privileged white group. Consequently, in the unitary white majority culture, images of leaders and leadership are formed and dominated by white male leaders. What are the images of white leaders and their leadership? How do they function and operate in the United States? What are the ineluctable impacts of these images on various ethnic groups, women, immigrants, and various other groups? How do these groups see and understand these images?

The concept of leadership has developed through conversation under preexisting sociopolitical, historical, and cultural milieu from the beginning of leadership studies in the United States. As the history of leadership's definition has shown, the concept of leadership has been formed and reformed in the power dynamics of class, race, gender/sex, and colonial/postcolonial discourses. In this sociopolitical context, the word "leader" often comes with several assumptions about the leader beyond the dictionary definitions. In a similar manner but from different approaches, the Christian religious context also has several assumptions about the concept of the leader. Before exploring images of leaders and leadership in the United States socioeconomic context, it is important to devote some attention to these hidden assumptions that already exist in both secular and Christian religious contexts. There are at least three assumptions.

First, the word "lead" has a connotation of "better." It implies the concept of superiority. From the perspective of unscrupulous US capitalism, "better" means faster, higher, bigger, broader, stronger, smarter, more intelligent, and having more capability to achieve. It indicates better abilities and qualifications. The image of the leader connotes a person who "leads" others with the presupposition that such a person is "in front of," "above," or "higher" than those who are led. It assumes the superiority of the leaders in the sense of their being able to better bring about measurable, quantifiable achievement. In terms of a Christian context, "better" means deeper spiritual maturity and mature moral/ethical development. The image of the leader in this context implies a person who leads others with more mature spirituality and moral/ethical integrity. However, in some contexts, spiritual leader means a person with more powerful spiritual gifts such as healing power and premonition. This kind of leadership presupposes being "for," and "over" others. It exists based on the concept of leaders having better ability in terms of spiritual, moral, and ethical maturity. These leaders are often assumed to demonstrate better involvement in interiority and exteriority. It unquestionably contains the concept of superiority in this sense.

Second, the current concept of leadership clearly assumes a different positionality between the leader and the follower. In the sociopolitical context, it inevitably implies the binary concept of the leader and the follower in terms of power. In the logic of capitalism, a hierarchal relationship between the leader and the follower is assumed. It seems necessary to give more power to the leader in the structure of capitalism. The difference in power between the leader and the follower legitimates inequality and privilege as a positional difference. It is accepted and exercised not as a problem, but as a necessity. In the Christian context, the word "leader" has a different connotation. Even though hierarchy exists in the position of leaders, spiritual leaders are not expected be privileged, because the traditional images of prophetic spiritual leaders portray them as seeking poverty and denouncing privilege. However, "leader" still assumes a position of superior spiritual power between leader and follower. In terms of depth of spirituality and spiritual power, it is believed that the leader has more spiritual authority than the follower.

Third, leadership assumes the singular form of the leader and the plural form of the followers. Structures of organizations and institutions have shown models of hierarchy in the form of a pyramid. The images of leadership are easily and traditionally pictured in this pyramid form. The image of the leader is represented as an individual person on the top, whereas the images of followers are portrayed as a mass of people on the bottom of this pyramid. Organizations and institutions give power to "a" leader who is physically, psychologically, spiritually, morally, ethically, intellectually, socially, politically, and culturally better than followers. Even though the various denominational church structures have instituted different forms of hierarchy, these religious structures commonly affirm religious order as a hierarchy. Various hierarchies between the clergy and bishops, between the clergy and the laity, and even between lay leaders and the laity exist. Traditional images of leadership presuppose a single clergy on the top and church members on the bottom. The common image of the leader is a shepherd and images of the followers are sheep. This single clergy is supposed to be superior to other church members in every conceivable way.

By creating a perfect individual who performs leadership perfectly in both secular and Christian contexts, the form of the pyramid is legitimated and models of hierarchy are admitted without endangering current structures. The individual leader becomes the protector of the structure. As the images of the individual leader are named and made visible, the images of followers become invisible and nameless. The individual leader is imbued with more power, whereas followers are treated as helpless and powerless. Followers are pictured as those who need to be saved and guided. Based on these preexisting assumptions in the United States, understandings of the leader and leadership in the US socioeconomic context is explored next.

White Leaders and Leadership in a US Socioeconomic Context

Leadership in the Nineteenth and Twentieth Centuries

A history of leadership studies shows that early leadership studies began with research focused on kings, warriors, and the aristocratic class and later introduced individual privileged white men. As colonial/postcolonial white European American history shows, most leadership positions have been continuously occupied by the privileged white group, an elite upper-class white Anglo European heterosexual male group without disability.

Many war heroes, presidents, and CEOs of large corporations, who were mostly from this privileged white elite group, were studied as the main subjects of the leadership studies. In the nineteenth and twentieth centuries, George Washington, Thomas Jefferson, Abraham Lincoln, Theodore Roosevelt, Andrew Carnegie, John D. Rockefeller, Henry Ford, and other white male leaders were recognized as the powerful leaders. Images of these leaders were tough, strong, paternalistic, bureaucratic, hierarchal, virtuous, charismatic, militant, independent, responsible, trustful, loyal, and authoritative. Jim Collins describes them as "disciplined, rigorous, dogged, determined, diligent, precise, fastidious, systematic, methodical, workmanlike, demanding, consistent, focused, accountable, and responsible."[1] Michael Maccoby characterizes them as "inner-directed, obsessive, and father-oriented, with values of loyalty, stability, and knowledge"[2] and "annoyingly stubborn and self-righteous."[3] These leaders set up the rules and demanded people follow them even though they themselves were innovative thinkers. They showed a great loyalty to institutions and dedicated their lives to these institutions. To protect the ideology of the institutions was novel in their view. Personal charisma was strongly emphasized, and hierarchical leadership was culturally accepted and encouraged. The individual, strong, militant styles of leadership became a predominant focus in leadership studies in this period.[4] In fact, these images are still popular as the ideal images of individual leaders, even in today.

A good example of the mentality of leadership in a socioeconomic context can be found in the research of Jim Collins and his team in 2001. In *Good to Great,* Collins and his team examine 1,435 of America's largest public companies from 1965 to 1995 based on *Fortune* rankings. By creating eleven elimination criteria, Collins selects eleven good-to-great companies: Abbott, Circuit City, Fannie Mae, Gillette, Kimberly-Clark, Kroger, Nucor, Philip Morris, Pitney Bowes, Walgreens, and Wells Fargo. From this research, Collins creates the concept of Level 5 hierarchy as the model of leadership: "Level 1—Highly capable individual, Level 2—Contributing team member, Level 3—Competent manager, Level 4—Effective leader, and Level 5—Executive."[5] Highly capable individuals from Level 1 demonstrate excellent ability to contribute individually. The limit of this highly capable individual is that this individual person's contribution cannot reach out to the team. People from Level 2 are not only highly capable individuals but also contributing team members.[6] They are able to contribute their talents toward the overall achievement of the team. Individuals from Level 2 are limited in that they do not know how to organize people and use resources toward the predetermined goal of the organization. Competent managers from Level 3 are those who know how to do these tasks but do not know how to bring a compelling vision and elicit people's commitment to the vision. Effective leaders from Level 4 are the people who have a clear vision, dedicate to commitment, and motivate a higher achievement.[7] However, they do not have what Level 5 leaders have. Collins's concept of leadership is a hierarchal, pyramid leadership with clear power and ability differences between the leader and followers. In fact, those from Level 1 to Level 3 are not considered as leaders, but only as followers. Each level has different limited abilities without the possibility of advancing to the next level. Level 5 is especially inaccessible. Collins calls the ideal leader a "Level 5 leader," who is

> an individual who blends extreme personal humility with intense professional will. . . . They were self-effacing individuals who displayed the fierce resolve to do whatever needed to be done to make the company great. . . . Level 5 leaders channel their ego needs away from themselves and into the larger goal of building a great company. It's not that Level 5 leaders have no ego or self-interest. Indeed, they are incredibly ambitious—*but their ambition is first and foremost for the institution, not themselves.*[8]

Collins labeled good-to-great leaders as Level 5 leaders and the attributes of these leaders as Level 5 traits. These traits have two emphases in duality; 1) humility and 2) fearless professional will. He summarizes the two sides of Level 5 leadership in the following;

> Professional will: Creates superb results, a clear catalyst in the transition from good to great. Demonstrates an unwavering resolve to do whatever must be done to produce the best long-term results, no matter how difficult. Sets the standard of building an enduring great company; will settle for nothing less. Looks in the mirror, not out the window, to apportion responsibility for poor result, never blaming other people, external factors, or bad luck.
>
> Personal humility: Demonstrates a compelling modesty, shunning public adulation; never boastful. Acts with quiet, calm

determination; relies principally on inspired standard, not inspiring charisma, to motivate. Channels ambition into the company, not the self; sets up successors for even greater success in the next generation. Looks out the window, not in the mirror, to apportion credits for the success of the company—to other people, external factors, and good luck.[9]

Collins believes that Level 5 leaders are different from other people in terms of professional ability and personal humanity. The expectation for the Level 5 leaders is this: Level 5 leaders should have all abilities of other levels, and more. In other words, they embody every single layer of the pyramid, whereas leaders at other levels do not have the ability to embody all these layers. Furthermore, a Level 5 executive has an ability to discern how to put "the right people on the bus and the wrong people off."[10] The right people mean those from Level 1 to Level 4. The wrong people are those who do not belong to any of these levels. They are outside of this framework. There is a clear value difference between the right people and the wrong people in this concept. Collins's hypothesis is that Level 5 leaders are not trainable, but are born with a seed, which is then developed under the right circumstances. In his concept of leadership, Level 5 leaders are born leaders and those from other levels are treated only as the followers with very limited abilities and many weaknesses.

Collins's research is one of the works that show the trends in images of leadership in the nineteenth and twentieth centuries. Images of leadership in that era were hierarchal and lineal. They all had a top-to-bottom framework in terms of power and unidirectional communication. Maccoby explains this leadership attribute as a bureaucratic personality. However, the images of leadership have changed as the times have changed, although it does not mean that those traditional leadership models no longer exist. They do exist, and they are still influential in modern American leadership. It is a very active model of leadership, even today.

Leadership in the Twenty-First Century

In the twenty-first century, there are many prominent white and black leaders who demonstrate various leadership styles. As large corporations such as IBM, Intel, Apple, Hewlett-Packard, Dell, Wal-Mart, Verizon, AT&T, Amazon, Facebook, Google, and other companies take over the American economy, media, politics, and culture, they influence the images of leaders and showcase different leadership practices. Bill Gates, Steve Jobs, Michael Dell, Larry Ellison, Lawrence Page, Barack Obama, Oprah Winfrey, Jeff Bezos, Mark Zuckerberg, Hillary Clinton, and other CEOs, politicians, and celebrities are recognized as prominent leaders in the twenty-first century. The strong paternalistic and independent images of white leaders are not entirely rejected, but these images are stretched to include additional characteristics like "encouraging dialogue and truth-telling, being transparent in their communications, and treating people as colleagues and collaborators rather than subordinates."[11] New images and new social characteristics of leadership are required.

The software/technology evolution is the main influencer of these leadership trends. As open communications are encouraged and empowered, styles of leadership need to be changed. Models of open communication are one of the newest and most important trends of leadership in the twenty-first century. The wider and broader networks in online communications, health care service systems, long-distance education systems, and even open, communicative talk shows create and demand new styles of open interactive communication leadership. Unlike the authoritative and bureaucratic top-down communicative traits of leadership, the interactive, transparent, mutual dialogical traits of leadership are emphasized.

Maccoby describes these traits as a form of interactive social character. In his understanding, these characteristics are "interactive," show "identification with peers and siblings," and are "experimental, innovative, and marking" whereas bureaucratic social characteristics are "inner-directed," show "identification with paternal authority," and are "precise, methodical, obsessive."[12] The strengths of these social characteristics lie in "their independence, readiness for change, and quick ability to connect with others and work in a self-managed team," but their weaknesses can be "inauthentically ingratiating and self-marketing."[13] Individuals having these social characteristics are not loyal to the institution or trust people, but take the responsibility to work for meaningful goals or projects. In other words, the images of this style of leadership represent responsibility in terms of work, but not trustworthiness in terms of organizational and/ or personal relations. They are quick to connect with people, but at the same time, quick to move on to others. In some senses, people with this characteristic are more individualistic, independent, and goal-oriented because their socioeconomic base is mostly in "entrepreneurial companies," "internet," "new technologies," "global markets," "employment uncertainty," and "diverse family structures."[14] They are interactive collaborators, coworkers, and coleaders as long as they have a common goal to achieve.

Even though an open, communicative style of leadership is the most critical change in models of leadership currently, it has critical challenges for the following three reasons. First, the characteristics associated with these images (individualistic, independent, lack of loyalty to the institution or people, and moving quickly to other relations depending on the projects) are deeply associated with the culture of individualistic capitalism. Individualistic capitalism is one of the most dangerous factors influencing the mentality of current leadership and its practices. It places the individual "I" at the center of leadership and "others" as followers. It nurtures the privileged group to be more independent and autonomous without any moral or ethical responsibility or guilt. It legitimates the polarization between the privileged group to be more privileged and the deprived group to be more deprived based on individualistic approach to independence and autonomy. It supports individualistic independence and devalues communal interdependence. This individualistic capitalism elevates indifference and apathy as the virtue of independence and autonomy and perceives communal interdependence as the problems of totality. This elevation and perception becomes the fundamental root of the privileged white leadership. In the current postcolonial era, colonial/postcolonial European structures and individual capitalism interplay within the context of US democracy to dismiss the communal values of other worldviews and cultures and eventuate in white leadership.

Second, open, interactive, communicative styles of leadership are often recognized as the independent and free communication styles of leadership. They are accepted as the "good" and "advanced, modern" style of leadership. The question is *who* is good at these styles of leadership. In the analysis of stereotypes, both white, privileged, male and female groups are recognized as better at open, interactive communications than other ethnic groups, particularly Asian immigrant groups.[15] In fact, these communication styles are commonly exercised by privileged white *liberal* groups. The predominant interpretation supporting white stereotype theory explains that even though middle-class Americans grow up in the bureaucratic social environment, they naturally feel conflicted about their submission to bureaucratic bosses, resisted them, and changed.[16] Despite the given environment, the white group challenges bureaucratic society and creates a new, open horizontal relationship with others. Based on this relationship, independent and free communication styles are established. This interpretation implies that other ethnic groups who do not have this natural feeling cannot perform independent and free communication styles. In other words, Asian immigrant groups and other immigrant groups who cannot create horizontal relationship with others under colonial and postcolonial oppression are not able to practice the open communication styles of leadership. Consequently, the open, interactive communication styles of leadership only belong to the privileged white liberal group. Again, it is assumed that the good and advanced modern styles of leadership are predominately and persistently created only by this white group.

Third, the liberal, independent, interactive, free styles of communication are often presented in the form of self-confidence with the mentality of positive thinking, and an excessive optimism.[17] Practices of these mentalities are often exercised from the experience of the privileged white group. Based on the higher educations, economic advancements, political advantages, and hierarchal socioreligious privileges, many white leaders easily imagine themselves as positive thinkers and engage in excessively optimistic behaviors without reference to the harsh reality that other groups face. Their positive experience of being white naturally leads into positive thinking and excessive optimism that again allows white groups to cultivate more self-confidence along with egoistic attitudes more easily than other groups. Positive thinking and excessive optimism are the flip side of white leadership. They experience positive thinking and excessive optimism as a good motivation to develop their self-confidence as leaders. From this experience, they have cultivated liberal, independent, interactive, free styles of communication without fear of systematic challenges. Then, how about other groups? Is it possible for non-white group leaders to develop the liberal, independent, interactive, free styles of communication without positive experience and optimism? Can these styles of communication be effective in every context? Are these styles really "good" and "advanced and modern" leadership that everyone is allowed to practice equally?

As these three reasons demonstrated, development of this open, communicative style of leadership has been deeply engrained with white privileges. Even though this leadership has been developed and exercised in other ethnic groups, especially among various women's groups, it has been predominantly recognized as a style of white leadership only. Therefore, it is important to explore what other styles of leadership have been developed and nurtured in various immigrant groups analyzing their colonial/postcolonial immigrant history and socioeconomic cultural contexts. These styles of leadership will be explored later in this chapter.

It is true that after the civil rights movement, many African American national leaders such as Martin Luther King Jr., Howard Thurman, Rosa Louise McCauley Parks, and currently Barack Obama and Oprah Winfrey have challenged the images of this white leadership and have created new, powerful images of black leadership. Their characteristics can be described as "physically and emotionally whole, spiritually disciplined, intellectually astute, and morally anchored."[18] Their images are more holistic and integrative in all dimensions of their personal and public lives. In the case of King, his leadership is recognized as a powerful prophetic legacy beyond the Christian context. His leadership is discussed in more detail in the next section. Barack Obama, deemed to be one of the greatest presidents and leaders in US history, has brought change and made a difference in many ways for various groups. He tried to reorient "the American perception of identity from division into unity."[19] Using elegant but direct and powerful speech, his rhetorical leadership shows a "process of discovering, articulating, and sharing the available means of influence in order to motivate" all American citizens to collectively participate in change for unity and well-being.[20] His concept of "change" bypasses individual transformation by individual excellence and lies in transformation through "collective work" and "collective effort."[21] He and many black leaders have demonstrated remarkable leadership. They critically challenge models of white traditional leadership to become prophetic voices for justice in this society.

Despite great African American leadership, sacrifices, and the paradigm shift from traditional leadership styles to an interactive, transparent, mutual, dialogical leadership, there are many common traits of leadership that are still formed and controlled under strong white elite influences. As racism persists and most socioeconomic lives are still controlled by the hands of an elite, upper class, white, Anglo-European heterosexual, male group without disability, the identity and images of leadership are also in the hands of this group. The research of Mahzarin R. Banaji and Anthony G. Greenwald shows that people feel safer and more comfortable with white people.[22] Particularly when people have to choose their leaders, this preference becomes clearer. It is not a preference anymore, but an absolute necessity. An analysis of stereotypes in terms of gender and race can explain this phenomenon. In fact, it is impossible to explain leadership dynamics without explaining the dynamics of gender and race in the forms of prejudice and discrimination.

Prejudice against Female Leaders

Prejudice against female leaders is still rampant. There are several ways to explain the persistence of this prejudice. One of them considers stereotypes of female leaders. As was discussed earlier in this chapter, until the twentieth century and even in this twenty-first century, the strong preference for male leaders was deeply correlated with stereotypes based on trait/personality theories. Paul S. Rosenkrantz, Susan R. Vogel, Helen Bee, Inge K. Broverman, and Donald M. Broverman in 1968 found 122 traits that males and females exhibit in terms of stereotypes. Among the 122 traits, twelve were defined as female and twenty-nine were identified as male. Some characteristics of leadership, such as "active, competitive, logical, independent, dominant, acts as a leader, self-confident, ambitious, able to separate feelings from ideals, and knows the way of the world," were only found in males.[23] This research concluded that male traits were seen as desirable characteristics, and women held negative self-concepts about themselves.[24] In another study, Broverman, Broverman, Frank E. Clarkson, Vogel, and Rosenkrantz claimed in 1970 that mental health professionals described male stereotypes as clinically heathier traits than female stereotypes.[25] Much clinical research has discussed male traits as the norm for clinical health including the areas of psychology and psychiatrics. In all aspects of life, including clinical health and spiritual development, female traits were associated with negative images.

However, thirty years later, Muriel N. Nesbitt and Nolan E. Penn, in 2000, reprised the research of Rosenkrantz and colleagues and came to a different conclusion. They claimed that the female traits were associated with much more positive images than thirty years before. The female stereotypes were not considered to be less objective, logical, direct, ambitious, competent, and effective. They concluded that female-associated traits were, in fact, more valued than male-associated traits.[26] In terms of clinical health, Thomas A. Widiger and Shirley Settle in 1987 reevaluated the research of Broverman and colleagues and claimed that "the findings were the result of an imbalanced ratio of male-valued to female-valued items in the dependent measure that forced the subject to display a sex bias."[27] They interpreted the previous results as due to an embedded prejudice against women. Both research projects demonstrated that female traits were no longer less-desirable social characteristics. Female traits were equally valued, even preferred in some contexts, such as nursing and educational settings, and especially in work with small children, work that has been traditionally associated with women's gender roles.

Both studies concluded two things. First, many research projects were conducted on gender-biased frameworks, with the implication that if these biased frameworks were changed, the results would be different. Second, despite both men's and women's preference for male traits in the past, this preference has now changed. Many research projects like these two try to demonstrate how male traits are deeply embedded in the United States as the norm, but they are greatly challenged over time. However, these research studies still could not explain prejudice against women leaders. Though female traits came to be increasingly valued, when it comes to leadership positions, much research in the twenty-first century still shows visible prejudice against female leaders.

Alice H. Eagly and Steven J. Karau have created a role congruity theory to explain this gap between the positive images of female traits and the negative images of female leaders. In 2002, they observed that "perceived incongruity between the female gender role and leadership roles leads to 2 forms of prejudice: (a) perceiving women less favorably than men as potential occupants of leadership roles and (b) evaluating behavior that fulfills the prescriptions of a leader role less favorably when it is enacted by a woman."[28] Even though stereotypes of females are viewed more favorably and some female stereotypes are more favorable than male stereotypes, described in words like "warm," "communal," and "caring for others," prejudices toward female leaders persist.[29] Male traits are still viewed much more favorably in terms of leadership and are often associated with successful managers more than female traits.[30] If female leaders show a more task-oriented character, they are criticized as less congenial and low on interpersonal skills.[31] They must demonstrate the traits of expertise on the job like effective, successful "male" managers, while at the same time acting as women within expected female roles. Particularly when women use self-promotional tactics, they are often evaluated more negatively, specifically by other female workers.[32] For men, self-promotion is encouraged and valued, but for women, it is socially and culturally discouraged. In terms of culturally assigned female roles and virtues, women are expected to show humility and modesty instead of self-promotion. Therefore, when women promote themselves in the workplace, other female workers perceive this behavior as problematic and react negatively. When the incongruity between female gender roles and leadership roles are intensified, women have increased difficulty attaining and experience more barriers to leadership. Even if they become leaders, they have a hard time being successful in their leadership roles.

This incongruity can be also explained by the mentality of the male privileged experience in the workforce. The workplace has been traditionally dominated by men. Many men did not have much experience with women as leaders or managers. In the past, they had seen women as subordinates, secretaries and assistants, not as managers and executives. With this background of privilege, men wanted to retain leadership positions only for themselves, especially in higher leadership positions.[33] A preponderance of male executive positions can be seen as evidence of this mentality. For example, even though women held 51.5 percent of management, professional, and related positions in 2015, they currently hold 20 (or 4 percent) CEO positions at S&P (Standard and Poor) five hundred companies. In the same report, 19.2 percent of women in 2014 held S&P five hundred board seats. Among these women, 80.2 percent are white, 11.7 percent are black, 4.4 percent are Latina, and 3.7 percent are Asian.[34] Despite great improvement in women's participation and promotion in the workforce, strong resistance continues to arise, especially from men when women become leaders. As women enter new positions as leaders, they experience strong resistance from both men who were used not to having female leaders and women who perceive female leaders as not conforming to female gender roles.

In conversation with the role congruity theory, Anne M. Koenig, Eagly, Abigail A. Mitchell, and Tiina Ristikari analyze three prominent leadership paradigm studies ("think manager–think male paradigm," "agency-communion paradigm," and "masculinity-femininity paradigm").[35] Based on this research, they confirm that this mega-analysis established the masculinity of the cultural stereotype of leadership. Even though these three paradigms used different methodologies to measure this meta-analysis, it led to the same conclusion in favor of male leadership.

> In conclusion, this meta-analysis establishes a strong and robust tendency for leadership to be viewed as culturally masculine across three paradigms that use different methods. The implications of the masculinity of leader roles for prejudice against female leaders are straightforward: Men fit cultural construals of leadership better than women do and thus have better access to leader roles and face fewer challenges in becoming successful in them. Despite some overall change toward more

androgynous beliefs about leadership, stereotyping continues to contribute to the labyrinthine challenges that women encounter in attaining roles that yield substantial power and authority. Given the strongly masculine cultural stereotype of leadership quantified by this meta-analysis, these challenges are likely to continue for some time to come.[36]

Continuously producing stereotypes through these three paradigms in favor of themselves, men have fewer challenges than women, so they have better chances of success. As a result, men are seen as better managers and leaders than women. Even though many women keep fighting prejudice against women leaders, these stereotypes keep producing the image that men fit better than women in positions of leadership, so women's struggles continue.

Stereotypes of the LGBTQIA community are another critical example in explaining the incongruity of the gap between gender and leadership. As the stereotype has been formed on the clear binary concept of male and female traits, the existence of the LGBTQIA community itself is a threat to this concept. It shows the problems of heterosexuality and its conflicts. In 2015, the research of William T.L. Cox and Patricia G. Devine found stereotypes of gay men with words such as with "feminine," "fashionable," "flamboyant," "wear tight clothing," and others.[37] In this research, most traits exhibit incongruity between male roles and supposedly female attributes in male bodies. Maylon Hanold argues that current views of the body in leadership literature are based on two assumptions: "1) the body is adequately understood as a biological phenomenon, and 2) uniquely the site of a 'true self.'"[38] These assumptions deny the possibility that the body is a social product. These limited views bring the body into a "docile" assigned process, producing the heterosexual body as the norm and supporting heterosexual structures as the basis of leadership.[39] Mismatch between expected "male gender roles and female attributes in the male body," "female gender roles and male attributes in the female body," and "both gender roles in binary gendered body" not only challenges these assumptions but also causes more conflict in current privileged white leadership. LGBTQIA members and their bodily presence in these mismatched gender roles shake the foundation of the privileged white leadership.

This mismatched gender role causes ambiguity in heterosexual society. It is one of the main reasons LGBTQIA leaders are ignored. This "lack-of-fit" evokes more prejudice and discrimination against LGBTQIA groups and gives them much less chance to be leaders in most sociocultural settings.[40] Many LGBTQIA members experience strong prejudice and discrimination in the job market. In a similar manner, promotion and job advancement are denied in many cases with hidden or overt discrimination. As current leadership images are predominantly tied to masculine traits, this mismatch brings suspicion and anxiety about the leadership abilities of LGBTQIA members under the heavy influence of toxic heterosexual systems. As LGBTQIA members enter the workforce or school system, prejudices and discrimination against them become more visibly violent and dangerous. They are hardly ever given opportunities to be leaders, and even when they are, they have a hard time becoming successful as leaders under harsh, biased judgment and evaluation.

Prejudice against Racial Ethnic Groups

The current construals of leadership are more likely to strongly favor white groups for leadership positions over other racial ethnic groups. Racism is, perhaps, the most critical barrier for racial ethnic groups to hold leadership positions. It requires countless sacrifices from various racial ethnic groups. As racism exists and persists, leadership positions are difficult to attain for these racial ethnic groups. Racial ethnic nonwhite women confront a triple barrier. Prejudice and discrimination against racial ethnic groups occur in many sociopolitical contexts just as prejudice against female leaders occurs everywhere. Despite the visible growth in terms of access to and success in education and economic advancement for racial ethnic groups, most leadership positions are overwhelmingly occupied by white elites. As negative stereotypes of female traits were strongly correlated with negative images of women leaders, negative stereotypes of racial ethnic groups are one of the most difficult barriers that racial ethnic groups experience in leadership positions in the United States.

The study of racial ethnic stereotypes began with the research of Daniel Katz and Kenneth Braly in 1933; G.M. Gilbert in 1951; and Marvin Karlins, Thomas Coffman, and Gary Walters in 1969. These three studies laid out many traits and asked people to choose images for African American groups. The most frequently selected traits for African Americans are similar in these three studies, but there are some traits that generally decreased or disappeared over time. In 1933, Katz and Braly selected the top ten traits describing African Americans:

"1) superstitious, 2) lazy, 3) happy-go-lucky/ignorant, 4) musical/ostentatious, 5) very religious, 6) stupid, 7) physically dirty, 8) native, 9) slovenly, and 10) unreliable."[41] Both Gilbert's study in 1951[42] and Karlins, Coffman, and Walters's study in 1969[43] showed similar findings. Most stereotypes of the African American group in this study were extremely negative and biased. There was clear prejudice and discrimination against the African American group in these studies. Considering US history at that time, it was not surprising to find this result. In these three studies, eight traits continuously recurred: superstitious, lazy, happy-go-lucky, ignorant, musical, ostentatious, very religious, and stupid. As these research studies used the same traits for the research, these eight traits were consistently selected by participants as images of African Americans. Most of these stereotypical traits had very negative and even dangerous implications. Considering the sociopolitical history of the United States in terms of racial struggles from the 1930s to the 1980s, the results of these studies were the historical products of racism. Strong racism produced severe prejudice and discrimination against African Americans as a group, and this prejudice and discrimination were systematically and institutionally embedded in many aspects of academic studies in the name of science.

Stereotypes of African Americans have changed in recent studies. In 1994, Yolanda Niemann, Leilani Jennings, Richard Rozelle, James Baxter, and Elroy Sullivan surveyed students free style, not listing categories, and found different stereotypes. For African American males, "athletic" is ranked as number one[44] and for African American females, "speak loudly" is ranked as number one.[45] In 1995, the research of Patricia G. Devine and Andrew J. Elliot illustrated that many of the top eight traits shown in the studies of Katz and Braly, Gilbert, and Karlins, Coffman, and Walters had disappeared.[46] In 2015, using a theory of stereotype directionality instead of providing trait categories, the research of William T.L. Cox and Patricia G. Devine found other stereotypical traits for African American males: "poor, athletic, criminal, tall, basketball, threatening, good at sport, secretive, poor articulation, likes hip-hop, wears baggy clothing, rapper, and others."[47] In these recent studies, there are two prominent positive traits: musical and athletic ability. These two traits are recognized as positive images for African Americans as a group by the media and culture. However, as shown even in recent studies, the stereotypes of African Americans, especially African American males, have remained negative. Images of African Americans as "criminal" and "low in intelligence/non-college" are particularly persistent negative images of African American males.

These negative images produce prejudice and discrimination against the group in many aspects of their daily lives. Many suffer from injustice in public and private spheres. Consequences and impacts of these negative stereotypes are strong barriers for African Americans as a group to be seen as leaders in socioeconomic political contexts.

In the case of African American females, women leaders are challenged by many more complexities in proclaiming leadership. Because of African American women's distinctive experience, many African American women leaders face different types of prejudice and discrimination from white Anglo women and men and from African American males. Patricia S. Parker in her research argues that women are treated as a homogeneous group based on white female experience and racism and sexism are treated as parallel processes with common effects.[48] Analyzing the leadership of African American women executives (AAWEs), she finds a different approach to understanding leadership from African American women's cultural points of view. Comparing the socialized leadership traits of female Anglo-Americans and of male Anglo-Americans with the traits of African American female leaders, Parker finds the socialized traits of African American female leadership as "self-confident, independent, autonomous, and nurturing."[49] In terms of leadership behaviors, African American female leaders demonstrate androgynous and direct communication behaviors, whereas female Anglo-Americans show collaborative and interdependent behaviors and male Anglo-Americans exhibit instrumental and assertive behaviors. In terms of leadership styles, "democratic, directing/participative, 'strong' influence strategies, and transformational" are descriptors of African American female leadership, whereas "democratic, participative, 'weak' influence strategies, altruism-based strategies, and transformational" describe female Anglo female leadership and "autocratic, directing, 'strong' influence strategies, punishment-based strategies, and transactional" are used to characterize as Anglo male leadership.[50] In this analysis, African American female leadership does not fit the binary structure of Anglo male and female leadership. Rather, they exhibit mixed as well as distinctive leadership traits, behaviors, and styles. Parker claims that the reason African American women have this distinctive leadership is rooted in their unique sociocultural experience. Because of the oppression of African American history and culture, African American mothers emphasize to their daughters that they must "possess a degree of autonomy, strength, independence and self-confidence in ability," and they socialize them to be confident, resilient, self-reliant, and assertive as they teach their daughters to resist the dominant white culture.[51] This distributive training, communal mentality, and family education form positive images of self-esteem and emotional stability for African American female adolescents.

In Parker's AAWEs study, African American executives demonstrate amazing leadership traits, behaviors, and styles even though these leaders face double or triple discrimination and biases. In order to fight against this discrimination, they develop "biculturalism, avoidance, and confrontation" as their leadership strategies and perform "creativity, risk-taking, boundary spanning, divergent thinking, and behavior complexity."[52] The case of African American women's leadership exemplifies how African American female leaders overcome stereotypes and create their own type of leadership. Despite the social context, they develop a unique leadership style from survival skills. At the same time, this case discloses how African American female leaders struggle differently from white female leaders. Under the discrimination of race, sex, and gender and its side effects, they are uniquely situated to struggle with stereotypes of the white structure.

In fact, much stereotype research was exclusively focused on African American groups because of unpredictable timelines of immigration to the United States by various ethnic groups. Early racial ethnic stereotype studies, other than those focused on African Americans, did not describe traits of racial ethnic groups as ethnic minority Americans, but as traits of *foreigners* from the different countries from which various ethnic immigrants came. In Gilbert's study, two Asian immigrant groups are selected: Japanese and Chinese. Stereotypes of Japanese were determined as "intelligent, industrious, progressive, shrewd, sly, imitative, extremely nationalistic, and treacherous" while stereotypes of Chinese were determined as "superstitious, sly, conservative, tradition-loving, loyal to family ties, quiet, reserved, and industrious."[53] Later, there were some other studies that considered stereotypes for racial ethnic groups as ethnic Americans. For example, in Niemann and colleagues, there are different stereotypical images of various ethnic groups. The top 20 percent of synonyms used for Mexican American males: "lower class (first ranked), hard worker, antagonistic, dark skin, non-college, pleasant, black/brown/dark hair, and ambitionless"; for Mexican females: "black/brown/dark hair (first ranked) attractive, pleasant, dark skin, lower class, overweight, baby makers, and family oriented"; for Asian males: "intelligent (first ranked), short, achievement-oriented, speak softly, and hard worker"; for Asian females: "intelligent" (first ranked) speak softly, pleasant, and short."[54]

Interestingly, unlike other groups, for Asian American male groups, there was one distinctive item on the list: speak with accent.[55] Even though it is not listed within the top 20 percent, it is listed in the top fifteen responses in order of frequency. It is a distinctive item in the list that only Asian male groups have.

In Gilbert's study, the stereotypes of (white) Americans are listed as "industrious, intelligent, materialistic, ambitious, progressive, pleasure-loving, alert, efficient, aggressive, and individualistic."[56] In the research of Niemann and colleagues, the top 20 percent of synonyms used for Anglo-American males are listed as "intelligent, egotistical, upper class, pleasant/friendly, racist, and achievement-oriented," and the top 20 percent of synonyms used for Anglo-American females are "attractive, intelligent, egotistical, pleasant/friendly, blonde/light hair, and sociable/socially active."[57] In comparison with the stereotypes of the white male group, the stereotypes of racial ethnic groups have many more negative images, regardless of national origin. Traits such as criminal, non-college, ambitionless, lower class, baby makers, speak softly, speak loudly, speak with accent, and unmannerly are the opposite of traits suitable for leaders. Reflecting on the stereotypes of racial ethnic groups, most traits are related to economic and educational disadvantages, cultural behaviors, and language issues. For African American groups, low economic status and less educational opportunities are projected on the negative images of their stereotypes such as criminal, ambitionless, and non-college. For Latinx groups, the recent national focus on the immigrant issue is deeply associated with their immigrant status being perceived as negative. Seen as "illegal" immigrants, their presence is denied. As their presence is denied, their leadership is not considered legitimate. For Asian Americans, lack of communication skills indicated by stereotypes of speaking softly and speaking with an accent is often evaluated as a problem for their leadership. Seen as foreigners or tourists, their presence in the United States is not recognized. Therefore, despite their economic improvement, their leadership is hardly discussed.

As discussed in this chapter, many people think that leaders or managers should be "ambitious, confident, self-sufficient, and dominant, that is, well endowed with agentic and competent qualities."[58] Common images of leaders in the leadership theories discussed earlier are based on intelligence, efficiency, achievement, ambition, independence, and communication. As we have shown, these images of leaders are much closer to the stereotypes of the white, elite, privileged upper class, male group without disability than to any other racial ethnic groups. Each racial ethnic group experiences different disadvantages of negative stereotypes and negative leadership images. The correlation between negative stereotypes and negative leadership images are closely associated with prejudice and discrimination against women and various racial ethnic groups. Consequently, women and various racial ethnic groups have fewer opportunities to be in positions of leadership. In the case of racial ethnic women's groups, opportunities to be in positions of leadership are very rare.

However, even though this reality prevails, some leadership scholars, such as Eagly and Chin, claim that women and racial ethnic group members have demonstrated a higher quality of leadership because of their racial ethnic experience and female experience. Because women and racial ethnic groups have learned how to negotiate between white and ethnic cultures and/or between male and female values, women and these groups have practiced how to solve problems and to find a vision for collaborating, and to embrace flexibility and openness to change in any circumstances.[59]

It is true that as the privileged white group holds the most sociopolitical and economic power positions, the good and positive images of leaders are continuously produced in the stereotypes of this white group. As the good and positive images of leaders become the images of this group, they have much better chances of receiving opportunities to be leaders in power again and again. However, despite the vicious circle of white power, in US history there are many powerful racial ethnic male and female leaders who overcame barriers, challenged the vicious circle of the white power structure, brought change to this history, and transformed this society for others in many ways. Looking into the leaders and leadership of African American group and Latinx groups in the next two sections, we will clearly recognize divergent and powerful leadership approaches that are different from those that are dominated by the privileged white group. Exploring African American leadership and Latinx leadership shows the existence of various powerful leaderships in the current US context and embrace different models of leadership. At the same time, by reflecting on leadership of these groups, it helps us have a better and deeper understanding of Asian immigrant leadership and its development process.

African American Leaders and Leadership in a US Socioreligious Context

Ethical Leadership in African American Leaders

Even though the images of leaders and leadership are predominantly painted by the images of white groups, African American leaders have led the way in US history and permanently changed the landscape of leadership in the US. Many African American religious leaders and civil rights activists have paved the way to reimagine the images of leaders and the concept of leadership in the United States. Through the civil rights movement, African American leadership was undeniably recognized in public. Their accomplishments not only changed the history of the US civil rights movement but also lifted countless African American people's lives from overt and degrading forms of oppression.

As discussed in the previous section, the public images of African Americans are perceived as criminal and dangerous. Even though recent studies show some positive changes in the stereotypes for African American groups, a long colonial history of slavery has prevented white culture from imagining African Americans as leaders. The remnants of colonial mentality cast doubt on African Americans' leadership capability. They distill from the experience of slavery the image of permanent followers. The destructive character of these images manipulates the public to sweep away sociopolitical prejudice and discrimination against African Americans and perpetuate their image as "Slave Americans."[60] The heritage of colonial/postcolonial constructions regenerates the dominance of white leadership over African American lives in the form of capitalism. Capitalism legitimates the heritage of colonial/postcolonial constructions as "norms" of the society in laws, principles, customs, and infrastructure. Many African American leaders express critical concern over these oppressive structures as they struggle with these "legitimated" laws and principles.

Many African American leadership scholars criticize the public images of African Americans from the toxic colonial history of slavery and try to find new foundations for African American leadership based on their own culture and religious traditions. Even though they understand African American leadership in various ways, many of them recognize African American leadership in the framework of moral and ethical leadership because many African American leaders, such as Martin Luther

King Jr. and Malcolm X, are profoundly connected with religious belief and ethical traditions.

Peter J. Paris defines the foundation of African American leadership from the perspective of the ethics of moral development. Based on "the dialectical relationship between person and community," he claims that individuals form their moral characters.[61] Depending on the communal values and norms in a particular context and the relationship with others, individuals develop their morality and ethics. To develop good moral character, there is a precondition: it is the will to be trained.[62] Not everyone has this desire. No one is just born a leader and naturally moral. Leaders should have the will to be trained voluntarily. Understanding community values, and experiencing communal support and individual personal mentoring, moral training is a crucial part of the process of becoming leaders. Without moral training in the dialectical relationship between person and community, it is impossible to develop ethical leaders. Paris sees moral training as necessary to the process of becoming a leader, but he does not see it as sufficient. Becoming a leader needs something more.

> Along with being moral, leaders must understand the rules on which moral practice is based and be able to guide the actions of others in accordance with those guidelines. Moral leaders not only must have the capacity to regulate their own lives in accordance with moral virtue, but also must be able to lead others to do likewise. In other words, they must display the capacity for good judgement, that which Aristotle called "practical wisdom." . . . Thus, good leaders are those who faithfully embody the basic traditions and values of those who are being led, and who have the ability to inspire the loyalty of the latter.[63]

Paris's definition of good leaders is within the paradigm of transformational leadership. Like transformational leaders, good leaders are required to have higher standards of morality and ethics, inspire others, stimulate them, and make them follow.[64] However, there is a difference between Paris and the transformational scholars. Whereas the transformational scholars define transformational leaders as those who raise "followers' level of awareness and consciousness about the importance and value of designated outcomes, and ways of reaching them,"[65] Paris's definition of good leaders includes the requirement that they have to know and embody the traditions and values of their followers, regardless of the will or goal of the leaders. Good leaders are not in a position to persuade followers to understand the designed outcome or the goal of the organizations, but rather they are in a position to embody the traditions and virtues of the people who are led. They are the embodiment of the community. In the case of African American leadership, good African American leaders need to embody African American traditions and values that African Americans believe and practice. Even though African American leaders perform different styles of leadership and have different thoughts, they share one thing in common, "namely, loyalty to the cause of serving the good of the African American community."[66] Serving the good of the African American community is the most important purpose of African American leadership. Many African American leaders have demonstrated their best effort serving the good of African American communities, whatever it takes. Practicing leadership virtues such as "honesty, truthfulness, forgiveness, forbearance, courage, generosity, faithfulness (loyal to the cause), and justice," many African American leaders fight against injustice and sacrifice their lives for their communities.[67]

In the research of Walter Earl Fluker, the ethical leadership within the African American context is defined as "the critical appropriation and embodiment of moral traditions that have shaped the character and shared meanings of a people (an ethos)."[68] Like Paris, Fluker also seeks the meaning of African America leadership from African American traditions, values, and norms for serving the collective communal good. Focused on African American moral tradition, experience, and history, Fluker reconstructs the formation of African American leadership in the intersection of personal and social transformation. Analyzing the leadership legacies of Howard Washington Thurman (1899–1981) and Martin Luther King Jr. (1929–1968) and lifting up the names of female leaders such as Ida B. Wells, Mary Church Terrell, Mary McLeod Bethune, Nannie Helen Burroughs, Fannie Lou Hamer, Pauli Murray, Ella Baker, Marian Wright Edelman, and Vasthi McKenzie, he claims that African American leadership led and constituted the foundation of American democracy and created the ethical leadership model.

Fluker understands ethical leadership as being based on a triangular model: self, social, and spiritual. He sees these three areas as dynamically interrelated dimensions of human existence. Based on these dimensions, he addresses character, community, and civility. As the self is formed, there are three characteristics that are necessary for ethical leadership: integrity, empathy, and hope.[69] Leaders should examine their selves and their personal life experiences in terms of these three characteristics. Civility is the main challenge with which leaders struggle. To lead a healthy civic life, Fluker suggests that leaders should practice reverence (spirit), respect (public), and recognition (personal).[70] Community is the primary concern of this model and leadership in community quests for courage, justice, and compassion from leaders.[71] Each dimension interrelates with the other. By "remembering, retelling, and reliving" African American personal and collective stories, Fluker claims that African American leaders, especially religious leaders, have practiced leadership and empowered individual communities and the broader society.[72]

Leadership of Martin Luther King Jr.

Both Paris and Fluker and many secular and religious leadership scholars agree the leadership of Martin Luther King Jr. is the model of leadership par excellence. When King appeared in public as a leader of the Montgomery bus boycott, no one imagined that he would be the most famous leader of the civil rights movement and would change the image of US leadership. Since King grew up as a pastor's son and became an ordained clergy, it is not difficult to imagine that his leadership was deeply rooted in his religious practice and faith. Paris claims that King's concepts of leadership such as nonviolence, love (agape), justice, human dignity, reconciliation, freedom, and morality, are formed from his understanding of God and humanity.[73] King's theological belief and spiritual faith based on African American Christian traditions shaped his leadership practice. Civil disobedience is one of his well-known nonviolent leadership practices, which shows his theological understanding of the unjust law in relation to the African American historical and cultural context.

> How does one determine whether a law is just or unjust? A just law is a man-made code that squares with the moral law or the law of God. An unjust law is a code that is out of harmony with the moral law. To put it in the terms of St. Thomas Aquinas: An unjust law is a human law that is not rooted in eternal law and natural law. Any law that uplifts human personality is just. Any law that degrades human personality is unjust. All segregation statutes are unjust because

segregation distorts the soul and damages the personality. It gives the segregator a false sense of superiority and the segregated a false sense of inferiority. Segregation, to use the terminology of the Jewish philosopher Martin Buber, substitutes an "I-it" relationship for an "I-thou" relationship and ends up relegating persons to the status of things. Hence segregation is not only politically, economically and sociologically unsound, it is morally wrong and sinful. Paul Tillich has said that sin is separation. Is not segregation an existential expression of man's tragic separation, his awful estrangement, his terrible sinfulness? Thus it is that I can urge men to obey the 1954 decision of the Supreme Court, for it is morally right; and I can urge them to disobey segregation ordinances, for they are morally wrong. . . . An unjust law is a code that a numerical or power majority group compels a minority group to obey but does not make binding on itself. . . . A law is unjust if it is inflicted on a minority that, as a result of being denied the right to vote, had no part in enacting or devising the law. . . . Sometimes a law is just on its face and unjust in its application.[74]

Disobeying the law and accepting the penalty of imprisonment, King showed his leadership in loyalty to his Christian faith. As he firmly believed segregation is a sin, he practiced his belief in the action of civil disobedience, school boycotts, and civil rights legislation changes as the leader of civil rights movement. Through his leadership, he recognized the African American moral and ethical tradition of the black church and faith as a foundation to transform white US society—a new force to bring social change that challenged the white—dominated structures. "As a Christian, he believed that as coworkers with God, leaders are called to create a just and loving society through redemptive suffering."[75] King called these leaders transformed nonconformists, who could never be in a comfortable position and persistently work "through the valley of the shadow of suffering, losing a job, or having a six-year-old daughter ask, 'Daddy, why do you have to go to jail so much?'"[76] A transformed nonconformist is the leader who is willing to work with others until the end. His sermon "The Dimensions of a Complete Life" is a good example of how leaders should practice leadership.

> As long as there is poverty in the world I can never be rich, even if I have a billion dollars. As long as diseases are rampant and millions of people in this world cannot expect to live more than twenty-eight or thirty years, I can never be totally healthy even if I just got a good checkup at Mayo Clinical. I can never be what I ought to be until you are what you ought to be.[77]

King himself practiced this kind of leadership in his life as he led the civil rights movement as a prophetic leader. He saw how the constructions of racial segregation brought economic injustice and exploited not only African American groups, but also poor white groups.[78] Because he was aware of varieties of injustice, he was not afraid to work with white persons who had goodwill. His leadership was practiced on the principles of inclusivity and harmony. He inspired others to work together to fight against racial segregation from their own positions of privilege and challenged the African American church to be the place of transformation for social action against injustice. He was a charismatic leader who demonstrated a higher standard of leadership.

However, there are some criticisms of his leadership. Thandeka argues that King failed to recognize the complexities of white shame because he "assessed this white shame from the standpoint of Negro shame and dignity."[79] Thandeka claims that King made this mistake based on three factors: First, King interpreted "unmerited suffering" as a necessity and "made it (the) virtue of love" based on his own experience of the transformative power of "unmerited suffering."[80] Second, "[H]e believed that the Negro protester could transform the humiliation of their own unmerited suffering into dignity."[81] Third, he concluded that "the newfound courage, esteem, and dignity of the Negro protester would stir the moral conscience of whites," who would "discover the moral cost to themselves—the wages *for* whiteness—of their mistreatment of the Negro."[82] As King transformed his own unmerited suffering into dignity, he strongly believed that other African American protesters would have the same transformative experience and inspire other whites to be enlightened. Because of this belief, he trusted the capacity for self-awareness and moral conscience of white groups and built the relationship and friendship with them. King's strategies, especially including working with white groups, had been the cause of many debates among different groups and even in African American groups about how to approach the civil rights movement. His strategies were adopted or rejected in other groups in this movement.

Despite the debates and disagreements among African American leaders such as Malcolm X, King became an ideal, beloved, ethical leader who was honest, truthful, courageous, faithful, and willing to take risks. He recreated the images of African American leaders as trustful and prophetic in the white-dominated culture and set up a higher standard of African American leadership in public. Because of King's leadership, the colonial constructions of racial privilege were exposed, and many discriminatory practices and laws were changed. Not only many African American leaders but also other social activists and leaders followed him as their role model.

African American Religious Leadership and Its Challenges

Many African American leadership scholars agree that African American religious leadership was the foundation of African American leadership. They claim that African American communities, especially churches, are the main resources of their leadership formation. However, there is a serious concern: the African American church has lost its leadership role in African American communities. Dale P. Andrews argues that black churches were impacted by the American revival movement and assimilated themselves to American individualism, adopting individual religious practices such as personal salvation and individualistic morality and responsibility.[83]

> The prominence of American individualism in the black religious culture, most vivid in evangelicalism, subverted a mutuality between black churches and their communities. Personal salvation and religious piety emphasized an individualistic morality in black churches. Undoubtedly this religious individualism contributed intensely to the displacement of black churches from their historical centrality in black communities. . . . The fragmentation of the African American community and the displacement of black churches complicated and even undermined any secular or religious attempts at social redress.[84]

Moreover, he claims that black churches lost touch with middle-income groups as well as with lower-income groups.[85] Many members of both groups do not have any connection, or have only a minimal connection, with the church. Neither group trusts black churches and their leadership roles in society, as they encounter racism in their own positions of privilege or oppression. American individualism collides with white racism to dismiss the importance of the communal values of African American culture and history. As black churches lost their historical and social role, many African American religious leaders have had a hard time practicing leadership against racism based on the communal sense of justice. Rather, they are asked to claim a justice defined as a sense of individual human rights and freedom.[86] Because racism became more difficult to fight in the form of American individualism, the communal sense of African American leadership was disrupted and displaced. Historically, black churches functioned as major connectors or mediators of black communities. However, as the chasm between African American middle-income groups and lower-income groups deepened, and as black churches lost touch with these two groups, African American leaders experienced more severe segregation and miscommunication in their own black communities.[87] Consequently, their leadership practice faces more difficulties in working collaboratively together with black communities as a whole toward racial justice through social action.

Besides this challenge, there is another challenge that African American leadership needs to address. It is the inner struggles of the African American self-identity as leaders. Lee H. Butler points out that as many African Americans have struggled with racism, classism, sexism, and genderism, they have suffered from forced internalization of these harmful dynamics unconsciously and consciously. Under the power of colonial and racial oppressive structures, many African Americans have internalized the values of colonial/postcolonial white capital culture as the norm for society even though they have consciously resisted and fought against these values. While the white worldview embraces the mentality of "I am because you are not," the African American worldview teaches "I am because you are."[88] Colonial/postcolonial white capitalist culture tries to implant otherness as the enemy to destroy, but African American traditions and culture teach otherness as a part of the community. However, as African Americans have lived as the other, not as a part of US white society, they experience otherness in marginalization.

In the historical memory of the experience of slavery, many African Americans have been forced to live by the historical, cultural, and sociopolitical manipulation of "being chattel, 'slave for life,' powerless, hopeless, helpless, and being degraded."[89] Having their African American heritage denied and being forced to accept the position of "Slave Americans,"[90] they have difficulty seeing themselves as leaders. Being a leader in white society means being white. To be a leader, African American and other ethnic groups are forced into the process of "learning to be white" based on the white expectation of assimilation.[91] However, because of the models of innovative and charismatic African American leaders, African American and ethnic leaders have fought this process. "The new 'rules of the game' thus contain *both* the legacy of movement efforts to rearticulate the meaning of race and to mobilize minorities politically on the basis of the new racial ideologies thus achieved, *and* the heritage of deep-seated racism and inequality."[92] These new rules of the game were achieved by the suffering and sacrifices of countless African American leaders and other ethnic leaders.

Butler explains this achievement in the paradigm theory of African American communal identity formation (TAACIF). It is neither dualistic nor stage theory. He creates this developmental theory as "an issue-oriented paradigm" that is based on two periods in life: a foundational period and a constructive period.[93] In a foundational period (the early life), historical self is formed and this self is continuously formed and directed by African Spirituality at a deeper level as this person meets a constructive period (the latter period of life). The ideas of both periods are "mediated by the energies of *Rage/Creativity*."[94] He captures rage not as a destructive force but as a transformative energy to change a way of life. Because "African American culture was founded and established upon the interaction of the Historical African Self, African Spirituality and the Creativity to maintain an identity of courage and integrity, rather than being overtaken and destroyed by Rage," African Americans are not buried under rage.[95] Rather, Lee claims that they are encouraged to transform rage into creativity.

As he analyzes on the side of the foundational period, he illustrates "emotional development," "existential longing," "learning the rules," and "identity and play" as the issues of the historical self.[96] For the side of the constructive period, he sees "relational development," "existential search," "living the paradox," and "identity and work" as the issues of African spirituality.[97] These pairs of issues are always correlated and interact with each other at every level. From these correlations and interactions, both the historical self and African spirituality constitute a collective past that African Americans lived. At the same time, both are critical resources for African Americans' future. Lee believes that three distinctive ideas (Historical Self, Rage/Creativity, and African Spirituality) form and support African American's communal identity formation and help them restore their humanity and integrity. This formation process in terms of personality is not necessary development only for African American leaders. However, African American leaders are the main ones to show the example of this process. Even though it is true that many African Americans, including African American leaders, have suffered with their self-images and the stereotypes under the toxic influence of white colonial/postcolonial culture, they have transformed their rage into creativity and challenged this society to pursue the communal and individual well-being of the African American community.

African American Women's Leadership

Along with African American leaders' identity issue, African American women's leadership has been an important issue for African American leadership studies. Few African American leaders are recognized and respected in public, and fewer African American women leaders get such attention. African American women have worked hard on both racial oppression and the oppression of womanhood simultaneously, but public images of African American leadership do not include African American women. However, in recent decades, many female African American scholars have introduced into the literature African American women's leadership and their activism in social movements and other fields.

In a search of African American women's leadership, Ruth L. Hall, BraVada Garrett-Akinsanya, and Michael Hucles study African American women's leadership from black feminist leadership in the time of slavery to contemporary black feminist leadership in various fields, such as social activism, politics, health professions, religions, and others. They believe that "black feminism is the space where race, gender, class, and activism converge and emerge creating a positive and powerful multi-dimensional vision of how to implement strategies and opportunities for Black women."[98] Many African American women see leadership and create a vision for African American women based on black feminism. Beverly Guy-Sheftall, Patricia Hill Collins, Alice Walker, bell hooks, and other African American women similarly state that black feminism is the place to consciously fight against oppression and create a vision for fostering community from the unique perspective of African American women.[99] Understanding marginality as the transforming place, many African American women leaders use their marginalized experience as transforming power. Hall, Garrett-Akinsanya, and Hucles define these black feminist leaders as follows:

> Black women activists who, from the intersections of race and gender, develop paths, provide a direction, and give voice to Black women. Black feminist leaders lead by example and generate opportunities for change, provide encouragement and skills to others, and ignite a desire in other Black women to create conditions for success. The ultimate goal of a Black feminist leader is to eliminate the multiple oppressions that compromise the lives of Black women. Race and gender anchor Black feminism and form the divining rod that makes Black feminist leadership unique.... Many Black feminist leaders' roots are in low income families and poor communities. Consequently, Black feminist leaders have always recognized the compromising conditions facing a disproportionate number of poor Black women who lack access to resources.[100]

Hall, Garrett-Akinsanya, and Hucles in their research illustrate how these black women leaders struggle and work in US history. Lifting up Harriet Tubman, Sojourner Truth, and Maria Stewart and their work in the suffragist and abolitionist movement, they demonstrate how these leaders led slave women to be free and challenged the roles of slave women in relation to white women socially and politically. After analyzing the legacy of slavery and its influence, they explore the lives of Ida B. Wells and Mary Church Terrell, who worked against lynching and formed the National Association of Colored Women (NACW) in the black women's club movement as core leaders.[101] For the early twentieth century, they illustrate achievements of many African American women leaders in various fields such as Mary McLeod Bethune in politics; Madam C.J. Walker in industry; Dr. Dorothy Ferebee in medicine; and Minnie Smith, Ma Rainey, Bessie Smith, and Billie Holiday in entertainment.[102] For the mid-twentieth century and the civil rights era, many African American women leaders joined the civil rights movement, the Black Power movement, the modern women's rights movement, and the modern gay rights movement.[103] Activists such as Rosa Parks, Fannie Lou Hamer, Ella Baker, Barbara Smith and Angela Davis, were the prominent leaders in these social movements. In the same era, many other African American women led and formed various organizations to support African American women's professional lives, such as Martha Franklin, who formed the national Association of Colored Graduate Nurses (NACGN); Shirley Chisholm, who was "the first black woman elected to Congress"; Patricia Roberts Harris who was cochair of "National Women's Committee on Civil Rights during the Kennedy administration," the first black woman to hold an ambassadorship, and "the first black woman in history to serve on a president's cabinet"; and Pauli Murray, who was "the first black woman ordained as a priest in the Episcopal Church."[104] Even in the twenty-first century, many African American women have been the first women in many different fields.

Hall, Garrett-Akinsanya, and Hucles conclude that black feminist leaders still struggle with "the Big Four Barriers-racism, sexism, classism, heterosexism/homophobia" but continue to create pathways and change the system, demonstrating the ability to adapt and transform under harsh circumstances and creating a space to connect with others with a positive cultural consciousness of African American values and culture.[105]

In the research on African American women's leadership in relation to ethical leadership, Marcia Y. Riggs gives more attention specifically to the black women's club movement. Understanding religion, education, and social reform as the interconnected spheres for the ethical tradition of African American women, she researches black women's leadership, especially that of the elite among them, by analyzing the National Association of Colored Women (NACW) and its ethical terms.[106] The NACW was founded in 1896 and became a leading agency for African American women's socioreligious movement against race, gender, and class oppression. This movement was a coalition of various women's organizations, such as prayer circles, literary societies, and professional groups in deep relationship with the black church.[107]

Riggs analyzes this movement using three ethical terms: "renunciation, inclusivity, and responsibility."[108] Renunciation is a critical part of African American female elite leadership. It is one of the most important leadership disciplines for African American female leaders. As African American female elite leaders understand commonality, construct shared understandings, and work together in solidarity with various class groups, they should be aware of their own "privilege of difference" and renounce it.[109] This privilege of difference is not the difference that is used to exclude others, but the difference that understands others. This privilege is not the same kind of privilege as the privilege of white groups. Recognizing the gap between middle-income and lower-income classes within African American groups, African American female elite leaders need to renounce their own privilege in terms of class and education and understand others in equally different positions. This renunciation deeply interrelates with inclusivity. Riggs sees inclusivity as a principal value and requirement of the black women's club movement to break through boundaries to recognize interrelationship.[110] It is not a unity forced by dominant groups. It comes from interrelationship. "Inclusivity means that any quest for unity must be premised upon interrelationships between the different 'we's' we are rather than upon homogenization to create an 'us' or domination to maintain unity."[111] In order to have inclusivity, African American female leaders as moral agents have to mediate two opposing sides, that is, between "accommodative and aggressive political activism, between religious radicalism for and the socioeconomics of societal change, between progress for individual Blacks and progress for Blacks as a group."[112] This mediation requires these leaders to *live in tension with*, not to aim at an end.[113]

As Riggs criticizes the lack of an adequate consideration of the need for intragroup accountability in the black church and the distorted moral vision of the black church tradition, she emphasizes the need for African American female leaders to embody renunciation, inclusivity, and responsibility as the moral vision of the beloved community, developing the following characteristics:

> 1. These leaders will be interpreters who exhibit moral courage . . . 2. These leaders will be facilitators who are guiding a process of mediating differing ethical positions so as to engender creative moral responses . . . 3. These leaders have committed but not absolutist moral postures, leaving themselves open to transformation in and through the very process of mediating the moral debate and agency that they are seeking to facilitate.[114]

Riggs illustrates the roles of African American leaders as moral agents, interpreters, and facilitators based on the distinctive contribution of the ethical tradition of African American women. She claims that these African American female leaders have used leadership to encourage the African American church and African American community to work not only for racial justice in society but also gender justice as God's justice.

Though African American women's leadership is invisible and hardly recognized, it has been always present to counter stereotypes of African American women in their roles of mother, daughter, friends, great queens, warriors, teachers, farmers, weavers, artisans, musicians, mystics, activists, and other positions. Reflecting on the actions and roles found in African American women's history, Toni C. King and S. Alease Ferguson recognize four basic pillars that undergird black feminist and black female leadership: "(1) the legacy of struggle; (2) the search for voice and the refusal to be silenced; (3) the impossibility of separating intellectual inquiry from political activism; and (4) the direct application of empowerment to everyday life."[115] Finding African American women's leadership from the motherline in the lives of transgenerational African American women such as Harriet Tubman, Sojourner Truth, Ida B. Wells, Rosa Parks, Fannie Lou Hammer, Alice Walker, Toni Morrison, bell hooks, Delores Williams, and countless other African American women, they define African American women's leadership as "the desire, ability and efforts to influence the world around us, based upon an ethic of care for self and other and fueled by a vision that one sustains over time."[116] African American women's leadership starts from the survival of family and community. Based on the motherline knowledge that helps African American women learn how to resist oppression and engage in the leadership of social change, African American women know how to understand who they are and what they can be as leaders. Understanding African American women's lives as a conflicted text to both lifting up their powerful voices and endangering to reveal African American women's survival knowledge, King and Ferguson rediscover African American women's leadership in the space of their history, work, and social actions.[117]

As many African American leadership scholars demonstrate in their research, African American women's leadership as well as African American men's leadership are always exercised for the African American community and on its behalf. Their leadership was never intended for individual achievement or privileges. The legacy of black leadership is based on the well-being of the whole community. From the slavery era to the present day, one of the major goals of their leadership is to achieve racial justice in the United States. As many African American male leaders work for the rights of African American men and their communities, many African American female leaders work in the intersection of race, gender, and class for their families, children, communities, and womanhood. The current goal of both African American male and female leadership is still the well-being of the entire black community. Even though many African American leaders are aware of how American individualism and capitalism disrupt their communal values and the morals of black tradition and culture, and even though they know how much the black church is weakened in the connection with the current generation and community, they do not lose faith in the black community as their own. Countless African American leaders recognize African American religious traditions and the black church as the main resource for their leadership and work toward justice through this network. Even though many African American leaders struggle with their own self-identities as leaders, and even though the images of African American stereotypes challenge African American leaders and leadership, they create a way where there was none to work for freedom and affirm the humanity and integrity of all people. They have been the voice of the marginalized and the oppressed in US history and have inspired others to see the hope in their path. Their leadership becomes a model for many other movements, including the immigrant rights movement.

Latinx Leaders and Leadership in a US Immigrant Context

Challenges of Latinx Immigrant Leadership

Even though many leadership positions are primarily occupied by white male elites, there is one place in which non-white/non-male national organizational leadership thrives. That is the immigrant rights movement leadership. The immigrant rights movement is a recent phenomenon. However, as was shown in the massive 2006 street marches and protests across the nation, the immigrant rights movement is nationwide. As was discussed earlier, many racial ethnic groups are exposed to more severe racism and sexism in multidimensional layers of the US sociopolitical system and economic structure and experience serious prejudice and discrimination against them. The immigrant rights movement is a movement for the survival of immigrants in the face of these prejudices and discriminations.

The public image of immigrants in the first decade of the twenty-first century is "a working class Mexican or Central American man," even though immigrants originate from 140 countries.[118] In fact, whether immigrants are Mexican or Chinese, and whether they are documented or undocumented, the word "immigrant" is spontaneously correlated with being "illegal" in the US context. Many current immigrants, regardless of their nationalities and immigrant status, are labeled as illegal or harboring the potential danger to be illegal. In other words, the public pictures immigrants as a group of illegal, dangerous people. This illegal immigrant status, or probability of being illegal in the past or future, induces white groups' feeling of anxiety and fear for their safety and privileges. Under the eyes of white racism, being an immigrant implies being undocumented and being undocumented means being illegal and being illegal implies being dangerous. Immigrants are seen as a threat to society. In this logic, the stereotype starts with a working-class Mexican or Central American man and ends with being dangerous.

Although these images are relegated to all non-white immigrant groups such as Asian immigrants, they are often more directly related with Latinx population and many white political leaders show serious offence against this population. Creating an electrified fence told by Herman Cain is a good example to show how white leaders reveal and cultivate anti-Latinx sentiments in the public square.

> I got back from China. Ever heard of the Great Wall of China? It looks pretty sturdy. And that sucker is real high. I think we can build one if we want to! We have put a man on the moon, we can build a fence! Now, my fence might be part Great Wall and part electrical technology. . . . It will be a twenty foot wall, barbed wire, electrified on the top, and on this side of the fence, I'll have that moat that President Obama talked about. And I would put those alligators in that moat.[119]

Later, Cain claimed this statement as a joke. However, when he had this talk, the audience was cheering, not laughing.[120] Even though his 'joke' involved mass killing against Latinx groups, it was enthusiastically supported, not discouraged. This anti-Latinx sentiment has furiously been accelerated by President Trump. He called undocumented immigrants animals and targeted Mexican immigrants specifically.

> President Trump used extraordinarily harsh rhetoric to renew his call for stronger immigration laws Wednesday, calling undocumented immigrants "animals" and venting frustration at Mexican officials who he said "do nothing" to help the United States. We have people coming into the country or

trying to come in, we're stopping a lot of them, but we're taking people out of the country. You wouldn't believe how bad these people are," Trump said. "These aren't people. These are animals." Trump's comments came in a freewheeling, hour-long White House meeting with local California leaders opposed to so-called "sanctuary city" policies. "California's law provides safe harbor to some of the most vicious and violent offenders on Earth, like MS-13 gang members putting innocent men, women, and children at the mercy of these sadistic criminals," he said. His comment about "animals" came after Fresno County Sheriff Margaret Mims complained that state law forbids her from telling U.S. Immigration and Customs Enforcement about undocumented immigrants in her jail—even if she suspects they're part of a gang . . . Trump's remarks were reminiscent of his first press conference as a presidential candidate in 2015, when he said the United States had become a "dumping ground" for people other countries didn't want." When Mexico sends its people, they're not sending their best," he said then. "They're bringing drugs. They're bringing crime. They're rapists. And some, I assume, are good people."[121]

Trump portrayed not only MS-13 gang members but also Mexicans in general as drug deals, criminals, and rapists. He demonstrated strong anti-Latinx sentiments in public and challenged local leaders to dismiss so-called "sanctuary city" policies.[122] He called this nation's immigration laws "the dumbest laws on immigration in the world."[123]

Cain and Trump are not the only ones who demonstrated strong anti-Latinx sentiment. Strong anti-Latinx sentiment is fostered by many political leaders, nurtured by media, and insinuated within laws in undistinguishable connection with racism and postcolonial mentality. Especially, stereotypes of undocumented immigrant images are specifically overlapped with stereotypes of Latinx images and further accelerate this sentiment in public. Stereotypical images of male immigrants are discussed as "contributors to criminal and economic instability," while the images of female immigrants are described as "welfare mothers" who bear "anchor babies" to gain residency and public benefits in the United States.[124] On the one hand, the images of male immigrants are presented as criminals. Portraying male immigrants as thieves in this country evokes fear and prejudice in a white society. Everything about immigrants is mediated through this fear and prejudice, which reduce the presence of immigrants into objects of danger. This fear and prejudice generate discrimination and violence without the feeling of guilt. On the other hand, the images of illegality lead to thoughts of welfare and economic benefits being taken from those who are "legal" in the white system. Being a welfare mother who is illegal in the US system means taking advantage of US economic benefits without contributions. This stereotype of female immigrants was used to dismiss their right to economic advancement. Producing images of female immigrants as free riders on US economic benefits and welfare prevents female immigrants from the recognition of any hard labor and work that they provide. They are treated only as promiscuous and uncontrollable bodies in terms of fertility. Both these images of male and female immigrants mislead the public to see immigrants as a dangerous and uncontrollable group. These images escalate prejudice and discrimination against immigrants.

What is the main ideology behind this prejudice and discrimination? What paradigms might it employ? In what sense are the stereotypes or public images of immigrants equivalent to the categories "terrorists" or "criminals"? There are many theories to explain this relation. One of the theories is the "nation-based paradigm."[125] Despite severe racism and sexism, many people (including some racists) reluctantly, but still mostly, agree that America needs to grant democratic equality and justice to everyone, regardless of their race and ethnicity. Based on this agreement, racial integration is encouraged. However, even when racial integration or assimilation is used as a justified ideology to treat everyone equally for the sake of racial justice, these images of immigrants are used as a fine line to exclude immigrants because they are not "Americans." Only US citizens can enjoy justice. The logic is this: as long as they are not Americans, no matter what circumstances they face, it does not matter to "us." The nation-based paradigm gives US citizens the permission to persecute immigrants. All bias, prejudice, and discrimination toward immigrants is justified. Racial equality does not apply to immigrants. Sexism or any other form of discrimination against female immigrants are no longer applied to them. Exploitation of immigrants is not counted; instead, the use of cheap labor to build a strong *white America* is legitimated.

This nation-based paradigm has a long tradition, which we can examine to analyze the relation "between racial separation and white supremacy."[126] It is essentially entrenched in the undercurrents of colonialism and colonial structures. Internal colonialism in particular has cooperated with this paradigm. Even though the anticolonial movement won national independence in many countries in the world, the power of the internal colonialism was embedded in many political and social systems, including the US sociopolitical system, after European colonialism ended. Michael Omi and Howard Winant identified internal colonialism by four elements in relation to racial formation:

1. A colonial geography emphasizing the territoriality or spatial arrangement of population groups along racial lines;

2. A dynamics of cultural domination and resistance, in which racial categories are utilized to distinguish between antagonistic colonizing and colonized groups, and conversely, to emphasize the essential cultural unity and autonomy of each;

3. A system of superexploitation, understood as a process by which extra-economic coercion is applied to the racially identified colonized group, with the aim of increasing the economic resources appropriated by the colonizers;

4. Institutionalization of externally based control, such that the racially identified colonized group is organized in essential political and administrative aspects by the colonizers or their agents.[127]

Using these tactics of internal colonialism originating in white colonial history, cultural nationalism/patriotism in the US targets immigrants as the existing, internal, colonized group. It becomes the main ideology controlling immigrants. As the visible and invisible geographical regions against immigrants within the US territory are imposed in each city and each state, many immigrants are beleaguered and exploited by the white colonial system as economic resources and political objects. International unequal exchange of labor and goods, colonial exploitation and control of resources, racial violence, and white cultural nationalism constitute fundamental elements of US capitalism. Based on unequal white domination and its cultural colonial heritage, racial prejudice and discrimination against immigrant groups are produced. The Eurocentric colonial sense of white race and white identity is centered at the core of US sociopolitical culture; colonial structure, rules, and systems easily implant nationalism as the legitimated rationale to protect white privilege. A long history of colonialism and postcolonialism shapes the culture of internalized, colonial, imperial racism in the United States and beyond. Playing on internalized colonialism within the nation-based paradigm, racism was transformed into the anti-immigrant movement.

In summary, creating these stereotypes is a result of white colonialism in the name of national security. Based on the strategies of internalized colonialism and the nation-based paradigm, these stereotypes of immigrants are used to justify and legitimate prejudice and discrimination against them. As the image of male immigrants is seen as criminals who threaten American national security and the images of female immigrants are treated as free riders to threaten American economic security, the public image-making process concerning immigrants fuels fear and anxiety about immigrants in white culture. Even though the labor of immigrants built the US economy from its earliest years to its most recent years, the contribution of their labor is not recognized but criticized and blamed as taking work away from US citizens. In the consciousness and unconsciousness of colonial/postcolonial minds and nationalism, the correlation between public images of immigrants and the feelings of white fear incorporate in discriminations and violence against not only Latinx groups but also against all racial ethnic immigrant groups.

Whether immigrants have legal status or not, the negative images of immigrants coalesce into destructive behaviors and attitudes for white society. These images of immigrants are discussed repeatedly in American political debates, not just as stereotypical images or behaviors, but as facts or truths. In these debates, male immigrants are frequently discussed as those who steal jobs from poor, white, working-class Americans, and female immigrants are repeatedly presented as those who jeopardize the welfare system and, on a deeper level, threaten white national identity. In these political disputes, immigrants are not seen as human, but as "animals" to dismiss and eliminate. The presence of both male and female immigrants is seen as a serious and dangerous threat to the nation. In the name of protecting the country, many systematic policies and restrictions against undocumented and/or documented immigrants were created and exercised. Since the Chinese Exclusion Act of 1882, immigration law and policy, domestic or even international surveillance, detention, deportation, board control, visa policy, and other policies are used to control immigrants. In fact, these strategies are created to target undesirable, unwelcome, non-white immigrant groups.

Latinx Leadership in the Immigrant Rights Movement

Although the immigrant rights movement was born in every ethnic immigrant group to protect their human rights, it became more active within Latinx groups. Geographical closeness from Latin American countries to the United States gives many Latinx groups more opportunities to access the US boarder than that of other groups. Because of this accessibility, the population of Latinx immigrant groups grew quickly and became the largest immigrant group in the United States. "In 1900, 84.9% of immigrants originated from Europe and only 1.3% were from Latin America and Caribbean; by 2010 only 12.1% were from Europe and 53.1% originated from Latin America and the Caribbean."[128] Under anti-Latinx sentiment, their visibility of being the largest immigrant group is easily the target of nationalism. The media often depicts the Latinx immigrant groups as the illegal undocumented group that endangers national security. Because of this circumstance, Latinx groups are one of the most active groups leading the immigrant rights movement.

The best-known immigrant organization was the United Farm Workers of America (UFW), founded and led by César Chávez and Dolores Huerta in the 1960s and 1970s. Their leadership was focused on labor laws, such as the pro-immigrant Agricultural Labor Relations Act, as a way to improve immigrant lives. During the 1980s, many immigrant organizational leaders tried to build alliances between immigrant organizations, labor unions, nonprofit organizations, religious organizations, and other transnational organizations.[129] In the 1990s and the early 2000s, immigrant rights movement became more visible in the public square. Many labor unions, such as Los Angeles County Federation of Labor (LACFL), The American Federation of Labor and Congress of Industrial Organizations (AFL-CIO), and Service Employees International Union (SEIU), intensively started to join and participate in the immigrant rights movement. They organized campaigns such as the Active Citizenship Campaign in 1995 (immigrant voter registration drive) and the Immigrant Workers Freedom Ride in 2003 (a national immigrant rights event designed to resemble civil rights freedom rides).[130] Many immigrant rights leaders have worked for immigrants, supporting their status, providing workshops, networking, fundraising, and organizing the immigrant rights protests and consumer boycotts.

After September 11, 2001, discrimination against immigrants became more violent. Both the Immigration and Naturalization Service and the

Department of Homeland Security developed "special registration" programs to reinforce more detentions and deportations, arrest more suspected terrorists, incarcerate them, and set up "a network of secret military prisons for indefinite incarceration and torture without trial."[131] From September 2001 to 2006, more severe discrimination and violence toward immigrants occurred in the name of national security than ever before.

In 2006, the Republican-controlled House of Representatives tried to pass H.R. 4437, known as the Sensenbrenner Bill. The purpose of the Sensenbrenner Bill was to make eleven million undocumented immigrants as felons rather than as people who had committed civil infractions, and it prohibited the act of providing shelter or any support or aid to undocumented immigrants.[132] If any family members, friends, clergy, service workers, or supporters would try to provide shelter or supply any aids, they would be charged with felony. The intention of this bill was to cut off any opportunities for undocumented immigrants to have access to health care or education and, at the same time, to raise fear by punishing any providers and supporters who could provide any help to undocumented immigrants. If this bill had passed, millions of these people would have become felons.

Because of this harmful violent act, many immigrant rights organizations such as the Coalition for Humane Immigrant Rights of Los Angeles (CHIRLA) and the New York Immigration Coalition started to organize massive protests in 2006. This grew into the biggest wave of mass movements in US history. The National Capital Immigration Coalition organized a rally on March 7 at Washington, DC, and thirty thousand protesters participated, and in downtown Chicago, one hundred thousand demonstrated on March 10.[133] In Los Angeles, between two hundred thousand and five hundred thousand rallied on March 25.[134] Countless mass marches occurred in March, April, and May 2006. On May 1 (May Day), "A Day without Immigrants" was promoted nationally, a one-day economic boycott to show how much immigrants contributed to the American economy. "Half a million people took to the streets in Chicago, a million in Los Angeles, and hundreds of thousands more in New York, Houston, San Diego, Miami, Atlanta, and other cities across the country."[135]

Through the 2006 mass marches, the immigrant rights movement's leaders' works became more visible and their existence known in the public sphere. Immigrant rights leaders work for immigrants in multidimensional ways to protect their human rights: "lobbying, petitioning, protesting, contacting public officials, joining campaigns, doing community work, and participating in labor unions, churches, nonprofit organizations, and voluntary associations."[136] Their work is concentrated in two parts, gaining immigrants' legal status ("civil rights movement") and obtaining immigrants' economic advancement ("labor movement").[137] Gaining legal status for immigrants is the most important work for immigrant rights movement leaders. Most of their work is to find a way to change immigration law and policies. "Emphasizing immigrants' contributions ('We pay taxes'), their allegiance to the U.S. ('I am an American, too'), family unity ('Please don't tear my family apart') as well as emphasizing their humanity ('No human being is illegal')," many immigrant rights leaders demand human rights for undocumented immigrants.[138] Their goal is to change the public images of immigrants by bringing attention to immigrant contributions to the American economy and allegiance to the United States. They fight prejudice and discrimination against immigrants, pointing out to the public that undocumented immigrants are also important contributors to the American economy as they demand immigrants' economic advancement.

The emphases on family unity and humanity are not only the main theme for the immigrant rights movement, but also form the foundation for the New Sanctuary Movement in which many religious leaders participate. Through the New Sanctuary Movement, many immigrant rights movement leaders are deeply connected with religious leaders and communities. They collaboratively work with religious leaders to protect family unity for undocumented immigrants using sanctuary as a means to that end. These leaders proclaim that undocumented immigrants are also humans who have the right to live together as a family under God's care. Immigrant rights leaders work with many other community leaders and religious leaders. They actively participate in national networking and create coalition activities with many other domestic, international, and transnational organizations and communities beyond their local community. At the same time, most of them are also active in local communities changing local conflictive policy and actual, current employer practices.[139]

As many immigrants move to metropolitan areas such as Los Angeles, New York, Chicago, and other cities, many headquarters of immigrant rights organizations are concentrated in these areas. In fact, many are female leaders with top leadership positions in these areas. Each city has disproportionately different concentrations of immigrant populations and various immigrant rights organizations. However, most immigrant rights organizations are oriented toward service to Latinx populations. From the late twentieth century to this twenty-first century, the majority of immigrants are from Latin America and Asia. From 1960 to 2016, the majority of immigrants are from Mexico (26.5 percent, 11,574,000), followed by India (5.6 percent, 2,435,000), China (4.9 percent, 2,130,000), the Philippines (4.4 percent, 1,942,000), and El Salvador (3.2 percent, 1,387,000).[140] The number of immigrants from Mexico are four or five times more than even India, the second-ranked in terms of population. As a natural consequence, many immigrant rights movement leaders are Latinx.

Discovering the prominent work of female leaders in unions or other immigrant workers' organizations is common in the immigrant rights movement. One of the early female immigrant leaders was Mary Harris Jones (Mother Jones), who was an Irish-born American immigrant woman. Her nickname was Miner's Angel. She was a powerful labor organizer to support rights of miners, steel workers, and child textile workers in Chicago, Pittsburgh, and elsewhere and cofounder of the Industrial Workers of the World with William D. Haywood, Eugene V. Debs, Danial De Leon and other founders in the late 1800s and the early 1900s.[141] Dorothy Jacobs (later known as Dorothy Jacobs Bellanca) is another female immigrant leader in the early 1900s. She was a garment worker who suffered from long hours of work and harsh working conditions. She organized strikes in Maryland and became the first full-time organizer for the Amalgamated Clothing Workers of America.[142] However, despite the hard work of the early female immigrant leaders, the power of patriarchy buried the names of female leaders. Leadership positions of unions and other immigrant organizations have been occupied mostly by male leaders within their own ethnic groups. However, in the recent immigrant rights movement, the visibility of female immigrant leaders is growing. LA immigrant rights movement organizations are a good example of this.

Southern California, especially Los Angeles, is one of the most active areas for Latinx immigrant advocacy. Many immigrant leaders have gathered to initiate the Los Angeles immigrant rights movement. There are various immigrant rights movement organizations within this movement. Ruth Milkman and Veronica Terriquez classify them in four major segments: "(a) Service-sector labor unions with substantial foreign-born memberships; (b) Immigrant hometown associations (HTAs) and ethnic organizations; (c) Community-based organizations (CBOs), including "worker centers" as well as umbrella organizations that function as coalition-builders; (d) Student immigration rights groups" and, arguably, (e) "church- and faith-based organizations."[143] Many women have various leadership positions in these organizations, including many religious ones except "the Catholic Church, which formally excludes women from its leadership structure."[144] Many forerunners, such as the United Farm Workers and the Chicano movements in the 1960s and 1970s, chose men exclusively for high-level leadership positions. Even though many female leaders and workers participated in these movements, they were not accepted as leaders and their work and leadership were not recognized by the public. However, in this recent immigrant rights movement, many female leaders occupy top leadership positions. Even though there is still a strong presence of male leaders in top leadership positions in unions and HTAs, many female leaders are present in CBOs and student immigrant rights groups in top leadership positions, and females occupy many middle and lower leadership positions in unions and HTAs more frequently than before. Why do these organizations have many female leaders? How have these female leaders risen through the ranks?

In the research of Milkman and Terriquez, there are three extensive explanations for this new phenomenon: First, the migration process allows female immigrants to advance their status and pulls them out from their private domain.[145] As they work outside of the home, they earn income. As they earn more income and have economic independence, they achieve better positions and increased power in the public sphere. In these circumstances, female immigrants gain access to educational opportunities. With these educational opportunities and job possibilities, women have learned how to overcome patriarchy and exercise leadership in the public domain. Because of the improved status of female immigrants in recent years, female leaders have more opportunities to exercise leadership. In this exercise, they have learned how to be good leaders.

Second, because the immigrant rights movement is a new movement, it demands a new style of leadership.[146] Unlike other organizations such as unions and HTAs that have a long history of patriarchy, organizations such as CBOs and student immigrant rights groups are new in this movement and haven't been influenced by a long history of patriarchal oppression. Rather, the immigrant rights movement has been supported by the feminist movement and feminist leadership. Since the late 1980s, the trend of the sociocultural demand is focused on gender equality. However, traditional leadership cannot accommodate this change. New leadership development is required, and many female leaders are equipped to follow this task. Many female leaders exercise different styles of leadership that are in collaborative efforts with others.

Third, "the *feminist consciousness* of immigrant women leaders" is the major reason for the rise of female leaders in the immigrant rights movement.[147] This feminist consciousness inspires many female leaders including immigrant women leaders to understand who they are as leaders and how to overcome patriarchal barriers. Milkman and Terriquez claim that this feminist consciousness is the critical resource for female immigrant leaders to perform in leadership roles with success and confidence.

As the example of Los Angeles indicates, many female immigrant leaders are visible in the public sphere. Their leadership is exercised at all levels of the organization. What is their leadership? How do people evaluate their leadership? How do these female immigrant leaders practice leadership differently? Susan C. Pearce, Elizabeth J. Clifford, and Reena Tandon illustrate the life stories of several female immigrant leaders in activism and characterize their leadership as "charismatic authority."[148] They claim that these female immigrant leaders are individual, heroic, inspiring visionaries who challenge traditional authority and norms. These female leaders fit the mold of transformative leadership, especially in their charismatic leadership that demonstrates extraordinary abilities, tenacious perseverance, tireless resilience, great competencies, firm determination, and the willingness to take risks. "They can be counted on to do the right thing, demonstrating high standards of ethical and moral conduct."[149] However, many female immigrant leaders shared that their leadership was not given from their innate characters. They found themselves becoming leaders in the process.

> We went to Tallahassee. . . . But I was afraid because of the dangerous situation in my country. It was dangerous for my family in my country. So I wanted to remain anonymous. My co-workers and the union gave me the strength, because I used to be a coward. One day, I put my name and picture out there. My daughter called me [from Guatemala]: "Mommy, do you know what you're doing?" I said, "Yes, I know."[150]

Their stories show that they did not believe they could be leaders at the beginning. They did not believe that they had the leadership ability to change their lives as well as the lives of others. They did not know who they were and what they could do as leaders. Many female immigrant leaders experienced fear before they became activists. However, when they met challenges or when they saw suffering in their communities, they wanted to change the unjust circumstances. Their leadership is often formed from their challenging but transformative life experience. Going through this life experience, they often find a vision for what they really want to do and they work not only for themselves but also for others and their communities. Fighting with these challenges, they learn how to change and transform their local and transnational conditions.

María Elena Durazo (US-born) is the best example of this case. Even though many female immigrant leaders occupied and even sometimes outnumbered men in the middle level leadership positions, it is still almost impossible for women to hold the top leadership positions. However, Durazo is one of few Latina women who broke this impossibility. She became president in Los Angeles's main UNITE HERE (the organizing drives of the LA hotel workers union) in 1989 and was the first woman appointed as Executive Secretary Treasurer of the Los Angeles County Federation of Labor, AFL-CIO, "the single most visible labor leadership position in the region" from 2006 to 2014.[151] She has been a key leader of immigrant movement history: I come from a family of eleven children . . . I remember the day I left . . . He (father) said, "I'm really sorry that I could not have provided more for you. I'm really sorry that I couldn't have made more money in my work to be able to send you through college so that you wouldn't have to go through all the struggles of getting scholarships and financial aid and everything else." I started thinking, how could it be that my father, who worked from sun-up to sun-down six days a week, working in the fields of this country—how it is that he ends up feeling this way? It seemed so wrong.[152] Her life experience led her to be a leader of the immigrant movement. Seeing both parents working all day but constantly struggling financially and witnessing the treatment that they received from white employers, she chose to work for union instead of being a lawyer. She made her decision to be a union organizer who could work with immigrant workers for their equality and justice. For me, there is nothing more extraordinary than being a part of men and women learning to take charge of their lives. There is nothing more important than being a part of the transformation from being very hardworking men and women who feel powerless against injustice to being hardworking men and women who feel dignity and fight for their rights. There is nothing more challenging than confronting the corporate system that controls so much in our lives.[153] Her leadership was formed from her second-generation immigrant family life experience and transformed the experience to work for equality and justice for all immigrants. She collaboratively worked with countless numbers of local and national union groups to change unjust circumstances for immigrant families and their communities. For example, in 2003, Durazo mobilized one thousand immigrants from nine western cities to New York and Washington to support undocumented and documented immigrants not only for their legalization but also for their human rights and well-being.[154] Her family experience confirms that immigrants came to the United States to work hard and they deserve to be treated equally, not exploited.[155] She is "a voluble, hands-on leader, as likely to show up on a picket line with workers as in the offices of the politicians and business leaders she sought to influence."[156]

There are many Latinx immigrant leaders like Durazo who have demonstrated transformative leadership despite racial and sexual discrimination and barriers. They overcame double barriers of sexism and broke glass ceilings with their own hands. They made an impossible dream into a possible reality. They showed the world that ethnic women were greater leaders and their leadership was vibrant and innovative in the consistent forms of resistance and resilience. They transform their painful suffering into extraordinary leadership. To overcome these barriers, they work hard on building a great support and networking, developing strong mentoring relationships, finding good resources and sharing information.[157] By constantly challenging racial, sexual, colonial, and postcolonial discrimination against immigrants, many female immigrant leaders keep taking risks. Even when they fear to do so, as the stories above show, they still take risks and meet the challenge. The leadership that they demonstrated proves that these immigrant female leaders hold high standards in their ethnic and moral beliefs while demonstrating those beliefs in action. Exhibiting charismatic authority, their leadership is not hierarchal but collaborative. As they are careful with the power dynamics in their relationship with coworkers, they use their charismatic authority in the determination to be collaborative. The life stories of many female immigrant leaders show their efforts to work with others in collaboration, sharing visions and the meaning of this work. From a coward to a freedom fighter and from an invisible anonymous follower to a visible leader, many female immigrant leaders experience great transformation in their immigrant lives. That experience becomes the pivotal element for their leadership.

Leadership in the New Sanctuary Movement

As many immigrant leaders fight for immigrant rights, there is another immigrant rights movement led by many religious leaders—the New Sanctuary Movement. This movement originated in the Sanctuary Movement, active during the 1980s in many religious organizations. According to Hilary Cunningham, even though Arlington Street Unitarian Church in Boston was the first sanctuary church that publicly declared its support for asylum for Vietnam War resisters on October 16, 1967, the origin of the immigrant Sanctuary Movement started from a public declaration of sanctuary from Southside Presbyterian Church in Tucson, Arizona, in March 1982.[158] In this first immigrant Sanctuary Movement, many religious leaders worked for refugees mainly from Central America, especially from El Salvador and Guatemala, to provide food, clothing, temporary housing, transportation, and other assistance. They housed immigrants on in churches and synagogues to protect undocumented immigrants from deportation until they could find safer places. The religious leaders in this movement had two goals: "first, the short-term goal of having the immigration status of 'extended voluntary departure' granted to Salvadorans and Guatemalans, and second, the long-term goal of bringing peace and economic justice to the region."[159] More than seventy thousand US citizens participated in this movement through churches to support refugees from Central America despite the fact that many of them had to violate federal immigration laws.[160] One of the most serious cases is *United States V. Aguilar*. In 1984, four undercover agents from Immigration and Naturalization Service (INS) entered churches and reported activities to the United States government by recording private conversations, copying documents, taping phone conversations, and collecting personal information.[161] From this report, sixteen Sanctuary Movement leaders were indicted and more than sixty people were arrested.[162] However, this kind of official violence could not stop the movement. Rather, many religious leaders of the Sanctuary Movement more diligently fought with the United States governments and wisely broke federal immigration law to protect immigrants until the amendments were adopted. After this struggle, in the early 1990s, the Sanctuary Movement became somewhat legally allowed as a religious practice.[163]

The New Sanctuary Movement is the second incarnation of the immigrant Sanctuary Movement. It is an interfaith movement in collaboration with the secular immigrant rights movement organizations. Clergy and Laity United for Economic Justice—California (CLUE—California), Interfaith Workers Justice (IWJ), and the New York Sanctuary Coalition/*Asociacion Tepayac* are the main organizations supporting this new Sanctuary Movement.[164] As the current immigrant situation seriously escalated due to more restrictive policies and harsher enforcement against undocumented immigrants, interfaith leaders gathered in Washington, DC, on January 29–30, 2007, for the first national gathering. Interfaith leaders were from "fourteen states, nine regional and national denominational offices, and two national interfaith coalitions" including "Interfaith Worker Justice, United Church of Christ, Union of Reformed Judaism and representatives from the Lutheran, Roman Catholic, Evangelical Christian churches, and the Jewish and Muslim faiths."[165] In this gathering, they reached a conclusion on the guiding principles and goals of this movement.

The New Sanctuary Movement was officially launched on May 9, 2007, with joint press conferences in New York, Chicago, Los Angeles, Seattle, and San Diego, politically aiming at the Comprehensive Reform Act of 2007 (S. 1348).[166] At the launch, many clergy and mixed-status immigrant families stood together. "Welcome the stranger" was proclaimed, and Golden Rule was emphasized. Interfaith leaders share this Golden Rule teaching and its necessity for faith.[167] They called for love and compassion for immigrants as they demanded political changes closely establishing their new network in the coalition between faith communities and immigrant rights organizations.[168] This movement takes place at the intersection of politics and religion. Many religious leaders claim the love of God must extend beyond the bounds of religious institutions.

Even though the New Sanctuary Movement was the second incarnation of the Sanctuary Movement, there is a difference between the two. Whereas the Sanctuary Movement worked with more recently arrived immigrants for their immediate physical needs, the New Sanctuary Movement focuses more on immigrants who have settled here for some time and need support for legalization and naturalization. Many religious leaders in the New Sanctuary Movement urge churches to perform *"prophetic hospitality"* that demonstrates their congregational practice of "hospitality" and "protection" for certain numbers of immigrants facing complications and injustice in the system.[169] To be eligible for sanctuary, there are several conditions to meet legal requirements.

> An undocumented immigrant must be in deportation proceedings, have a good work record, and agree to undergo training to overcome fear of public exposure in order to articulate their cases at news conferences and public gatherings. They also must not have committed any crimes, and they must have US-born children to make the case that to separate them would destroy a family. That more undocumented immigrants are not taking advantage of sanctuary is related to the significant amount of resources a congregation has to spend on each harbored individual and the reluctance of undocumented immigrants to live in confined environments where they are not permitted to leave under the likelihood that they will be arrested.[170]

The New Sanctuary Movement established these criteria partly for strategic reasons. However, some religious leaders exercise power to select immigrants whom they prefer. In this process, sometimes they debate over hidden prejudices and discrimination against immigrants. In the research of Grace Yukich, there are cultural, religious, racial, and ethnic distinctions drawn by immigrant rights activists. Many immigrant rights activists intentionally prefer "mixed-status family" over "single" persons, "heterosexual" over "LGBTQIA" ones, those who are "law abiding" over those with "criminal records," those with "good work records" over the "unemployed," those with "community connections" over the "socially isolated," those with "winnable cases" over those with "difficult cases," "brothers/sisters" in families or congregants over "strangers," "prophetic leaders" over "victims," "nonthreatening/polite" immigrants over "threatening/angry" immigrants, "nonterrorists" over those "critical of US policies," and "Latinos/Asians" over "blacks," and "Christians" over "Muslims."[171] They unconsciously or consciously divide the immigrants into two different groups: "good/deserving undocumented immigrants" and "bad/undeserving undocumented immigrants."[172] Uplifting the images of good/deserving model immigrants, immigrant rights leaders and religious leaders in the New Sanctuary Movement try to leverage public opinion toward granting immigrants immunity based on their good, deserving backgrounds.[173] These leaders want the public to recognize how much good, deserving immigrants have contributed to society, and how fast these immigrants have integrated themselves into society.[174] Many religious leaders and immigrant rights workers insinuate to the public, perhaps unconsciously, that some immigrant groups are more deserving than others. They want to demonstrate that these immigrants *deserve* to stay. Depending on how well and quickly the immigrants integrate into white norms and culture without being seen as a threat and depending on which immigrants fit best into the construction of this stereotype, preference is given only to certain groups.

Yukich argues that by emphasizing goodness/deservingness, these leaders dismiss the message to the public that *all* immigrants as human beings deserve basic civil liberties and human rights.[175] She criticizes that even the immigrant rights movement and the New Sanctuary Movement leadership are affected by this stereotypical prejudice. Their unconscious and conscious prejudice undercuts the very meaning of human rights, rights which by definition are based on the mere fact of someone's humanity, not ability. This leadership practice perpetuates another white-dominated strategy to institutionalize prejudice against immigrants.[176]

Fortunately, many immigrant rights leaders of the younger generation are aware of this prejudice within the movement and challenge it in their leadership. They often criticize this stereotype and its danger and demonstrate a new leadership. There is one amazing example of this new leadership.

> In 2010, queer undocumented youth activists Mohammad Abdollahi, Yahaira Carrillo, and Tania Unzueta occupied the Arizona officers of Senator John McCain, and in 2011, Dream Team Los Angeles activists Adrian, Francisco Javier, Nancy Meza, Neidi Dominguez, and Tony Ortuño staged and live-streamed a sit-in at Immigration and Customs Enforcement (ICE) officers in Los Angeles. By 2012, the movement had grown stronger and the networks of DREAM activists more robust; their media connections across platforms were much broader, and they had developed a degree of leverage over the Latin@ vote. On June 15, 2012, President Obama announced the Deferred Action for Childhood Arrivals (DACA) program, which provided a two-year, temporary permit that allows some DREAM Act-eligible youth to remain in the United States without fear of detention and deportation.[177]

"Prerna Lai, the undocuqueer founder of DREAMActivist.net," reported that "DREAM activism and the broad new wave immigrant rights organizing have not only been led by undocumented youth, they have been disproportionately led by young, undocumented queer people of color."[178] This new leadership was powerfully demonstrated in the movement to approve the Deferred Action for Childhood Arrivals (DACA) program. The approval of this program was victoriously achieved through immeasurable effort and collaborative work by countless immigrant rights activists, especially many young queer people of color. Organizing and utilizing the network of family relations, friends, church connections, community organizers, and movement leaders, the undocumented youth including LGBTQIA members became a crucial part of this movement as leaders. They effectively use media, distribute valuable resources and information, create networks, and organize and participate in protests in many forms. Their leadership was effective and powerful not only in the approval of the DACA program, but it also made a great impact on Dream Act legislation, especially for higher education. Because of their leadership, many undocumented youth have a better chance for higher educational opportunities.

The leadership of the immigrant rights movement and the New Sanctuary Movement present different images of leadership. It has changed the images of leaders and has created the new images of leadership. It generates and integrates more images of leaders from adults to youth, from men to women, from heterosexual members to LGBTQIA members, from white to black, yellow, gray, pink, and purple, from the able-bodied to those with disabilities, from US citizens to undocumented immigrants, from the rich to the poor, from the upper class to the grassroots, from educated elites to people with no formal education, from secular leaders to religious leaders. In the immigrant rights movement and the New Sanctuary movement, these leaders all work together to find "*pathways to participation*," as they take on their roles as leaders without coercion.[179] Whereas the images of leaders available in white elite culture expect something from leaders based on individual excellence in the qualities of competitiveness, efficiency, and fastidiousness, the images of immigrant rights leaders create expectations for leaders, as well as for the collective efforts of all participants, of openness, network building, and creativity.

The issue of what to do about undocumented immigrants has been a major controversial issue in US society for at least the last decade. As hundreds of millions of people take to the streets for this issue, whether they are pro-immigrant groups or anti-immigrant groups, the leadership of this immigrant community is more critical than ever. It creates serious questions about the nature of leaders and leadership in this era, and many immigrant leaders have responded to these questions in courageous action.

Chapter 4

Challenges of Asian Immigrant Leadership

Immigrants from different ethnic groups experience diverse challenges and perform diverse styles of leadership, and Asian immigrants are no exception. How do they create their leadership? What are the main influences and resources? Chief among influences are Asian culture and its heritages originating from Asian countries. As discussed above, African American leadership has been formed in between African American culture and its communal concerns. Asian immigrant leadership is formed in a similar way. It has been formed originally in between Asian culture and its communal concerns and delivered to the US immigrant context with many conflicts and challenges. Like African American leadership, Asian immigrant leadership cannot be discussed without involving community. Moreover, like Latinx leadership, it always deeply concerns immigrant rights and their well-being. One of the key issues of developing Asian immigrant leadership is how to deal with the daily challenge of being immigrants in the United States. As the formation of Asian immigrant leadership is explored, the uniqueness of Asian immigrant leadership is not found from how different characteristics of leadership styles are in the comparison with white, African American and Latinx groups necessarily. Rather, it would be found in the analysis of Asian immigrant contexts that Asian immigrants face distinctively. In other words, Asian immigrant leadership is different from African American leadership and Latinx leadership not because it has unique features, but because Asian immigrants encounter different sociocultural and political challenges and these challenges lead them to create different types of leadership.

Before the formation of Asian leadership in the United States is discussed, it is important to understand how Asian leadership is known and perceived in US culture and beyond. What are values of leaders in Asia? What are practices for leadership in Asia? Are they deeply related to any specific religious practices? How are these values and religious practices understood in Asian leadership? How does Asian leadership differ from Asian immigrant leadership? The continent of Asia encompasses many different countries, cultures, worldviews, and religions. The approach to Asian leadership is not monolithic—there is no one universal form and practice of Asian leadership. Therefore, in this chapter, we explore and discuss Asian leadership in the limited scopes and values of disciplines such as Confucianism, Buddhism, and some aspects of Taoism, and their impact on how leadership is practiced.

Images of Leadership in Asian Cultural and Religious Values

Asian Leadership

Images of Asian leadership are studied and evaluated usually in the context of global leadership studies. In the Global Leadership and Organizational Behavior Effectiveness research program, Robert J. House and his research team studied 951 organizations of 17,300 managers from sixty-two countries.[1] Based on language, geography, religion, and historical accounts, they classified the sixty-two societies into ten regional clusters ("Anglo, Germanic Europe, Latin Europe, Sub-Saharan Africa, Eastern Europe, the Middle East, Confucian Asia, Southern Asia, Latin America, and Nordic Europe") and define nine cultural dimensions ("uncertainty avoidance, power distance, institutional collectivism, in-group collectivism, gender egalitarianism, assertiveness, future orientation, performance orientation, humane orientation").[2] This study also identified twenty-two positive leadership attributes as desirable and eight negative leadership attributes as undesirable.[3]

In this research, the cluster of Confucian Asia (South Korea, China, Singapore, Japan, Hong Kong, and Taiwan) shows high scores in "in-group collectivism," "institutional collectivism," and "performance orientation."[4] These countries emphasize results and work as a group over individual goals. They are loyal to their families. House and his research team described the leadership profile of the Confucian Asian countries as "self-protective, team oriented, and humane oriented."[5] Leaders from these counties do not invite others to get involved with goal setting or decision-making. They are self-protected. Even though they deeply care for others, are sensitive to others, and emphasize communal relationship, they as leaders make executive decisions without consulting others.[6]

The cluster of Southern Asian (the Philippines, Indonesia, Malaysia, India, Thailand, and Iran) achieves "high scores on humane orientation and in-group collectivism" as leaders from these countries demonstrate "strong family loyalty and concern for their communities."[7] Like Confucian Asian leaders, the leaders from these countries exhibit self-protective leadership along with "charismatic/value-based, humane-oriented, team-oriented" leadership.[8] Southern Asian countries characterize effective leadership as "collaborative, inspirational, sensitive to people's needs, and concerned with status and face saving."[9] Even though they do not want others to get involved with the decision-making process or the process of forming the goal for organizations, they emphasize collaborative work in team-oriented leadership.

House and his research team conclude that both clusters see participative leadership as ineffective and prefer autocratic leaders.[10] They culturally prefer humane-oriented leadership to encourage individuals to be fair, just, altruistic, gracious, and caring for others. "Countries with stronger humane orientation consider the interests of others, affirm belonging and affiliation, and embrace norms and responsibilities for protecting well-being of others."[11] Unlike the individualistic culture of the United States, many Asian countries show a strong tendency to exercise collectivism over individualism. Consequently, leaders from these countries exhibit strong cultural tendencies toward humane leadership along with exclusively hierarchal leadership. More to the point, these leaders place collaborative, communal, humane team-work over individual goals without engaging in a collaborative leadership in which power and power positions are shared with others.

As reviewed in the previous chapter, current US leadership is more inclined to perform collaborative, interactive, participative leadership in a context of individual, democratic capitalism. The sharing of power in the form of collaborative, interactive, participative leadership appears to be encouraged as a form of advanced leadership, even though it is not in fact implemented in many US contexts under racial, sex, and gender prejudice and discrimination. In this perspective, the self-protective leadership, team-oriented leadership, and humane leadership cannot be understood as effective leadership by the standards of the US's individual capitalistic culture.

There are three different points to understand self-protective, team-oriented and humane leadership in relation to Asian immigrants in the United States. First, self-protective leadership is seen as the primordial form of old bureaucratic and authoritarian leadership in the US context. As it was mentioned earlier, the advanced form of leadership in the current US context is collaborative, interactive, participative leadership that tries to dismiss the boundary between leaders and followers. From this point of view, self-protective leadership that shows the clear distinction between leaders and followers is seen as an outdated leadership style in the US context. However, as House's research above demonstrated, self-protective leadership in Asia is currently exercised as a normative, orderly, predominant leadership style inherited from Asian culture and history. This oppositional evaluation on self-protective leadership can cause more confusion to Asian immigrants who live in both cultures and receive different messages from these cultures. Second, team-oriented leadership that exercises in Asian contexts is viewed differently from the team-oriented leadership that is understood in the US context. Considering the trend toward individual democratic participatory styles of capitalism, team-oriented leadership in the US includes sharing power in decision-making and forming institutional goals. The team as a collective unit is a natural labor force in Asian communal culture, so team-oriented leadership is also expected. However, as House's research showed, team-oriented leadership in Asian contexts, does not include the concept of sharing power in decision-making or forming goals together for the institutions, even though Asian communal culture embraces collaborative and integrative team-oriented leadership. Therefore, team-oriented leadership without distribution of power is an odd concept in the United States. It directly challenges Asian hierarchal sociocultural structures and brings more ambiguous positions for Asian immigrant leadership. Third, reflecting individual democratic styles of capitalism and its influence, humane leadership is seen as ineffective leadership in terms of efficiency of work in a socioeconomic context in the United States. Rather, this leadership is understood as appropriate for religious contexts. It is evaluated quite positively and even encouraged in religious contexts in the United States or in a nonprofit organizational context, but not in a socioeconomic political context. However, humane leadership is prevalent in Asian socioeconomic political contexts. It emphasizes relationship and concern for others in terms of communal social values beyond religious teachings. This leadership is also greatly exercised both in Asian immigrant religious and non-religious US contexts. It is considered one of the most important leadership styles in terms of efficiency of work in Asian immigrant contexts.

In summary, Asian leadership is presented as self-protective, team-oriented, and humane and leaders in Asia give more attention to the needs of the community. The values of leadership differ from those in the United States. How do the leadership values differ? Why do Asian leaders perform different styles of leadership and on what basis? The concepts of leadership in Asian countries require an understanding of Asian values and culture based on various religious practices. Without an understanding of the practice of religious beliefs in Asia, it is impossible to understand Asian immigrant leadership and its practices.[12]

Virtues of Asian Religious Leadership

Confucianism is not only a religion but also a cultural, social, political ideology in many Eastern Asian countries. It is a foundation of Eastern philosophy and sociopolitical thought. The practice of Confucianism centers on the cultivation of virtues. These virtues are not necessarily only for leaders to cultivate. All people are called to cultivate these virtues to be fully human. However, "in Confucianism, the ultimate goal of human life is to cultivate oneself to be a fully human being to become a *jūn zǐ* (i.e., a superior man or woman)" who "loves and cares for his(her) people, understands their needs as human beings, lives and acts according to righteousness, and observes appropriate rites and rituals."[13] The ideology of Confucianism requires a superior being, a *jūn zǐ* who is the ultimate person to build and rule. If one wants to be a leader in many East Asian countries, one is expected to become a *jūn zǐ* or at least to embrace the characteristics of the *jūn zǐ*. Where did these characteristics come from in the East Asian context? How do people perceive them? What are the virtues and practices that form these characteristics?

In a study on Confucian virtues and East Asian leadership practices, LingLing Lang, Beverly J. Irby, and Genevieve Brown chose eight Confucian virtues that relate to East Asian leadership: *rén* (benevolence or humaneness); *yì* (righteousness); *lǐ* (rites and rituals, propriety); *zhì* (wisdom); *xìn* (honesty and trustworthiness); *zhōng* (loyalty); *shù* (reciprocity, altruism, and forgiveness); and *xiào* (filial piety).[14] Even though these virtues are profoundly philosophical concepts of religious beliefs, they are commonly known virtues for many Asian leaders. Asian leaders are encouraged to practice these virtues in their daily lives as the form of Asian attitudes or attributes for leaders.

Rén in Chinese or *In* in Korean is represented in all Confucian virtues. It is the fundamental Confucian virtue. All other Confucian virtues are rooted in *rén*. The character for *rén* originated from the figures of "two persons" together in an ideogram. Two persons are next to each other. The meaning of *rén* is found in the notion that when people relate well and work together, they can be truly human and demonstrate good humane behavior.[15] The meaning of *rén* includes "benevolence, love, kindness, charity, compassion, altruism, goodness, perfect virtue, moral perfection, righteousness, propriety, loyalty, forgiveness, filial piety, and courage."[16] It is both the starting point and ending point of the practice of leadership. If anyone practices *rén* completely, that person is the perfect leader.

If *rén* is interpreted as the humane duty of leaders as individuals, *yì* (righteousness) is understood as the public duty that leaders as members of society must perform in the public domain.[17] In *yì*, people are moral subjects who can deliver justice and perform righteousness regardless of given systems and structures. It must be practiced beyond social constructions. It is the right thing to do. It is justice. Many Asian leaders are required to put *yì* before *lǐ*. They perceive *yì* as the center of public leadership.

Lǐ are rites and rituals that reflect the order of society through the construction of formality. All virtues are actualized in the form of *lǐ*. They cannot be delivered without *lǐ*. If *yì* is the inner discipline required to elicit justice from individual human beings, *lǐ* is the outer disciplines that actualize justice within the systems and institutions of society. They are found in laws, rules, dogmas, customs, traditions, and propriety. *Lǐ* constructs social orders and systems. It creates social relations and gives an individual a name and a position, such as "ruler, minister, father, mother, son, and daughter" with "different responsibilities and duties."[18] Because of *lǐ*, leaders know how to behave and perform in their leadership positions in public. The public expectations of leadership are reflected and shaped by *lǐ*. Even though the original teaching of *lǐ* emphasizes modesty and humility in each given leadership position, it in fact creates a clear hierarchy and boundary of positions for each person. As it allocates duties and responsibilities of leaders, it assigns obligations and obedience of followers.

Zhì is wisdom. This is not only a Confucian virtue but is also found in Buddhist, Taoist, Hinduism, Islam, Christian, and other religious traditions. It is found in every culture and religious tradition. From ancient times to the present day and from Eastern culture to Western, wisdom is one of the most essential qualities for leaders. In Buddhism, *zhì* means absolute knowledge achieved by enlightenment. Through absolute knowledge, people can be liberated. *Zhì* can be translated as *prajñā* in Sanskrit, which means "a mental event, a state of consciousness, normally in the Indo-Tibetan Buddhist context a state of consciousness which results from analysis, investigation."[19] It is an understanding of the way things really are beyond visible reality. It interconnects conceptual and nonconceptual understanding and leads to ultimate awareness. *Prajñā* is "a Wisdom supremely compassionate, rescuing humans from their ignorance and suffering."[20] Ultimately, *prajñā* is the perfect form of wisdom. It has power to emancipate all people and all things. In the Confucian tradition, if *zhì* does not carry out the action of *yì*, it is not true wisdom. *Zhì* must accompany *rén* and *yì*. However, in the Confucian tradition, wisdom is a virtue that not everyone can have. Wisdom is one of the distinctive qualities that only leaders should have or cultivate. Only the select few who know how to learn and investigate can obtain this virtue.[21] In other words, it is the virtue that only *jūn zǐ*, leaders or sages, can obtain. Leaders without wisdom are not true leaders. However, there is a question about how to obtain wisdom. In fact, it is not clear whether wisdom can be learned or not. If wisdom is a quality that people are born with, only the select few can be leaders. If wisdom can be practiced by learning, anyone can be a leader. As long as people can learn, they are allowed to be leaders. However, in the Confucian system, learning is not permitted for certain classes under different religious and social circumstances. It means leaders can be trained and nurtured only within the privileged class. Western culture also shares this phenomenon. There, wisdom is understood in terms of intelligence or having higher education, it is perceived as one of the most important traits for leaders in modern Western leadership studies. However, still only certain classes of people have the privilege of accessing higher education opportunities.

Xìn is honesty, trustworthiness, and faithfulness. Leaders should be honest and keep their promises in words and deeds. *Xìn* searches for truth and authenticity not only in leaders themselves but in others as well. The precondition of this virtue is a relationship. Without a relationship with others, *xìn* does not have any value. *Rén*, *yì*, *lǐ*, and *zhì* are the leaders' inner qualities in themselves, whereas *xìn*, *zhōng*, *shù*, and *xiào* are qualities that leaders need to nurture in a relationship with others.[22] *Zhōng* and *xiào* are somewhat distinctive qualities that Asian leadership strongly requires. The concept of *xiào* is not limited to children's obedience to their parents. As parents have responsibilities to take care of their children, their children also have also responsibilities to support their aged parents after they grow up, not only psychologically but also financially.[23] Despite modern social changes and industrialization, this virtue is strongly practiced in many Asian countries. Both *zhōng* and *xiào* demand a sincere heart to and for others, including families and communities. Respect and veneration are important parts of these virtues. *Shù* is similar to the concept of the Golden Rule. It asks one to do for and with others as one would do for oneself. It means leaders need to respect others' will, rights, and boundaries without imposing their power.[24]

These virtues are not limited to the Confucian tradition. Taoism has similar virtues (*te*). In the Taoist tradition, the Great Man or the Sage must practice these virtues. To dwell in the Way (*Tao*), these leaders must venerate the Way and honor virtues. One of the most important virtues of leadership predominantly taught by Taoist traditions is the emptiness of self. The concept of the emptiness of self is not the most important concept in Taoist tradition alone; it is found also in Confucian and Buddhist traditions. In the Taoist tradition, it is best described as follows:

> By not elevating the worthy, you bring it about that people will not compete.
> By not valuing goods that are hard to obtain, you bring it about that people will not act like thieves.
> By not displaying the desirable, you bring it about that people will not be confused.
> Therefore, in the government of the Sage:
> He empties their minds,
> And fills their bellies.
> Weakens their ambition,
> And strengthens their bones.
> He constantly causes the people to be without knowledge and without desires.
> If he can bring it about that those with knowledge simply do not dare to act,
> Then there is nothing that will not be in order.[25]

In the Taoist tradition, the duty of the Sage or leaders is to teach people how to empty their minds as well as emptying their own because "the Way is empty."[26] The concept of emptiness is an essential part of Taoist practice. Emptiness applies both to one's mind and deed. It is empty but not depleted. It is empty but not exhausted. It is empty and dwells in the Way. Practicing being in emptiness is becoming the Sage and becoming true leaders.

In many Asian countries, emptiness of self is also deeply related to Buddhist virtues. In fact, emptiness of self is also one of the most important and critical teachings in Buddhism. To understand emptiness of self, it is important to understand the Four Noble Truths[27] and to practice the Eightfold Path[28] and how these Truths and Path relate with absence/emptiness of self. As the Four Nobel Truths explain what suffering is and how to end suffering, the Noble Eightfold Path shows how to end suffering by practice.[29] Knowing the Four Nobel Truths and practicing the Noble Eightfold Path, emptiness of self naturally follows.

Emptiness of self is the ultimate stage of self. It encourages all people to practice. In a Buddhist understanding, the self is not composed of psychophysical constituents. Rather, it is an existing entity that is in neither mind nor body. It originates from the perfection of wisdom (*prajñāpāramitā*) that dismisses all discursive thought and brings true peace. "The principal ontological message of the *prajñāpāramitā* is an extension of the Buddhist teaching of no-Self to equal no essence, and therefore no inherent existence, as applied to all things without exception."[30] Without an understanding of emptiness, it is impossible to understand the way things really are and to recognize ultimate existence. It is to know how to completely let go, cut discursive thought, and to experience "existential relaxation."[31] Absence/emptiness of self is the precondition to discovering the true nature of reality. "Emptiness does not mean nonexistence. It means Interdependent Co-Arising, impermanence, and nonself."[32] It is the first door of liberation from the three doors of liberation (emptiness, signlessness, and aimlessness) and "the Middle Way *between* existent and nonexistent" and "*beyond* existence and nonexistence."[33] Emptiness of self is the way to see life as it is. It is a way of liberating suffering.

Absence/emptiness of self has been taught and practiced as the basic but most difficult teaching of Buddhism. The goal of this practice is to see life as it is. When someone arrives at the stage of emptiness of self, and when someone has trained to have a right view, this person can see life as it is and be in the present moment. Even though these trainings are taught as the principles for training all believers, they are known as hard principles to achieve. Very few sages and religious leaders could fully practice these principles and become liberated from suffering like Buddha and the Bodhisattvas who attained perfect wisdom and compassion for others. These principles were not just religious principles; they became cultural, social principles that people expected their leaders to naturally embody.

Like Bodhisattvas who "are able and willing to help sentient beings in whatever ways may be of greatest benefit"[34] and even "postpone *nirvāṇa*, or turn back from *nirvāṇa*, in order to place all other sentient beings in *nirvāṇa* first,"[35] leaders in Asian countries are expected to help others in whatever ways may be of greatest benefit and postpone their own benefits until all others share benefits together. Under oppressive colonial and postcolonial institutional histories, many Asian leaders, including sociopolitical, economic, and religious leaders, have claimed that their goal of leadership is to end suffering and bring liberation for others. As they claimed this goal and exercised these practices in their sociopolitical, economic, and religious daily lives, this practice became a part of their leadership. As these religious practices are highly encouraged and cultivated, it can clearly be seen that they correlate to traits of leaders in Asian countries.

These Asian religious virtues are taught, developed, distorted, reinterpreted, practiced, and re-practiced by many religious thinkers and leaders in East Asian countries. They form the core of Asian societies' understanding of human beings and their relations with one another. Even though they originate from religious teachings, they are not considered religious virtues any more. Rather, they have become standard virtues of all human beings. Especially, for leaders, these practices are not optional but required. These virtues have been present in Asian countries for hundreds of years. They have established the formal and informal economy in many Asian countries.[36] Rules, regulations, laws, customs, traditions, and systems are formed and influenced by these virtues in the actualization of *lǐ*. Based on these religious virtues, many leaders from various Asian cultures demonstrate love, care for others, benevolence, justice, righteousness, compassion, wisdom, trustworthiness, honesty, and loyalty as leadership traits.

A study of Hong Kong CEOs' Confucian and Taoist leadership is a good example for this phenomenon. From this study, Chau-kiu Cheung and Andrew Chi-fai Chan claim that Chinese leadership is established "based on relationship building, virtuous practice, hierarchical and centralized organization, humility and self-effacement."[37] Confucian Taoist religious leadership is commonly practiced as the secular CEO's leadership in a socioeconomic context.[38] CEOs see these leadership features not as religious virtues, but as moral ethical characters for themselves. These virtues are already understood as a cultural expectation of all leaders, not just religious leaders.

In a study on East Asian leadership based on Confucian virtues, Lang, Irby, and Brown also claim that several leadership models in a socioeconomic context are developed and widely conducted with Confucian virtues in East Asian countries. Based on *rén* (benevolence or humaneness) and other Confucian virtues, they elaborate "1) humane and benevolent leadership, 2) ethical and moral leadership, 3) transformational leadership, 4) expert and professional leadership, 5) paternalistic leadership, and bureaucratic and authoritarian leadership" to be part and parcel of East Asian leadership.[39]

Humane and benevolent leadership is a prominent leadership style deeply rooted in the Confucian virtue *rén*.[40] In many Asian organizations, leaders care about their people like family, protect their people, and even are concerned about their people's personal matters because they expect respect and loyalty from their people as followers within Confucian sociocultural order. In this Confucian order, *rén* is also closely connected to paternalistic leadership/fatherly benevolent leadership, including characteristics like trust, friendliness, forgiveness, sympathy, and paternalism.[41] Unlike the US where this humane and benevolent leadership is often exercised in nonprofit and religious organizations alone, in Asia this leadership is exercised also in socioeconomic and political contexts. However, this leadership is not practiced there equally throughout the classes. Only certain social, political elite classes are expected to exercise this leadership.

Ethical and moral leadership is founded on "*rén* (benevolence or humaneness), *yì* (righteousness), and *lǐ* (rites and rituals, propriety)."[42] Leaders, such as *jūn zǐ*, need to demonstrate moral character as qualification for being leaders. Ideally, being leaders in Asian societies means being moral leaders. They must be morally good. They never perform *lǐ* at the expense of *yì*. They care about people first. In fact, the moral character is the most important factor of leadership in many Asian organizations.[43] Leaders in many Asian organizations are expected to perform ethical and moral leadership as their duty and obligation.[44] Demonstrating the ethical and moral standards of a leader is a precondition of leadership in Asian culture. Without exhibiting proper moral character, leaders are not recognized as leaders.

Elements of transformational leadership are commonly found in Asian leadership based on Asian religious virtues. Since leaders are expected to be moral, they must transform themselves and encourage others to do so. Being role models of organizations, leaders lead others by example, exercise their charisma to inspire others, support them, and help them achieve more and better.[45] They encourage followers to achieve the higher-level moral values and ideals such as justice and benevolence.[46] Asian leaders are always expected to put others' needs or organizational needs before their own needs. However, some transformational leadership scholars point out that transformational leaders are not necessarily expected to make others into leaders who are better than themselves. In both United States and Asian contexts, the concept of transformational leadership does not include equality of positions and power between leaders and followers. Especially in Asian contexts, the more transformational leaders are respected, the more they are seen as superiors. This is due to the influence of paternalistic leadership.

Professional and expert leadership is related to wisdom. The wisdom tradition in Asian religious cultures encourages Asian/Asian immigrants to master knowledge, so education is always the most important aspect of their lives. Because learning and wisdom are important Confucian, Buddhist, Taoist, and Hindu virtues in many Asian countries, many leaders in Asian countries and in an Asian immigrant US context work in higher education and become experts in the field. They are expected to be knowledgeable and acquire new knowledge before others.[47] They are not just experts, but masters. Professional and expert leaders in an Asian context are masters, who have transformed themselves into top-notch experts in every dimension. In this leadership, leaders are the masters and followers are the students in a clear hierarchical order. Leaders are expected to not only master skills and demonstrate excellence but also to master knowledge and go beyond. Leaders need to show the ability to transform knowledge into creation. In Western society, professional and expert leadership requires mastery to maintain the current order. It is not transformation that is expected, but more productivity. However, in Asian contexts, performing professional and expert leadership requires more than productivity. It requires two transforming processes. First, it requires a transforming process of leaders. Second, it expects a process of transforming knowledge into creation. If leaders do not transform themselves, the process of transforming knowledge into creation is not possible. Without these transforming processes, their leadership is not accepted as professional and expert leadership in Asian society. Asian society requires more than the professional and expert leadership that is known in US society. It requires creativity beyond professional knowledge. Many Asians in Asian countries as well as Asian immigrants in the US demonstrate their professional knowledge and skills with excellence in their work. Maybe this leadership perfectly fits in the images of model minority Asian leaders in the US context.

The images of Asian leadership are commonly described as paternalistic, bureaucratic, and authoritarian leadership. It is rooted especially in "*lĭ* (rites and rituals, propriety), *zhōng* (loyalty), and *xiào* (filial piety)."[48] Based on the concept of *lĭ*, Confucian patriarchal order established hierarchal regulations, policies, rules, and laws. Five cardinal relationships (ruler and minister, father and son, husband and wife, elder brother and younger brother, and friend and friend) have established hierarchal boundaries in each relationship. These hierarchal boundaries set the hierarchal order between leaders and followers.[49] "The leadership is one that requires an education, training, and culture; a 'breeding' that can be respected by the people, emulated only to a certain degree by those less culturally advantaged."[50] Followers can emulate leaders within limits, but they cannot be leaders. Therefore, it is expected that leaders take care of followers, and followers are expected to obey and follow leaders in absolute trust. Sometimes sacrifices are expected of followers not as abuse, but as loyalty. Hierarchal order between leaders and followers conforms to class order. This order still exists in terms of economic wealth and sociopolitical power.

Various Asian leaderships are still actively practiced based on Asian religious cultural virtues discussed in this section. These virtues are predominately perceived as standard traits for leaders in many Asian countries. The norms and standards of Asian leadership are built and developed with these religious virtues and traditions. Virtues of many religious practices from Confucianism, Buddhism, Taoism, Christianity, Hinduism, Islam, Shamanism, and indigenous Asian religions become the requirements for Asian leaders to practice. It is a critical part of Asian leadership. Consequently, practices of these religious cultural virtues have been an important exercise of leadership training. These values strengthen the whole structure of Asian leadership in communication with Asian history and culture. Burns claims that "values are power resources for a leadership that would transform society for the fuller realization of the highest moral purposes";[51] these Asian values have likewise been power resources for Asian leadership. Practicing these values is training for Asian leaders to transform Asian society for the fuller realization of the highest moral purposes.

With current Asian leadership now under the strong influences of Western individual capitalism and globalization, the notion of Asian leadership is more complex. When Asians leave their countries and arrive on US shores as immigrants, the concepts of Asian leadership are particularly in question. Through a strong transnational dynamics and acculturation process, Asian immigrants start to reevaluate the concepts of Asian leadership. At the same time, they try to understand perceptions of US leadership in a deep conversation with complex dynamics of racial, sex and gender, class and colonial/postcolonial discourses. What are the results of this reevaluation under these discourses? How do these dynamics interplay to shape Asian immigrant leadership? What are the concepts of Asian immigrant leadership? How do Asian immigrant leaders themselves define and practice leadership? What are the challenges of Asian leadership? In the next section, these questions are seriously considered and possible answers are explored.

Challenges of Asian Immigrant Leadership in the Discourses of Race, Sex and Gender, and Culture

One of the common perceptions is that Asian immigrants are overly enthusiastic about education and obsessive about top-ranked colleges, but underrepresented in leadership positions overall.[52] "Many college-educated Asian immigrants engage in low-status, low paying occupations as taxi drivers, gas station attendants, or cleaners," whereas many Korean immigrants work in labor-intensive small businesses in relation to their ethnic community.[53] Even for American immigrants who work in high-paying jobs, there are few Asian immigrants in leadership positions. In a 2015 report on diversity in Silicon Valley, Asian immigrants were well represented in lower-level positions at five big tech firms (Google, Hewlett-Packard, Intel, LinkedIn, and Yahoo), but not in higher levels. "In these five firms, white men and women are 154% more likely than Asians to hold an executive role."[54] Asian immigrant groups are the second-largest immigrant groups in the United States, but "Asian Americans only hold between 1% and 4% of upper-management and decision-making position."[55] Despite their higher education, they do not get equal opportunities like white Americans and often end their careers in midlevel managerial positions or second-class leadership positions.

Images of Asian American leaders are commonly described as highly intelligent and educated, but lacking in social skills. In a study of assessment fit between stereotypes of minority managers and the successful manager prototype, Beth G. Chung-Herrera and Melenie J. Lankau describe the Asian American manager stereotype as "less self-confident, more intelligent, less articulate, more industrious, more educated, more technically proficient, less charismatic, more family oriented, more globally aware, more religious values, hide emotions more, more reserved, more quiet, more passive, more shy, more submissive, and more timid."[56] Even though Asian American managers are recognized with positive traits—more intelligent, more industrious, more educated, and more technically proficient in terms of their professional knowledge and technical skills—they are evaluated with negative traits such as less self-confident, less articulate, less charismatic, more passive, more shy, and more submissive in terms of leadership traits. They are good workers, but not good leaders. Several traits, such as hides emotions more, quieter, more reserved, more passive, shyer, more submissive, and more timid, are understood as indicative of a lack of social skills. Hiding emotions or performing less self-disclosure impression management tactics are particularly seen as features unsuitable for leaders. Katherine R. Xin also claims that Asian American managers often demonstrate "significantly lower levels of self-disclosure, self-focused impression management tactics, and supervisor focused impression management tactics, but more job-focused impression management tactics compared with European American managers."[57] These stereotypes and management tactics imply that Asian Americans are poorly equipped with the traits of the successful leaders in business settings. Rather, they better equipped with the traits of workers, followers, who need help and guidance.

In light of the virtues of Asian religious teachings that discussed earlier, hiding emotions or inhibited self-disclosure traits are quite understandable in the eyes of Asians. However, in the eyes of US culture, these traits are unsuitable for leaders. The low success rate for Asian Americans in leadership positions, especially for first-generation immigrants, is understood as the result of their lack of leadership qualities due to failures in the acculturation process. Stefanie K. Johnson and Thomas Sy believe that these stereotypes impede Asian Americans in two ways:

"stereotypes about Asians being highly competent can make Asians appear threatening in the workplace, and stereotypes about Asians lacking social skills make them seem unfit for leadership."[58] When Asian Americans or Asian immigrants demonstrate excellent skills and produce high levels of accomplishment, it provokes fear in elite, privileged white groups and incites envy among other racial ethnic groups. Elite, privileged whites feel particularly threatened. Out of fear, they use the negative stereotype (lack of social skills) to disqualify Asian immigrants for leadership in the same group.[59] Their discrimination and hostility toward Asian immigrants prevent them from taking leadership positions. White fear against Asian immigrants is one way to understand the challenges of Asian immigrant leadership.

How do we understand Asian immigrant leadership then? Even though there are many ways to understand the challenges to Asian American or Asian immigrant leadership, one of the most significant ways is to know how Asian immigrants recognize and understand leadership concepts within and beyond Asian values and white-dominated colonial/postcolonial cultural values in their immigrant contexts. As Asian immigrants understand certain leadership concepts as immigrants, they simultaneously encounter white concepts of leadership and are evaluated by them. Some Asian leadership concepts are perceived positively in an Asian immigrant context, but are quite opposite in the US context. Many Asian immigrant leaders experience the conflict in these concepts. What are these concepts? How are they perceived differently?

Self-Confidence in the United States

Self-confidence has been one of the most popular and well-known leadership concepts and traits in US culture. Self-confidence is understood as the key concept to be a successful leader. It is a "must have" trait for leaders in the United States. It is believed that "the leader's most important role is to instill confidence in people."[60] As discussed in the earlier section, it is defined as a trait that only top executive, elite, Anglo male leaders and African American female leaders have.[61] However, it is never demonstrated as a strong suit for Asian American and Asian immigrant leaders, especially for Asian American female leaders. Rather, Asian American leaders are often criticized as a group with "less self-confident" characteristics.

What is self-confidence? How is it defined? George P. Hollenbeck and Douglas T. Hall define self-confidence as "our judgement of whether or not we can do something," and they introduce six implications to understand the concept of self-confidence: "1) a judgment, result of our thinking," 2) "based on perceptions both of our capabilities and what the task or challenge requires," 3) "task specific," 4) "something that can be changed," 5) "*NOT self-esteem*," and 6) "develops in self-reinforcing, positive cycles."[62] Based on these implications, self-confidence can be understood as a judgment of one's ability to accomplish a specific task depending on the extent of the environment's support of change and development. It is not self-esteem but a judgment. In this study, Hollenbeck and Hall explain that when people take a risk, make an effort, and have a successful experience, they develop self-confidence. Hollenbeck and Hall introduce four basic resources to cultivate self-confidence; "1) actual experience, the things that we have done, 2) the experiences of others, "modeling," 3) social persuasion, the process of convicting by someone else, and 4) emotional arousal, how we feel about events around us and how we manage our emotions."[63] As people develop self-confidence based on these resources, they demonstrate better approaches of motivation, perception, and thought processes. As a result, they perform better. Self-confidence is not something that one is born with. It is developed in the cycle of one's individual and social experience. Ron Heifetz and Donald Laurie also claim that "self-confidence comes from success, experiences, and the organization's environment."[64] It is something to nurture and develop. When people experience success, positive experience, and a good organizational environment, they become confident. Both studies agree that self-confidence is derived from successful experience and from social communal environments. Without the positive experiences of success and encouragement from social communal environments, it is not possible to develop self-confidence.

The question then becomes who has self-confidence? What groups have it the most? What if there are people who do not have successful experience and do not receive any encouragement from their social environments? Is it possible for them to develop self-confidence? How? Is self-confidence really understood as Hollenbeck and Hall define? How is self-confidence understood in the United States? How is it perceived and performed?

In the Western culture of the United States, the concept of self-confidence is often performed in the forms of upbeat self-promotion, excessive positivism, and claiming authority.[65] It is not a judgment of one's capability or social environment. Rather, it is commonly articulated as "we can do anything with a positive attitude." The concept of self-confidence in the

United States is perceived not as a judgment, but as excessive positivity. In fact, self-confidence and positive thinking (optimism) are unified as two sides of one coin.[66] It is perceived neither as a perception of a leader's capability nor as the challenges of a task. It is not about confidence in a specific task. Rather, it is perceived as a leader's excessively positive attitude for all tasks. It is the expression of leaders to show how to produce happiness *no matter what*. Self-confidence is not about performing specific tasks but about accomplishing all tasks at all times. It is about how to promote a leader's agenda with authority. Imposing happiness on everyone in the group, leaders are expected to show a positive attitude as self-confidence under any given circumstance.[67] Self-confidence becomes excessive enthusiasm about success in the United States. It is a belief of the inevitability of good to great. Based on their successful experience, self-confidence becomes leaders' obsessive self-authority.

Who performs excessive positivism and authority as self-confidence in this society now? As Chung-Herrera and Lankau's study discovered, the trait of self-confidence is found only in white groups.[68] Asian American, African American, and Hispanic American groups are determined to be less self-confident. It seems that self-confidence is the exclusive purview of privileged, elite, heterosexual white males without disability. It has been developed and nurtured only within this group. This white group experiences success without barriers in terms of racial prejudice and sexual and gender discrimination. Its members have watched many white leaders as role models. The society as a whole endorses their existence as whoever they want to be. All social communities accept them as who they are. An emotional arousal naturally follows. The positive and supportive experience of being white in this society positions them to develop self-confidence. Based on the successful experience of being white and based on the strong influence of white individualistic capitalism, privileged whites perform extreme positivism to increase the pressure on others to produce more. Success gives them the right to claim authority over others. It gives them permission to lead others. Their success becomes the narcissistic white superiority named self-confidence, and the circle of the development of self-confidence is complete.

When the concept of self-confidence encounters white Christian evangelical spirituality, it is even more dangerous. White Christian evangelical spirituality in collaboration with positive thinking fortifies the concept of self-confidence in an absolute sense of authority. Norman Vincent Peale claims the practice of positive thinking techniques to be the power of faith in action. He believes that by practicing these techniques, people will learn how to "expect the best and get it, create their own happiness, believe in themselves and in everything they do, develop the power to reach their goals, break the worry habit and achieve relaxed lives, improve their personal and professional relationships, get people to like them, assume control over their circumstances, draw upon that higher power, and be kind to themselves."[69] These techniques are equivalent to the power of faith. Peale emphasizes keeping positive thinking in every thought and with every move. It is a commandment from God. Keeping positive thinking is identified with keeping faith in God. Positive thinking becomes faith itself. In this construction of belief, positive thinking fixes all problems. It removes the inferiority complex and brings confidence in oneself.[70] It is claimed in the form of divine authority. Many charismatic preachers and ministers adopt positive thinking as a part of a spiritual exercise to develop strong faith. They embrace positive thinking as God's will. Using God's language, they affirm excessive positive thinking as an absolute form of the power of faith. Excessive positive thinking boosts self-confidence in a spiritual sense. Self-confidence becomes an extreme form of self-belief and self-conviction. It produces superiority and nurtures grandiosity. It is perceived as a strong conviction from God. Many charismatic religious leaders themselves cultivate this extreme positive thinking as self-confidence:

> Weber argued that charismatic leaders typically believe in their divinely ordained mission, viewing themselves in overly positive ways as "the chosen ones" with a "destiny" and "higher purpose" differentiating them from others. Excessive positive thinking can therefore fuel leaders' inflated sense of superiority and excessively positive self-belief and self-conviction. Their grandiose self-image can be compounded by followers who attribute exceptional qualities to leaders through, for example, transference, or fantasy. Such excessive positivity in the dialectical dynamics between charismatics and their adoring followers can strengthen leaders' belief in their own power and invulnerability in ways that perpetuate their hubristic and narcissistic practices. The posthumous idealization of founding members of organizations and societies further reveals how followers' excessively positive attributions and romanticism may become even stronger after the charismatic leader dies.[71]

In this white, evangelical Christian context, self-confidence turns into faith in the form of extreme positivism and an absolute sense of authority. When excessive positive thinking from this evangelical belief encounters complexities of race, sex and gender, class, and colonial/postcolonial dynamics, it accelerates the privileged white group to believe themselves to be chosen leaders from God to protect society. The concepts of superiority and narcissistic practice are accepted as self-confidence and legitimately practiced by the privileged white group in a spiritual and psychological sense. Engaging with racial, sex and gender, class, and colonial/postcolonial discourses, the concepts of white superiority and white-centered narcissistic attitudes are perpetually equated to self-confidence.

For racial ethnic groups, the circle of development of self-confidence is not applicable. The complicated immigrant experience does not cultivate positivity in Asian immigrant and Asian American leadership. Racial ethnic groups, under the pressure of severe prejudice and discrimination, do not experience much success compared to privileged whites. They do not have many opportunities to develop self-confidence in society at large beyond ethnic boundaries. Struggling with various prejudices and discriminations, they have difficulty finding good role models within their ethnic groups in larger public squares. The absence of role models from their own ethnic groups and the invisibility of Asian immigrant leadership positions are what they experience. In fact, many of them are the first role models for other Asian immigrants and Asian Americans. They are the pioneers in their fields. Moreover, the society or the organization's environments do not encourage these racial ethnic groups to develop self-confidence. Rather, the message from white society is a denial of immigrants' or racial ethnic minorities' existence and their leadership.

Racial ethnic groups are discouraged by society to be leaders. Despite their excellence, they are not allowed to claim authority. Positive and successful experience of leadership is not a part of their immigrant experience. They are forced to stay in positions of permanent followers. As they experience serious disadvantages in advancement and discrimination from various social constructions, they encounter serious impediments to the emotional arousal needed to be leaders. Moreover, when Christian evangelical spiritual leaders encourage extreme positivism and enthusiasm, but racial, ethnic religious groups fail to maintain these attitudes, their failure is perceived as due to their own personal limits. When they are taught to expect the best, but they cannot get it, it is interpreted as due to their lack of faith. When they realize that they cannot assume control over their social circumstances, their frustration with social environment is understood as their personal misjudgment. Instead of developing superiority, they experience inferiority. Instead of fostering narcissistic attitudes, they experience shame. Without actual experience and modeling and without social persuasion and emotional arousal, they experience an endless series of frustrations. As they experience these frustrations, they cannot easily develop self-confidence. However, it does not mean they cannot develop leadership. Based on these individual and communal struggles and frustrations, Asian immigrant leaders develop their own way to form leadership. In fact, self-confidence converged with positive attitudes is not the way to develop Asian immigrants and Asian American leadership.

Self-Awareness in an Asian Context

The Asian way of developing leadership is not self-confidence but self-awareness, including self-evaluation, self-reflection, self-control, and self-completion. Self-awareness is a fundamental part of Asian ethnic cultural values for leaders. Dong Min Kim, Jang Wan Ko, and Seon-Joo Kim claim that in Oriental philosophy, the foundation of leadership starts with *Su-Gi-Chi-In*, which means self-cultivation first, then governing people next. *Su-Gi-Chi-In* is considered as to be the goal of leadership. In the *Great Learning*, "the process of development of *Su-Gi-Chi-In* is divided into four levels: *Sushin* (cultivate one's mortality)—*Jega* (manage the family)—*Chikook* (governing a country)—*Pyungchunha* (rule over the whole country peacefully)."[72] Kim, Ko, and Kim explain these four levels of the leadership process in comparison with the process of self-awareness of individuals and individuals in personal, social and global relationships. *Sushin* is the first stage of leadership training. It is self-awareness. In the concept of *Su-Gi-Chi-In*, training oneself in terms of self-awareness is the first development to be leaders. Without the proper training of *Sushin*, it is impossible for leaders to lead family, region, and the whole country.

Similar to the concept of *Sushin*, *Zhixin-Chijing* (cultivation of the mind and eternal piety), a concept advanced by sixteenth-century Korean philosopher Yi Toegye, is a form of self-reflection.[73] *Zhixin-Chijing* means keeping internal piety by mastering one's mind. It is about how to control one's mind to be in inner piety. In Yi's understanding of *jing* as "the best state of mind where one keeps one's balance and stays firmly committed to doing what one desires," in his book *Toegye Compendium*, book 7, he suggested four methods to cultivate the state of *jing*: "a) concentrating one's mind on one thing without having any other thought in mind, b) keeping one's appearance (e.g., posture and conduct) neat and dignified, c) ensuring that one's mind always stays alert and awake, and d) mastering one's mind such that other things or thoughts will not be allowed."[74] For Yi, keeping inner piety is the most important value and is achievable in the form of self-completion only though self-learning and self-awareness. Based on achieving self-completion, leaders can finally lead others and establish balanced social relations. Both *Sushin* and *Zhixin-Chijing* are concepts of self-training to develop leaders' morality and integrity. Without completing the process of self-awareness for moral integrity, leaders cannot be true leaders. Leaders must be aware of their own genuine and authentic self even when no one is aware. They should know who they were, who they are, what they are capable of, what their limits are, what they want to be and what they are willing to do. They must be in the state of self-awareness. They must control their self and stay in integrity. Through these Asian virtues and teachings, Asian immigrants and Asian Americans have tried to cultivate leadership.

Along with self-awareness, self-effacement or a humility that encompasses emptiness of self is another way of training oneself in Asian ethnic culture, which was discussed earlier in this chapter.

> Therefore in the Sage's desire to be above the people,
> He must in his speech be below them.
> And in his desire to be at the front of the people.
> He must in his person be behind them.[75]

> Therefore the Sage knows himself but doesn't show himself;
> He cherishes himself but doesn't value himself.[76]

> Therefore the Sage:
> Put himself in the background yet finds himself in the foreground;
> Put self-concern out of his mind, yet finds that his self-concern is reserved.[77]

The Asian ethnic cultural code of leadership is deeply related to self-effacement rather than self-promotion. Self-promotion is an immature behavior for leaders in Asian context. Leaders should not promote themselves but stay below and behind people. They should be in the background.

Instead of self-promotion, self-effacement is encouraged and nurtured in Asian context. The concept of self-effacement is deeply connected to the concept of self-control, such as hiding emotions and being quiet. It is expected that leaders should not display self-promotion or preference through emotions. They should stay in a neutral position. Being quiet and hiding emotions are often encouraged as the way of self-control, "self awareness," "self-regulated behaviors" and virtues for leaders.[78] It is believed in Asian context that being talkative and/or expressing emotions of anger or happiness might hurt others' opinions or bring fear in others. Therefore, leaders need to train themselves not to reveal their emotions. They are encouraged to practice "the wordless teaching."[79] They must control their emotions and keep a stable psychological state of minds. Meditation and yoga are encouraged as part of leadership training.

However, in the United States, being quiet and hiding emotion are secretive and dishonest behaviors. They are evaluated as a lack of self-confidence. In Asian culture, silence is a sign of respect for others but in the US culture, it is understood as a disrespectful behavior.[80] It is believed to be a sign of a lack of intelligence. It is treated as a communication problem. Leaders are supposed to talk less in Asian culture, whereas leaders are encouraged to talk more in the United States. Leaders in the United States are encouraged to demonstrate excellent skills of debate and public speaking as a sign of self-confidence: "If we know something, until it has been expressed—verbalized—we don't have it available for use in our conscious experience."[81] Many competitions of speech and debates are encouraged in Western educational settings. Speaking is a critical part of leadership formation in US culture, whereas silence is a crucial part of leadership training in the Asian ethnic culture. Many white leaders in the United States are trained to not hide their emotions, even anger, but many Asian immigrant leaders are trained not to reveal their emotions. Images of charismatic leaders in the United States are of someone who can speak eloquently and lead people with strong self-confidence and positive attitudes, whereas images of charismatic leaders in Asian ethnic immigrant culture is of someone who is serene and leads people with profound self-awareness. The characteristic of being quiet is more suitable for leaders in Asian culture. However, it is never encouraged in US culture.

"Harmony, respect for authority/elders, shame, humility, a higher standard of excellence (hard work and the importance of success), and eagerness to learn/be educated" are also deeply connected with self-awareness in Asian leadership values.[82] Harmony is one of the most important values in Asian leadership. It is deeply related with respect for authority/elders and humility. As the goal of leadership in Asian culture is to lead the community in harmony, respect for authority and the practice of humility are understood as not only the integrity of leaders but also their capacity for self-awareness. Respect for authority/elders and the practice of humility in terms of self-awareness means that leaders should, first and foremost, respect others' opinions and not put themselves before others. These characters are believed as a way to practice self-awareness for leading the community without conflict. In the same manner, a higher standard of excellence and an eagerness for education are understood as a way to develop self-awareness to enhance one's own ability to serve others and community in harmony. Therefore, self-awareness has been one of the most fundamental embodied concepts that empower many Asian leadership features.

However, in the United States, harmony can be understood as an "avoidance of conflict, unassertiveness," and respect for authority/elders and humility can be understood as "being reluctant to disagree or challenge."[83] Under the influence of individualistic capitalism and negative images of Asian culture in the US, harmony, respect for authority/elders, and humility can be interpreted as barriers to individual freedom and independence. In a similar manner, shame and humility can be understood as characteristics of overconcern for appearances, or lack of confidence, while a higher standard of excellence and eagerness for education are pictured as "overly demanding" and "not a good team player."[84] These negative evaluations can easily produce the stereotypes of Asian immigrants and Asian American leaders as "not being assertive, worrying too much about face, or being less social."[85] The problem is not the values of these characteristics. Some of these characteristics are evaluated as positive leadership attributes in recent feminist leadership studies and leadership trait study. The problem is who is practicing them in what contexts. If these characteristics are practiced by privileged, elite whites with self-confidence and American white accents, they might be interpreted as level 5 leadership traits. However, if they are practiced by Asian immigrants with self-awareness and Asian accents, they could easily be perceived as inefficient leadership traits.

In summary, Asian leaders cultivate leadership based on Asian understandings of self-awareness in relation to leadership characters like being quiet, hiding emotions, harmony, respect for authority/elders, shame, humbleness/humility, higher standard of excellence (hard work and important of success), and eagerness for education. However, these are often considered negative attributes of leadership for Asian immigrants in the US context. For example, hiding emotions is encouraged and silence is embraced for leaders in Asian ethnic culture, whereas hiding emotions is understood as shy and dishonest in the United States. Asian morals and values encourage Asian leaders to be aware of their behaviors in the sense of critical self-awareness/evaluation,[86] whereas the values of US leadership emphasize self-promotion, extreme positivism, strong self-authority, and expressive speech in the expression of self-confidence. Asian leadership does not promote self-confidence as the essential quality of leadership, whereas US leadership does not value self-effacement in practice. The concept of self-confidence, especially self-promotion and extreme positivism, is not perceived as positive traits for leaders in Asian ethnic context, whereas self-promotion and extremely enthusiastic positivism are now presented as crucial techniques for job interviews and promotion in the United States.

The concept of self-confidence shows an unbridgeable dilemma in these two cultures. On the one hand, self-confidence is required as the most important key concept for leaders in the United States.[87] If you want to be a leader, you must be self-confident. It is believed to be the essential, universal necessity for all leaders regardless race, sex and gender, class, nationality, ethnicity, and religion. Self-confidence is a collective psychological condition for being leaders in the United States. It is even endorsed and granted by religious ideology as an important part of spiritual practice. On the other hand, it is nurtured and encouraged by this society only within the privileged white group. The whole social and cultural environment supports only the white group's development of self-confidence. It is designed only for this group as preparation for leadership. Consequently, self-confidence belongs only to privileged whites.[88] The dilemma is that self-confidence is required as the most crucial concept of leaders by everyone, even though it only belongs to privileged whites in US society. It is implied that self-confidence is not achievable by or trainable for other groups. This is another vicious circle of white patriarchal leadership practice. As this dilemma is engaged by Asian values of leadership, it causes more struggles for Asian immigrant and Asian American leaders.

Self-Confidence and Self-Awareness in the Asian Immigrant US Context

When Asian immigrants move to the United States, they experience a discrepancy and confusion between leadership in the United States (self-confidence) and their ethnic cultural leadership (self-awareness). What Asian immigrants and Asian Americans learn from their ethnic culture is not what they see and observe in leadership in the United States. For example, the Asian cultural sense of quietness and hiding emotions are still recognized as stereotypes of Asian immigrants in the United States. However, this is not perceived as just a cultural difference. Further complication adds to these stereotypes of Asian American attributes. This is related, first, to difficulties in speaking English and, second, to speaking English with Asian accents.

Many first-generation immigrants are not comfortable speaking English. Most of them prefer to speak their native languages even if they can speak English well. Because of difficulties in speaking English, many first-generation immigrants avoid public engagement. They stay in their own ethnic community and speak their own Asian language. However, speaking ethnic languages provokes fear and anxiety in English speakers. It is interpreted as dis-communication in society, and their gathering in ethnic communities is recognized as a socially isolated and "dangerous" presence. These behaviors are seen as hiding in an ethnic cave and criticized as failure of acculturation.[89] Karthick Ramakrishnan and Celia Viramontes explain this experience as social isolation and linguistic barriers.[90] This linguistic barrier causes Asian immigrants to be silent. It increasingly induces behaviors of quietness and hiding emotions. Their embodied behaviors of quietness and hiding emotions converge with the embarrassment of not being able to speak English. To cover this embarrassment and to avoid provoking fear from others, they are forced to smile and not reveal their emotions. As Asian immigrants have embodied quietness and hiding emotions as a part of their cultural practices, this linguistic barrier reinforces this behavior. Out of survival, they learn how to smile beneath their frustration. Consequently, these attributes are portrayed as perpetual Asian immigrants' stereotypes and are interpreted as innate communication problems.

Second, even if Asian immigrants are fluent in English, speaking English with Asian accents is often disdained and recognized as unsophisticated and ineloquent speech. "Asian immigrants with strong Asian accents are subject to more discrimination in the labor market than those with less obvious accents."[91] People with Asian accents are met with "a combination of irritation, unease, distrust, and condescension."[92] Unlike the public adoration of European white accents, often accompanied by classical music and regarded as an educated, elegant high-class accent, public mockery of English spoken with Asian accents can be easily found, from politicians, talk-show hosts, newspapers, and news commentators to law makers, lawyers, and judges speaking to petitioners.[93] "Accent, when it serves as a marker of race, takes on special power and significance."[94] As a result of speaking English with an Asian accent, employment discrimination often occurs and the glass ceiling is employed against promotion of Asian immigrants.[95] Even though speaking with Asian accents is not ostentatiously measured as a communication problem in public domain, it is always scrutinized as "contested terrain."[96] Asian accents are perceived as miscommunication. Within these complicated social dynamics, Asian immigrants' communications is not encouraged. By hiding the embarrassment and shame, they become quiet and hide their emotions more. In this vicious circle, these perceptions are again fortified as stereotypes of Asian immigrants. When the meaning of quietness and hiding emotions enters an Asian immigrant context, its positive impact in Asian leadership turns into negative images of leadership for Asian immigrants. Colonial/postcolonial interpretation of Asian accents reinterprets the meaning of quietness and hiding emotions as lack of self-confidence in an Asian immigrant context. This is an example of how the Asian immigrant context changes the values and meanings of leadership for Asian immigrant in the United States.

Even though many Asian immigrants and Asian Americans are taught about self-awareness as a fundamental part of leadership from their ethnic cultures, when they enter an immigrant context in the United States, they encounter a serious dilemma and conflict. To overcome this dilemma and conflict, a reevaluation of the meaning of self-awareness in an American immigrant culture itself is inevitable. The concept of self-awareness needs to reflect the positionality of Asian immigrants in the complex discourses of race, sex and gender, class, and colonial/postcolonial discussion. It requires knowledge of the values and morals of both Asian ethnic communal culture and US individualistic culture within the interaction between local, national, transnational, and global contexts.

The roots of self-confidence in Western culture are derived from individual freedom and autonomy, whereas the roots of self-awareness in Asian cultures derive from communal goodness. The concept of self-awareness in an Asian immigrant context emerges from both these cultural contexts. It concerns both individualistic and communal contexts. However, it goes beyond just combining two cultures. The concept of self-awareness has been transformed from its original meaning into its creative contextual meaning in an Asian immigrant context.

From the long experience of colonial/postcolonial domination under white Euro-American power, from immigrant experiences of prejudice and discrimination against non-white groups, and from Asian cultural values and practices, self-awareness in an Asian immigrant context is conceptualized as a process of discernment for Asian immigrants' individual and communal abilities, limits, and possibilities based on interactions and reinterpretations of both Asian ethnic values and US culture locally, nationally, and globally. It is discernment for the transformation of immigrant identity in praxis. It is self-awareness beyond one's own self. It requires self-awareness about the individual and social contexts within and beyond one's own immigrant community. It asks for serious attention to who they are and what they do with others beyond their own ethnic boundaries under the consideration of psychological and spiritual sensitivities and socioeconomic positionality of Asian immigrants in the US. Therefore, self-awareness is one of the most important traits for Asian immigrant and Asian American leadership. Some Asian American leadership scholars such as Linda Akutagawa and Jean Lau Chin are keenly aware of self-awareness as the most fundamental part of Asian American leadership and introduce various models of Asian American leadership development processes.

In the Leadership Education for Asian Pacifics, Inc., program, Akutagawa introduces Asian American leadership development with five goals: 1) cultivating "an open, honest, nonjudgmental atmosphere"; 2) leveraging Asian values and developing new skills; 3) providing a "culturally relevant" and "sensitive" learning experience; 4) "keeping Asian Americans from falling behind the leadership curve in the workplace"; and 5) "benefiting the organizations that support Asian American leadership development."[97] To accomplish these five goals, she claims that self-awareness should be the foundation of Asian immigrant and Asian American leadership formation. Based on the concept of self-awareness, this program develops five components of a leadership framework. The first component is to "expand self-awareness." Instead of self-confidence, Asian immigrant and Asian American leaders should expand their self-awareness and meet others as who they are and where they are. Being aware of seeing themselves as "a community representative and a bridge to others," they should be "comfortable with themselves" and with others, a comfort that lies in "understanding relationships among perceptions, behaviors and values" between multicultural dynamics.[98] Following the expansion of self-awareness, Asian Americans should "lead and manage change" (second component); "learn continuously" (third component); "grow high-performing teams, coalitions, and partnerships" (fourth component); and "sustain energy and stamina" (fifth component) as the main components for developing an Asian immigrant and Asian American leadership framework.[99] This framework encourages Asian immigrants and Asian American leaders to develop their own concept of leadership and leadership skills, both between the two cultures and beyond.

In a study of Asian American leadership, Chin analyzes perceptions of incompatibility between Asian Americans and their potential for leadership roles and finds how Asian American leaders might respond to stereotypical threats. Reflecting these responses and prejudices and drawing on resilience and strength of Asian values and culture, she suggests "a model of diversity leadership" as Asian American leadership development.[100] She encourages creating this model for Asian immigrant and Asian American leaders to embrace diverse and inclusive perspectives beyond the prototypical Western white male model of leadership.

Thomas Sy, Lynn M. Shore, Judy Strauss, Ted H. Shore, Susanna Tram, Paul Whiteley, and Kristine Ikeda-Muromachi evaluate perceptions of leadership as a function of contextual factors of race and occupation. They suggest the connectionist model for Asian American leaders, "positing that leadership perceptions are generated at the moment of use, and are highly flexible, depending on one's experience, knowledge, motivation, purpose of judgement and goals (e.g., accuracy goals, social motives, accountability, power hierarchy, etc.)."[101] They believe that Asian American leaders demonstrate and develop more connectional styles of leadership with people, environments, and contexts.

Even though these scholars suggest different types or models of Asian American leadership development as a result of their studies, all of them observe the common problems of prejudice and discrimination against Asian immigrant and Asian American leaders in the complexities of race relations and start with these problems as the first step to understanding Asian immigrant and Asian American leadership. The common assumption is critical awareness of the uniqueness of Asian immigrant and Asian American positionality in a US context and the dual meanings of Asian immigrant leadership concepts. The more Asian immigrant and Asian American leaders are profoundly aware of their immigrant context, the better they perform as leaders. These scholars emphasize the deeper analysis of Asian immigrant context and its challenges. They demonstrate what both US leadership and Asian leadership really require, how Asian immigrant leaders understand both leaderships, and how they can transform those leaderships and create new leadership skills in the workplace and in public.

However, achieving self-awareness itself is not the goal of these leadership studies, even though it is an important part of leadership training. The goal of Asian American leadership training is to discover how Asian immigrants and Asian Americans understand leadership and transform the meaning of leadership in their local communities, society at large, and beyond. In other words, the goal of their leadership development is not transformation of Asian leadership styles into a US white context, but transformation of their leadership into their immigrant context that exists in the interactions between Western and Eastern local, national, transnational, and global contexts. To survive, it is inevitable for Asian immigrants to extend these concepts beyond Asian ethnic cultural boundaries, overcoming the criticism of Asian immigrant and Asian American leadership and transforming both Western and Eastern values into their own immigrant context and beyond with their own discernment.

PART III

POSTCOLONIAL LEADERSHIP IN AN ASIAN IMMIGRANT CHRISTIAN CONTEXT

Chapter 5

Asian Immigrant Christian Leadership

As Asian immigrant and Asian American leaders encounter a Christian context in the United States, it adds another dimension to leadership formation. Peter C. Phan points out that even though Christianity was born in (Southwest) Asia, originating in Palestine, and was centered in Asia until the seventh century, "it returned to its birthplace as a foreign religion, or worse, the religion of its colonizers, and is still being widely regarded as such by many Asians."[1] It became a Western religion when it moved to Rome. With colonial/postcolonial invasions, Christianity has been recognized as the most powerful colonial Western religion in Asian countries. Even though Christianity in Asia has a minority status, it has powerful influence on education, health care, and social services in many Asian countries.[2] However, when Asians migrate to the US, they recognize Christianity not as a religion of the minority, but as a religion of the majority. Some Asian immigrants became Christians by missionaries before they came to the United States, and others became Christians upon their arrival. Whether they were already Christians or became Christians after their arrival in the United States, they encounter Christianity in a different way from the Christianity of their native countries. The relationship between Christianity and other religious faiths in an Asian immigrant context necessarily adds a plurality and diversity to their faith practice, even though Christianity discourages plurality and diversity as a threat and promotes universalization and uniformity as absolute values.[3] As the understanding of Christianity changes, the expectations of the church change and so do the expectations of church leaders.

Images of Jesus in Relation to Leadership in an Asian Immigrant Christian Context

Images of Jesus as a Leader in a Western Christian Context

The model of Christian leadership originates with Jesus's leadership from the beginning of Christian history. Whether in East or West, whether through the eyes of Christians or the eyes of believers of other faiths, Jesus has been recognized as the primordial figure of Christian leadership. Christian leadership is often summarized as following Jesus. From the leadership of disciples to the leadership of priests and pastors, the model of Jesus's leadership is believed, confessed, claimed, and worshipped as the model of Christian leadership. What is the model of Jesus's leadership? How can it be examined? Burns claims that "from the days of Homer, the simplest way of understanding leaders and rulers was to examine their distinguishing characteristics. It is the same today."[4] Therefore, one of the most important steps to understanding Jesus's leadership is examining Jesus's distinguishing characteristics. What are these traits? How do we know?

Even though there is no physical evidence of Jesus's existence in history, many historians, biblical scholars, and theologians have proven his historical existence and provide numerous characteristics of Jesus. In fact, there are countless images of Jesus that have been created and believed throughout history. The images of Jesus are not images of the individual Jesus, but images of Jesus that people create and project from their own contexts. Depending on various traditions of theologians, biblical scholars, pastors, all believers and their methodologies, the images of Jesus have been discovered and rediscovered and claimed and reclaimed over the years. Depending on each sociocultural historical context, the images of Jesus are challenged and changed. To examine the images of Jesus is examining the traits of Jesus. However, it is not an analysis of the individual Jesus's characteristics, but *an analysis of communal belief and communal characteristics that people project on their ideal leaders through Jesus in each context*. In other words, examining the images of Jesus in terms of leadership is understanding the traits of ideal leaders that people hope to have in their own Christian contexts through the images of Jesus. Therefore, it is important to analyze how each image of Jesus relates to leadership traits in each different context.

Biblical scholars, theologians, and historical researchers examine the images of Jesus in theological, sociocultural, historical, and spiritual studies. Some historical studies introduce contemporary images of Jesus as the social prophet (Richard Horsley), the charismatic Jew (Géza Vermes), the magician (Morton Smith), the Jewish Sage (Ben Witherington III), the cynic philosopher (F. Gerald Downing), and others.[5] Other historians and theologians in Jesus Seminar describe the images of Jesus as a rebel leader, a charismatic holy man, a supernatural magician, a social and/or eschatological prophet, an eschatological sage, a healer, a spiritual person, a social movement leader, the Messiah, and others in historical studies of Jesus.[6] The Jesus Seminar captures the existence of Jesus not as a divine figure but as a historical figure. It tries to demystify some images of Jesus such as a divine savior, a miracle worker, or a magical healer in terms of physical illness, but to refortify human images of Jesus as a living Jew or a leader of a social justice movement. The emphasis of these studies is to picture Jesus as a historical human, a living person, even though it does not pay much attention to the skin color of this historical person. However, the common images of Jesus in a white Christian context claim Jesus in a different way. The most common and popular images of Jesus are a Divine Universal Savior with white skin and a white face. Jesus became the white-raced, male-gendered Christ. Through colonial art and postcolonial influences of the media, colonial and postcolonial ideologies and theologies, the images of Jesus are seriously tainted and distorted. As the white images of Jesus became *the* image of Christ, white Jesus's leadership became *the* leadership for all Christians. As Jesus's skin color and maleness are created as white in historical studies, the leadership of Jesus is effortlessly identified with white leadership.

Images of Jesus as a Leader in an Asian Immigrant Church Context

Many Asian immigrant Christians and churches also look up to Jesus as the model of Christian leadership. As many Asians encountered Jesus through white Western missionaries, their images of Jesus were deeply influenced by these missionaries and their theologies. It is undeniable that many Asian Christians and Asian immigrant Christians are still under the heavy influence of colonial and postcolonial Western theologies and ideologies. However, it is also true that images of the white Christ have been seriously challenged by Asian and Asian immigrant theologies and churches since the first day Christianity encountered Asian soil. The images of Jesus in Asian and Asian immigrant contexts have been claimed as radically different from the images of white Christ in a Western context. White Jesus has been uncolored in many Asian immigrant churches and recolored with their own beliefs. Many Asian immigrant scholars claim that Asian religious cultures have shaped the images of Jesus differently from white missionaries' theologies, and hardships of the Asian immigrant experience have promoted different images of Jesus.

Even though there are numerous images of Jesus that Asian and Asian immigrants created, there are two commonalities that are embedded in these images: suffering and Asian multireligious cultures. Every image of Jesus claimed by Asian immigrant Christians and theologians is deeply related to the suffering of Asian immigrants and resonant with Asian multireligious cultures. These two factors are deeply ingrained and intertwined in the images of Jesus in Asian and Asian immigrant contexts. It means that requirements for leaders of Asians and Asian immigrants are also deeply related to how to understand suffering and deal with it in a way that Asians and Asian immigrants could understand from their Asian immigrant cultural traditions.

Co-sufferer

The image of Jesus as co-sufferer is a common theme among Asian immigrant theologians and other Latinx immigrant theologians. However, the image of Jesus as co-sufferer is claimed differently in each Asian ethnic context. In the case of Andrew Sung Park, the image of Jesus as co-sufferer is deeply related with the Korean concept of *han*. Exploring the suffering of the innocent, powerless, marginalized, and the voiceless, Park defines the Korean concept of *han* as "a physical, mental, and spiritual repercussion to a terrible injustice done to a person, eliciting a deep ache, a wrenching of all the organs, an intense internalized or externalized rage, a vengeful obsession, and the sense of helplessness and hopelessness."[7] It is "frustrated hope, the collapsed feeling of pain, letting go, resentful bitterness, and the wounded heart."[8] He extends this concept beyond a Korean context and explains it in global colonial/postcolonial history. Analyzing the meaning of *han* in biblical traditions, Asian traditions, and Asian immigrant culture, he claims Jesus as "a man of *han*," who suffers among the innocent, the powerless, the marginalized, the voiceless, the untouchably unclean, the friendless, and the despised.[9] Instead of the images of Jesus as Victor or Conqueror and the images of traditional knowledge of God's attributes, such as all mighty and powerful, Park sees the images of Jesus as one who has "the wounded heart of God" profoundly rooted in suffering of Asians.[10]

One of the distinctive characteristics of Jesus in Park's description as well as other Asian American scholars mentioned later is togetherness. The emphasis of *co*-sufferer is suffering *together*. This characteristic in leadership has not often been found in other trait theories. Instead of leading up front, this characteristic calls for a simple coexistence, not by leading people out of suffering as savior, but by sinking in suffering together as co-sufferer. Even though it seems similar to some characteristics such as loyalty and solidarity from trait leadership, collaborative leadership, servant leadership, or team leadership, the concept of togetherness itself is not listed as a distinctly popular leadership characteristic in these theories. However, "just by being together" is one of the very important leadership characteristics that many Asian people expect in leaders in Asian traditions. Recognizing togetherness in the images of Jesus is a reflection of the needs of Asians and Asian immigrants from their leaders. They do not look for leaders as superiors from above but look for leaders among them.

The concept of togetherness in terms of suffering is an important one, especially to Korean women. Emphasizing Korean women's suffering in colonial/postcolonial history, Chung Hyun Kyung critically engages with the concept of *han* from a Korean woman's perspective. As she analyzes the process of colonial domination by looking into Western missionary theologies and androcentric interpretations of the Bible, she discovers the different images of Jesus that Asian women confess. She claims that even though "some Asian women's theologies on the surface look similar to Western missionary or Asian male theologies," she finds "the emergence of new meaning out of the old language" when she examines Asian women's treatment of the traditional images of Jesus.[11] In comparison with the traditional images of Jesus as suffering servant, Lord, and Immanuel that traditional white theology has taught to Asian women, she introduces new images of Jesus that Korean women believe. Reflecting on Korean and Asian women's suffering experience, she claims Jesus as "liberator," "revolutionary," "political martyr," "mother," "woman," "shaman," "worker," and others.[12] Focusing on the different experiences of Korean and Korean immigrant woman from Western women and men, she reinterprets the images of Jesus in the context of Korean and Korean immigrant women. Instead of the images of Jesus as white, male, father, and superior, she understands Jesus as Asian, female, mother, and liberator in colonial and postcolonial struggles. Transfiguring the images of Jesus from male to female, from father to mother, from white to Asian, and from above to below is an audacious but necessary movement, not only for Chung Hyun Kyung but also for many other Asian female theologians.

Asian Women as Leaders

Lifting up the images of Asian women as one of Jesus's images is another new concept that is hardly revealed in any leadership studies. Images of Asian women as leaders are scarce. The positions and roles of women in Asian and US culture are not those of leaders but followers. As has been revealed in many patriarchal Asian cultures, Asian women are hardly ever imagined as leaders, especially in public spheres. Despite Asian immigrant women's increasing economic advancement and social positions in the labor market,[13] Asian traditional gender roles perpetuate strong discrimination against Asian immigrant women as leaders. A strong male-centered religious leadership doubly oppresses Asian women and emphasizes women's submissiveness, especially in Asian Christian congregations. As the images of Jesus are identified with the images of Asian women, the position of Jesus's leadership transfers to the positions of Asian women's leadership in Asian immigrant contexts.

As a Japanese Puerto Rican American immigrant, Rita Nakashima Brock also demonstrates the necessity of this movement. As she examines the broken heart of male dominance in Christianity, she analyzes a unilateral understanding of power and explains how it operates with colonial and postcolonial white power. Criticizing traditional analogies of father-son patriarchal family relationships and identifying erotic power with the work of women and feminist insights, she understands that "Christ-the revelatory and redemptive witness of God/dess's work in history—is Christa/Community," which "is the church's imaginative witness to its experiences of brokenness and sacredness of erotic power in human existence."[14] Deconstructing the abuse of patriarchal images of Jesus, Brock not only claims the female image of Jesus, Christa, but also identifies Christa with community. Lifting up the importance of Asian women's work and communities, she transfigures the images of Jesus's maleness into femaleness and transforms the images of Jesus as individual Savior to communal Savior. Claiming the images of Jesus as Christa/Community, she reconstructs Jesus's erotic power to heal brokenheartedness "toward a whole-making life" and establishes solidarity with women.[15]

Brock's profound claim makes a shift of leaders' image from a male hero individual to a community that emphasizes the presence of females. The forms of leaders in Western culture are often associated with "a leader" or leaders as individuals. The traditional images of Jesus are often associated with an individual Jesus in the same way that the traditional images of leaders are often associated with an individual leader. Seeing Jesus as community itself is not imaginable in Western individualistic culture. However, in Asian culture, imaging Jesus as community, not an individual, is a reasonable and legitimate claim, even though it is not a common claim. As the images of Jesus are imagined as community, the images of leaders can be reexamined beyond the concept of individuality. In an Asian and Asian immigrant context, a leader is not seen as an individual leader, but as *a part* of the community (or the head of a community). Even if it assumes a hierarchy in leadership, the assumptions of being leaders still belong to community in Asian and Asian immigrant culture.

When Asian women become leaders, it is easier to recognize leaders as a part of the community, not as a separated individual on the top. When the images of Jesus are shifted from an individual male savior to Asian women/community, the images of Christian leaders are re-imagined and their leadership cannot be bounded with individualized leadership. The image of Jesus as Christa/community confirms an Asian women's communal leadership that many Asian women exercise throughout the history. Witnessing communal leadership is not rare in many Asian countries. Throughout colonial and postcolonial Asian histories, many Asian countries have demonstrated communal leadership in public, such as South Koreans' Candle Light Protest in 2016–2017, China's Tiananmen Square Protest in 1989, and other numerous student-led and grassroots-led movements. Many Asian women have been the active participants and effective leaders of this communal leadership. Even though Asian women are hardly recognized as distinctive individual leaders, the image of Jesus as Asian women provides a possibility to lift up the images of Asian women as individual and communal leaders.

Hybridity

Kwok Pui-lan is another scholar who demonstrates radical changes of the images of Jesus in an Asian and Asian immigrant context. As she critically analyzes how Western Christianity was reconstructed through the effort of Western missionaries, she scrutinizes how Chinese women consciously questioned traditional roles and images of women, became leaders as "agents of social change" in the Christian community, and were deeply involved with social change in China.[16] Closely examining the relationship between Jesus and women, she introduces Jesus as the salvific figure in both male and female forms in a pluralistic Chinese religious context.[17] Beyond a Chinese Christian context, she extends her understanding of the various images of Jesus in colonial and postcolonial immigrant and global contexts. In *Introducing Asian Feminist Theology*, she discusses four representative approaches of the images of Jesus as "a Fully Liberated Human Being" in the Filipino context, "a Priest of *Han*" in the Korean context, "one epiphany of God" (an organic model of Christology) in the Chinese context, and the "Embodiment of Feminine Principle" in an Indian context.[18] In *Postcolonial Imagination and Feminist Theology*, Kwok introduces five marginalized images of Jesus as "the Black Christ" from an African American and black context, "the Corn Mother" from an American Indian context, "the Feminine Shakti" from a Hindu Indian cultural context, "the Theological Transvestite" from the context between Judaism and Christianity, and "Bi/Christ" from a sexual theological context.[19]

From these intense discussions, she claims the concept of Jesus/Christ as the most hybridized concept in the Christian tradition. As Kwok observes these images of Jesus/Christ, she proposes five points: 1) the images of Jesus continue to hybridize as they encounter diverse cultures; 2) "the hybridized images of Jesus" were explosive in the second half of the twentieth century as formerly colonized and oppressed people struggled "for political independence and cultural identity"; 3) one of the "key debates concerning Christ will be in the interpretation of his passion and suffering"; 4) the need to guard against anti-Judaism; and 5) "the colonialist representation and anti-Jewish ideology have much to do with gender and sexual stereotypes."[20] Based on Asian and Asian immigrant women's stories and experiences, she warns that the images of Jesus have been formed by various colonial and postcolonial power groups and, at the same time, challenged and recreated by the oppressed and the colonialized.

One of the most prominent and distinctive characteristics of Asian immigrant leadership is hybridity. As Kwok claims the concept of Jesus to be the most hybridized concept in Asian and Asian immigrant context, this hybridized process in immigration is deeply embodied in the Asian immigrant experience. It is often confused with an assimilation process. As soon as immigrants move to the US, it is believed they need to participate in an assimilation process because it is assumed that this assimilation process is the standard process for all immigrants. However, the goal of an assimilation process is to adopt white norms and culture at the center of the immigrant lives,[21] whereas the process of hybridity is not to adopt the white culture as core values but to understand various cultures and adjust them in their own immigrant contexts. Many leaders in Asian Christian congregations also struggle to show how to exercise this hybrid ability more effectively in their immigrant lives. This ability is often presented as "adaptability" and "flexibility" in leadership studies. These are depicted as among the most important leadership characteristics for Asian American leaders to develop in their leadership formation.[22] Creating the images of Jesus in a space of hybridity is not a simple phenomenon. It reflects Asian immigrants' most difficult dilemmas and hopes to create the unknown but valuable path for their immigrant lives.

Wisdom

As Kwok indicates, the images of Jesus are closely developed based on Asian and Asian immigrants' experiences and Asian religious traditions that are the main resources to develop the valuable path for their immigrant lives. Asian wisdom tradition is one of these valuable resources. Using feminist and Korean women's theological traditions and experiences as main resources, Grace Ji-Sun Kim calls attention to wisdom traditions to define the images of Jesus. Drawing from various Asian religious traditions including Korean wisdom culture and comparing the texts of biblical Sophia, Isis, and *prajna*, she reveals how patriarchy has extricated Sophia from the Christian tradition.[23] As she consciously analyzes a white patriarchal framework of Sophia done by white feminists, she urges Korean North American women to develop liberative images of Sophia from Korean women's own religious and cultural roots. Seeking a distinctive and syncretic Korean North American feminist Christology, she criticizes the image of Jesus as the white male savior and claims that Korean North American women need to reimagine the images of Jesus as Sophia in Korean women's traditions and Korean North American women's immigrant lives. She believes that the grace of Sophia could release Korean North American women's *han* and bring healing.[24]

Wisdom is the foremost trait of Jesus's leadership. Kim along with many white feminists claim this wisdom tradition to explain who Jesus is. It is also the most popular trait that many trait theorists suggest when they define the characteristics of leaders. Many Asian Christian leaders do find wisdom not only in the Christian tradition but also in Asian religious traditions. Wisdom is often named as intelligence or education in leadership traits. It is usually presented as one of the typical stereotypes of men and characterized as a characteristic that belongs to the elite class alone. Therefore, claiming wisdom in the women's tradition is another move to nurture women's leadership. As images of Jesus are claimed as wisdom in Asian women's traditions, wisdom belongs to Asian women. As wisdom belongs to Asian women through Jesus, Asian immigrant women are able to perform leadership without shame. Reimagining Jesus as Sophia in the Asian women's tradition opens up the possibility to recognize wisdom as a woman's characteristic in leadership traits.

Relationality

As *han* is often used as the concept of suffering that needs to be released, for Wonhee Anne Joh, *jeong* is the concept that can release *han*. Situating *jeong* in comparison to *han*, she defines the Korean concept of *jeong* as "relationality of the self with the others" and argues that "*jeong* is the power embodied in redemptive relationships."[25] She understands *jeong* not as a binary concept, but as a more flexible and hybrid concept. Exploring Korean colonial and postcolonial history and Korean immigrant identity politics, she demonstrates how Koreans and Korean immigrants, especially through lifting up the experience of Korean women's embodied way of *jeong*, transform their suffering and create redemptive relationships with one another. Defining *jeong* as emancipatory praxis that is radically different from a male/patriarchal perception of *jeong*, she understands Jesus and Jesus's love on the cross "not as self-abnegation or sacrifice but as a radical inclusive love that is both transgressive and emancipatory."[26]

Emphasizing relation to community is another distinctive characteristic of Asian and Asian immigrant culture, which is deeply related to communal culture. It is diametrically opposed to Eurocentric, individualistic independent culture. The preconditions of Asian and Asian immigrant leadership are often exercised within exclusive relationships such as family relations or national ethnic relations. The strong boundary between in-group and out-group exists in personal ethnic or national differences. At the same time, under the heavy influences of American individualism, the emphasis of relationship in an Asian immigrant Christian context shifts from communal responsibility to individual responsibility. Many Asian immigrant churches join this privatization. With this double complicity, Asian immigrants tend to embrace more exclusive forms of relationship for survival. However, this new image of Jesus challenges the form of exclusive relationship. It requires inclusivity and communality. It calls for a more flexible and hybrid boundary in relationship. It encourages a new form of inclusive leadership for Asian immigrant leaders.

Asian Jesus as Asian Leader

One of the prominent but distinctive images of Jesus in Asian and Asian immigrant cultures is the images of Jesus with an Asian genderless face. Understanding the reign of God as Jesus's vision in the context of the contemporary history of Asia, Choan-Seng Song sees Jesus as a "prophet," "dreamer," and "visionary" who transforms people to overcome the suffering of life and lead them to liberation.[27] Using the Chinese sources and other Asian resources, he transposes "Jesus with a Chinese face."[28] Instead of the image of Jesus as the Davidic Messiah that white Christians confess, Song claims Jesus as crucified people in relation to the suffering of Asian and Asian American people and beyond.[29] From Jesus to Christ, from Christ to Christa, and "from the pointed-nosed Christ to the flat-nosed Christ,"[30] he denies "European" Jesus and understands Jesus in perpetual solidarity with those who suffer.[31] In each Asian immigrant context, immigrant theologians identify the images of Jesus with their own Asian faces based on their own specific Asian faith in relation to suffering.

Collecting resources from the stories of Asian people, the stories of Asian women, the sacred texts and practices of Asian religions, and Asian monastic traditions, in *Christianity with an Asian Face: Asian American Theology in the Making*, Phan situates Jesus within the context of Confucian family ethics and family relations in a Vietnamese tradition. As he analyzes the Confucian, Taoist, and Buddhist cultures of Vietnam, he portrays Jesus as the eldest son and an ancestor.[32] Exploring the concept of Vietnamese *truong toc* (the head of the family-clan) and analyzing the roles and expectations of the eldest son and ancestor in the Vietnamese tradition, as a Vietnamese American theologian, he regards Jesus as "the immigrant par excellence, the marginalized one living in the *both-and* and *beyond* situation" and "the elder brother and paradigmatic ancestor."[33] However, it is not the only image of Jesus that he defines. As he is aware of the images of Jesus as "the Universal, Unique, and Absolute

Savior" in the interfaith dialogue among Christianity, Judaism, and other pluralistic world religions, he introduces new images of Jesus. With deep understanding and appreciation of various Asian traditions and Christian traditions, especially the Catholic tradition, Phan defines the images of Jesus as "the Light," "the Enlightener," and "the Enlightened One" (or the Buddha) in *Being Religious Interreligiously: Asian Perspectives on Interfaith Dialogue*.[34] With an interreligious and multicultural perspective, he defines various images of Jesus in Asian and Asian immigrant contexts in the United States and transforms them into a transnational global immigrant space.

Like Phan and Song, many Asian and Asian immigrant theologians introduce Asian faces of Jesus. Comparing the concepts of Krishna in the Bhagavad Gita in a Hindu context, Buddha in a Buddhist context, Muhammad in an Islamic context, and others, Asian scholars such as Aloysius Pieris, Seiichi Yagi, Overy N. Mohammed, and Alexander J. Malik introduce Asian images of Jesus that are quite different from Western images of Jesus.[35] M. Thomas Thangaraj's crucified guru is a good example of these new images of an Asian Jesus. Engaging in a bilingual or cross-cultural Christology and reflecting on a Hindu theological tradition, Saiva Siddhanta, Thangaraj conceptualizes the meaning of guru in the framework of Christian Christology. He claims Jesus as the Crucified Guru in the image of a teacher who teaches with authority and enables disciples to act.[36] Making a bridge between South Indian traditions and Christian traditions, he attempts to transform the common vocabulary of the people of Tamilnadu into the concept of guru Christology for Christians in Tamilnadu and in a global immigrant Asian space. As Thangaraj explains the authoritarian character of the Hindi gurus in the West, he embraces the democratic understanding of the *guru-sisya* (teacher and disciple) relationship in the dialogue with Jesus's model of "self-sacrificing guruship."[37] He believes that this new image of Jesus "is rooted in commitment," "germinates in accountability," "branches out in conversation" between different cultural communities of believers, "blossoms in holistic vision," and "bears fruit in transformative praxis."[38]

Communicator

In the same way that Thangaraj contextualizes Indian tradition in a dialogue with the Christian tradition through images of Jesus, Kosuke Koyama engages in this conversation with Thailand and the Japanese tradition. Based on personal missionary experiences in Thailand and Japanese immigrant experiences and focused on Israeli, Islamic, Hindu, Buddhist, and Confucian contexts, Koyama reroots the concept of Jesus's incarnation to "in-culturation and in-localization."[39] He describes Jesus as a communicator between heaven and earth, God and people, and immigrants and others.[40] Koyama believes that Jesus is the one who stands in the midst of all transitions.[41] In-culturation and in-localization are difficult but necessary processes to practice for Asian immigrants, especially for the first generation of immigrants. Locating the images of Jesus as the one who stands in this transitional process is the inevitable and natural move for Asian immigrants.

Claiming Asian Jesus is a paradigm shift from white Christianity to Asian Christianity, as well as from the white Western savior to the Asian savior, and from the white colonizer to the Asian liberator. Claiming Jesus with an Asian face is claiming Jesus with an Asian identity. As the flat-nosed Christ, Vietnamese eldest son, Guru, enlightened one and communicator, the images of Jesus are deeply integrated with Asian images of leaders. This identity shift symbolizes the process of in-culturation of Christianity in Asian and Asian immigrant culture, which is opposite the process of assimilation of immigrants. As Jesus stands both in and beyond space, Asian immigrant leaders are supposed to stand both in and beyond space. In fact, creating this space is another leadership ability that Asian immigrant leaders need to possess.

Marginality

Because assimilation operates as the main ideology of white culture toward immigrant communities, many Asian immigrants accept the process of assimilation as a necessary step for immigrant life, but they often find themselves at a place of marginalization in the end. Observing Asian immigrants and their marginalized positions in US white society, Jung Young Lee discovers this acculturation process as a marginalized process for many Asian immigrants. However, reflecting on Asian immigrant Christian experiences and faith, he claims the process of marginality not as a marginalized process but as making a new creative core from the margin in an Asian immigrant context. From this new meaning-making process of marginalization, he defines new images of Jesus. Based on new concepts of marginality such as in-betweenness, in-bothness, and in-beyondness, Lee believes that Jesus as a divine servant transforms the margin into a new creative core. He proclaims "Jesus as the margin of marginality."⁴²

Marginality is a historical and socioeconomic political category. Anselm Kyongsuk Min understands this marginality in relation to political economy:

> People are marginal only because they have *become* marginalized, and have become so, because they have lost the struggle for political-economic power. It is the political-economic power of white Europeans that led to their colonialist and imperialist domination of the world and the consequent marginalization of Native Americans, African Americans, and Hispanic Americans. It is the political-economic weakness of Japan, China, and Korea, and the need of the expanding U.S. market for cheap labor in the nineteenth century, that brought Japanese, Chinese, and Koreans to the United States and marginalized them as Japanese Americans, Chinese Americans, and Korean Americans.⁴³

Min explains that even though people are not born marginal, under strong US imperialism, they became marginal. When they lost the struggle for political-economic power, they became marginalized. Individual outstanding achievement cannot overcome collective marginalization of certain races. This marginalization continues until collective political economic power is restored and immigrants are strong enough to be competitive with those of the center. Analyzing the relations between political-economic power and the meaning of marginality in US race relations, Min agrees with Lee on the possibility for a transformation of "alienation and rejection" into a positive resource, but requests a realistic sense of historical reality and a moral sensitivity to its contradiction, which he calls "political love, the dialectic of love and power in the praxis of justice."⁴⁴ Min understands the historical Jesus in his solidarity with the marginalized others of society as the key to overcoming the marginality of others in a globalizing world. He proclaims "Jesus' crucifixion and resurrection as signs of his solidarity in suffering and hope" with the marginalized and "(his) incarnation as the solidarity of the human and the divine in their radical difference."⁴⁵

As Min claims, the space of solidarity of others in marginality for Asian immigrants needs to be in the dialectic of love and power in the praxis of justice in relation with others. Where is this space in Christianity? Many Asian immigrant Christians find this space of marginality on the cross. The cross is a space that many Asian Christian leaders try to reinterpret and recreate. Defining the images of Jesus and the meaning of the cross as the margin of marginality is another distinctive characteristic that is commonly presented in Asian and other ethnic immigrant Christian leadership. The position of Jesus has now radically shifted from the top to the bottom of the bottom as the space of the cross transforms its marginal space into the new core. The act of Jesus on the cross transforms the isolation and rejection of the society toward the marginalized into a solidarity of others toward society. Embracing in-betweenness, in-bothness, and in-beyondness, analyzing historical political economy and power, and creating solidarity of others, these new images of Jesus challenge not only spiritual leadership but also political and economic immigrant leadership as a whole. These new images challenge the expectation of Asian immigrant leaders who hold a strong sense of hierarchal spiritual leadership in an Asian immigrant context and of isolated economic political leadership from a white social context. Embracing these new images empowers Asian immigrant leaders to create a new core for Asian immigrants beyond their own communities.

Crossing Boundaries

In an Asian immigrant context, the margin of spiritual and political marginality is the Asian LGBTQIA (Lesbian, Gay, Bisexual, Transgender, Queer/Questioning, Intersex, Asexual, and others) community. Under pressure from a strong heterosexual Asian religious culture and evangelical Christian culture, Asian LGBTQIA communities are caught in between the racism of the LGBTQIA community and the queerphobia of Asian communities. Concerning the homophobia and heterosexism of ethnic churches and beyond, as an Asian American gay man, Patrick S. Cheng points out serious discrimination and violence within and beyond an Asian immigrant context, ethnic context, and US white context. Positioning Jesus in the heart of this community, he claims "Jesus as the recovery of radical love" and "embodiment of radical love."[46] He examines the suffering of LGBTQIA people and proposes the suffering and life of Jesus as the platform for the foundational change to cross divine, social, sexual, and gender boundaries. Dismantling binary categories of classification, he believes Jesus can be the one who crosses traditional gender boundaries to becomes a "multi-gendered body."[47] As he examines queer of color theologies, including theologies of queer blacks, queer Asian Americans, queer Latinx and Two-Spirit Indigenous theologians, he claims three themes of rainbow theology ("1. multiplicity, 2. middle spaces, 3. mediation") and defines the new images of Jesus as constituting the "Rainbow Christ."[48] Understanding both the rainbow and Jesus as symbols of God's covenant with God's people, he explores the images of Jesus as a symbol of "multiplicity," "homelessness," and "mediation."[49]

Boundary crossing is a dangerous concept for leaders. It requires great risks. However, it is a necessary trait for leaders, especially for Asian immigrant leaders. Boundary-crosser is a natural quality for Asian immigrants who live in-between cultures. They have to cross boundaries, overcoming many barriers and much discrimination. They have to consider multiplicity, middle spaces, and mediation not as a choice, but as a necessity. They experience homelessness being treated as permanent guests in the United States. As this new image of Jesus crosses divine, social, sexual, and gender boundaries and dismantles binary categories of classification, it creates new expectations of Asian and Asian immigrant Christian leaders who need to embody these expectations in action. Boundary crossing is not necessarily presented as a leadership trait in current leadership studies, but it is a necessary leadership trait for Asian American leaders. As these images of Jesus are developed in an Asian immigrant Christian context, they also reflect the expectations and hopes of Asian religious leaders who are able to cross these boundaries freely despite fear and conflict.

In summary, when images of Jesus encounter the reality of Asian immigrants, the traditional images of Jesus are challenged. Even if these images are defined by the same names, they are understood differently depending on the context. "Liberator" (or "savior") is a good example. Being called a liberator in the Korean church context is different from being called a liberator in a white church context. The images of Jesus as a white male savior, conqueror, and victor in a white Christian context are transformed into the images of Asian co-sufferer, liberator, grassroots leader, teacher, healer, the margin of the marginalized, and so forth in an Asian immigrant context. As the images of Jesus are changed based on Asian immigrant culture and Asian religious teachings, the models of Asian Christian leadership need to be challenged. From white to Asian, from savior to co-sufferer, from conqueror to grassroots leader, from the center to the marginalized, the positions and images of Jesus have changed from a vertical position to a horizontal position. Being a leader in a modern capitalistic society means being better and higher. Leaders are required to demonstrate better abilities than others in this society. The images of savior and victor are more suitable concepts for leaders. However, a shift from the image of Jesus Savior to Jesus Co-Sufferer in an Asian immigrant context requires different concepts of leadership. It does not deny the fact that the images of Jesus Savior exist in Asian immigrant churches. In fact, the image of Jesus Savior is a predominated figure. However, acknowledging the coexistence of both traditional and nontraditional new images challenges the existing leadership. As a consequence, it demands different forms of Christian leadership.

Exploring and rediscovering various images of Jesus can be one of the most important steps in developing new Christian leadership for Asian immigrants. As many Asian immigrant Christians and theologians discover the new images of Jesus that Asian immigrants already believed or re-interpret the images of Jesus in Asian immigrant contexts, they recognize what Asian immigrants need from their leaders. *The images of Jesus are the reflection of people's needs and wants from their Christian leaders.* Understanding images of Jesus in Asian immigrant church contexts is a way to understand Asian immigrant Christian leadership and the images of leaders. As positions and images of Jesus are challenged and changed, the expectations of church leadership are challenged and changed simultaneously. Then, the questions become who are those presently in church leadership and how does church leadership need to be changed. Who are those presently in church leadership? One of the main segments of church leadership is church officers. In the Protestant church, pastors are expected to lead congregations. In the Catholic Church, priests, bishops, and the pope are those who lead churches. However, they are not the only ones who exercise church leadership. Despite the fact that each Protestant denomination shows different leadership and the Catholic Church exercises a hierarchal order in leadership, many lay leaders carry out church leadership with and without support from church officers. Therefore, it is important to explore various leadership positions and to understand the dynamics between them. As these dynamics are explored, it is easier to imagine how church leadership needs to be changed in an Asian immigrant context.

Challenges of Asian Immigrant Christian Leadership

Traditional Clergy-Centered Leadership

As discussed in the previous section, Christian leadership is mostly studied in the roles of church officers such as ministers, pastors, priests, bishops, the pope, and so forth. Prior to Vatican II, a minister was commonly identified with a member of the clergy in Protestant churches, whereas a priest was identified as a celebrant of the Eucharist in Roman Catholic and Orthodox Churches. However, "minister" was also used in Roman Catholic sacramental theology and canon law "to distinguish between 'ordinary' and 'extraordinary' ministers of the sacraments."[50] As it is discussed in chapter 2, the meaning of "minister" is found in the word "ministry," which derives from the Greek word *diakonia* (service). A person who provides service is a *diakonos* in the Greek, which can be translated as "servant," "assistant," or "deacon."[51] Therefore, this usage reveals that one of the most important roles of ministers is providing service to others as servants or assistants in both Protestant and Catholic traditions. As leaders of church, ministers are required to demonstrate leadership to serve others in the church and beyond. How do Christian pastors and theologians define a minister? What are the expectations for ministers? James E. Dittes explains a minister as follows:

> To be a minister is to take as partners in solemn covenant those who are sure to renege. To be a minister is to commit, unavoidably, energy, and passion, self and soul, to a people, to a vision of who they are born to be, to their readiness to share and live into that vision. To be a minister is to make that all-out, prodigal commitment to a people who cannot possibly sustain it. . . . The minister is called to their need, by their fundamental inability to be who they are born to be, hence by their fundamental inability to share and live into that vision in which the minister invests all.[52]

Dittes understands roles of a minister as a partner, one committed to God and God's people, and a helper to meet people's need. Instead of minister, pastor is another name commonly used for church leaders in the Protestant church. Seward Hiltner understands a pastor as a leader who "organizes" the church to care about people, and protect them from threats and "communicate" with them in a matrix of sociopolitical and cultural relationships.[53] He sees a pastor as an organizer and a communicator. William H. Willimon describes the roles of a pastor as "priest, interpreter of Scripture, preacher, counselor, teacher, evangelist, prophet, leader, character, and disciplined Christian."[54] Timothy Keller understands a pastor as a person who can "turn passive laypeople into courageous and gracious lay ministers" by inspiring them through their godliness and demonstrating humility, love, joy, and wisdom.[55]

As these definitions describe, ministers or pastors are themselves located at the center of church leadership, and their roles are defined by their abilities and skills. What are the skills that they have to demonstrate? Ammerman describes the skills of congregational leaders, especially clergy, as follows: "understanding the environment (thriving congregations could describe the environment they were facing); organizational self-assessment/awareness (understanding what buildings, membership, traditions imply); creative use of resources (thinking outside the box about resources, scouring the environment for resources, mobilizing resources in creative ways); innovation (thinking creatively about new ways to carry out activities); use of stories, symbols, rituals, myths (doesn't matter what symbols but whether used); intentional training of outsiders to become members (a skilled leader helps the less skilled gain the skills they need for full participation in the organization and conflict management—because all organizations undergoing change have conflict)."[56] Understanding church as an organization, Ammerman finds these skills as the skills for congregational leaders. Actually, many clergy and church leaders are expected to perform all of these skills in church leadership.

With these kinds of specific roles and expectations, clergy leadership is encouraged and emphasized. However, it is not expected to be accomplished by training only. It requires the precondition. Based on I Corinthians 15:7 and Acts 1:5–26, and 6:1–6, clergy claim to be disciples of Jesus in the succession of twelve apostles. As is briefly discussed in chapter 2, the precondition of clergy leadership is God's individual personal calling. All clergy are expected to be called by God. They are chosen to follow Jesus by God. Their strong affirmation of leadership derives from this concept of being "called by God" or "chosen by God." They believe they are on a divinely ordained mission. It is the notion of being called by God or chosen by God that makes clergy differentiate themselves from others.

The problem is not the concept of calling, but the concept of differentiation through calling toward others. Some clergy strongly believe that this calling is not only given by God but also makes them superior to others. For them, this calling is often interpreted as higher spiritual authority granted by God. It gives them a validity to locate themselves in a higher position in relation to other members in the church. They understand this calling as an existential difference between clergy and church members. The more clergy believe calling as a validation to obtain positions of higher authority in the church with excessive positive thinking and belief, the more they feel the sense of superiority.[57] The more they feel the sense of superiority, the more they pose in higher positions of not only spiritual but also sociopolitical power and privilege. In this process, some clergy demonstrate a distinctly superior manner in their leadership. These clergy often recognize images of God as "Sovereign, Master, Lord, and Father."[58] As it is discussed before, many Asian immigrant clergy see others through the lens of a sovereign, parental, and bureaucratic relationship and exercise a sovereign, parental, and bureaucratic leadership.[59]

Martha Ellen Stortz classifies this leadership as "power over" leadership. Often these clergy who exercise power over leadership claim themselves as charismatic leaders and hide their dangerous narcissistic behaviors. Claiming a divine calling as their vocation, these clergy exercise more authority and power. They understand ordained clergy positions as higher positions of leadership.[60] In the Catholic Church, church officers are organized in a pyramid structure. At the summit, there is the pope. At the upper reaches, there are bishops. Priests are at the midlevel, and the laity is at the base.[61] This pyramid structure itself fortifies higher positions of leadership. In the Protestant church, many ministers also claim their ordination as spiritual superiority and see other church members as people in need. Both Protestant and Catholic churches locate laity at the bottom of leadership hierarchy.

Scott Cormode understands this leadership model as a builder's model. "It is an organizational approach in that it sees the minister as the head of an organizational structure."[62] Clergy in this leadership model insist on the prerogative of position rather than the abilities of integrity or performance. Clergy in this model emphasize strong organizational church structure and their own positions of power at the top of the church structure. Even though lay leadership is empowered and emphasized by pastors themselves, it is emphasized as a secondary leadership that assists pastors and helps others. The existence of this hierarchal leadership structure is undeniable in many Christian churches.

However, in recent years, there is some advocacy to embrace lay leaders. In Protestant churches, many lay leaders participate in the decision-making process as the final decision committee and share the pulpit by preaching and worshipping together with pastors. As lay pastors, lay preachers, lay elders, and lay deacons, the laity exercises leadership in the Protestant church. They are involved in various roles from Sunday school teachers, music directors, and worship leaders to church administrators and church representatives to other communities. In the Catholic Church, lay leadership is claimed on Vatican II's Decree on the Apostolate of the Lay People. Vatican II encourages the laity to participate in the lay apostolate and to collaborate with activities such as catechetical instruction, pastoral care for others, administering the resources of the Church, among others.[63] Because of declined numbers of clergy, many married men are ordained as permanent deacons to exercise all kinds of ministries. Many lay men and women leaders are involved with traditional roles, from ushers and sacristans to more recent roles such as Eucharistic ministers and pastoral care persons, and from ministers of music and education to church administrators.[64]

In an Asian immigrant context, both the Protestant church and Catholic Church also have similar discussions. Clergy-centered leadership is common in an Asian Christian church context. This leadership structure is inherited from a white Western Christian church structure. From the beginning of Christian missionary history, clergy-centered leadership has been institutionally practiced and exercised. However, the clergy-centered church leadership structure is not just an invention of Western Christianity. As many Asian countries demonstrated "paternalistic, bureaucratic, and authoritarian leadership" patterns in socioeconomic institutions, as discussed in the previous section, Asian patriarchal culture itself fortifies this leadership. Not only the Asian immigrant church but also other Asian religious organizations show similar patterns of this paternalistic, bureaucratic, and authoritarian leadership.[65] Under the strong Asian patriarchal culture and the powerful Western Christian hierarchal culture, many Asian immigrant Christian churches adopt clergy-centered leadership. Because many Asian clergy are predominately male, this leadership is often presented as a paternalistic, bureaucratic, and authoritarian male clergy-centered leadership. Especially in Korean Protestant churches, and multiethnic Protestant churches, male clergy predominately preserves strong authority over all decisions made by a lay board in some cases.[66]

Lay Leadership in Asian Immigrant Congregations

However, in comparison with the average US church, many ethnic immigrant worship communities, including Korean and Chinese Protestant churches, feature more involvement by lay leadership in worship and other leadership roles.[67] Furthermore, in comparison to Asian Christian congregations in Asia, there is more visible lay leadership in Asian immigrant congregations in the US.[68] Despite clergy-centered leadership in an Asian immigrant Christian context, many Asian immigrant Protestant churches share more leadership roles and responsibilities with lay leaders. There is one interesting explanation for this vibrant lay leadership in an Asian immigrant context. Many Asian lay members show strong ownership of their congregations. Not only in Asian immigrant Christian churches but also many other Asian immigrant religious organizations share this distinctiveness. As many first-generation immigrants participate in and build their congregations from the beginning of their congregational lives, they demonstrate strong ownership for and commitment to congregations. "The sense of ownership that comes from building an institution typically expands to significant commitment to its subsequent administration, which encourages the assumption of a congregational structure that incorporates lay authority as a central feature."[69]

As lay leaders show deep commitment and a strong sense of ownership of their congregations, clergy-centered leadership is challenged. Even though paternalistic, bureaucratic, and authoritarian leadership is still a strong feature of dominant leadership in many Asian immigrant congregations, under the strong influence of an American democratic atmosphere and the feminist movement, paternalistic, bureaucratic, and authoritarian leadership patterns have been increasingly criticized and discouraged. Because of this strong lay leadership and encouragement of democratic styles of leadership from the young second and third generations, incorporative and collaborative styles of leadership are more encouraged in recent years. Strong participation from lay leaders invigorates the Asian immigrant Christian context, and collaborative ministry between clergy and lay leaders is increasingly consciously empowered compared to Asian Christians in Asia and white Christians in the United States. Despite the strong presence of male clergy leadership, Asian immigrant Christian leadership has acquired a different leadership and sought more participation from church members.

Challenges of Asian Immigrant Church Leadership

Lack of Ordained Clergy Women's Leadership

Considering the problem of male clergy's patriarchal leadership, it is reasonable to identify that the first challenge of Asian immigrant Christian church leadership is lack of ordained clergy women's leadership. Lack of ordained clergy women's leadership is not just an Asian immigrant Christian problem. It is a major problem of Western Christianity in general. However, under complicity with the Asian patriarchal tradition, the Western Christian tradition, and the racial discrimination within white society, positions of ordained Asian clergy women's leadership are triply blocked. For example,

> In the Presbyterian Church (USA), 33 % (5,528) of clergy were female (Descriptive Statistics for PC (USA) 2002–2010). Of the 33% of female clergy, only 1.75 % (97) were Asian American clergywomen (*Race, Ethnicity, and Gender* PC (USA), 2010). In the United Methodist Church, 24.6 % (10,916) of clergy (includes elders, deacons, and associate members) are female. Of the 24.6%, the Asian American subset is 1.67 % (182) (General Council on Finance and Administration for United Methodist Church). These statistics show that less than 2% of female clergy in these two denominations are Asian Americans.[70]

As statistics show, numbers of Asian American ordained clergy women are less than 2 percent in mainline Protestant churches, and the presence of Asian American ordained clergy women is rare. Furthermore, the presence of Asian American ordained female senior pastors in their own ethnic churches is extremely rare. Most of these female pastors serve either in cross-cultural appointments or in specialized ministries such as chaplain or nonprofit organization leader.[71]

Su Yon Pak analyzes barriers to women's leadership of Asian American ordained female clergy with four points. First, "the double bind."[72] Pak argues that Asian American women are forced to choose between gender and race. If they choose gender over race, they usually end up serving Euro-American congregations where they have better opportunity to be ordained. In this choice, they lose the support of their own ethnic communities where they can fight against racism. If they choose race over gender, they would not have a chance to be ordained. Many Asian American women are frequently caught in this conflict. Second, "cultural norms and values."[73] Explaining the colonial and postcolonial exchanges between conservative Euro-American missionary Christianity and Asian Confucian culture, Pak argues that immigrants become more conservative and show more conservative attitudes toward women's leadership.

Third, "Confucian virtues."[74] Criticizing harmful Confucian virtues in relation to women, Pak illustrates how Confucian virtues are used as an ethnic identity to defend Asian culture while oppressing women's leadership. She claims that the Confucian moral code still remains as a major barrier to women in leadership:

> In the immigrant context of the United States, these Confucian moral codes become a way to claim ethnic and cultural identity. Faced with the threats of racism and discrimination, Asian Americans hold on to "the old ways" as a means to resist assimilation and protect themselves from insidious encroachment of the outside and "others." It is a way to be Asian. As a result, these Confucian moral codes can be even more rigidly observed in Asian American churches than in churches in Asia. The cost of letting go is higher in the foreign land than in their homeland. Asian American women attempting to access leadership positions in this context may be accused of "acting white" and not in touch with their Asian heritage. In a church context this makes it difficult, if not impossible, for Asian American women to be in traditional pastoral leadership where they have authority over men.[75]

Even though Pak indicates that there are some positive aspects of Confucian virtues as a part of Asian culture, she illustrates the harmful impact of Confucian virtues on Asian American women and their leadership. Fourth, "ecclesial barriers."[76] Analyzing the institutional limits of the calling system in the Presbyterian Church (USA) and the cross-cultural appointment system in the United Methodist Church, Pak explicates the ecclesial barriers in the Asian immigrant Protestant church for Asian American immigrant women.

Under the weight of the double bind between race and gender, cultural norms and values, Confucian virtues, and ecclesial barriers, Asian American ordained clergy women leaders suffer and are buried. In order to survive, many of them, including second- and third-generation of women, choose a "silent exodus" from their ethnic churches.[77] Lack of ordained clergy women's leadership is the most critical problem that all Asian American immigrant churches face. However, the worst problem is that most of these churches do not recognize this problem as a problem. It is not recognized as a problem but as a part of culture. Discussion about patriarchy remains only within the circle of Asian feminist women. There remains a strong resistance from the Asian immigrant Christian church and Asian culture in general.

However, it does not mean there is no Asian immigrant women's leadership in Christian congregations. Women exercise leadership regardless. Despite the lack of ordained clergy women's presence, women exercise leadership in the form of lay leadership in the church with alongside lay men. When lay leadership is considered, participation of women in church leadership is significant. "Relatively high percentages of worship communities report that women are in the majority of lay leadership positions within the community."[78] As lay elder, lay deacon, Christian educator, church accountant, and church administrator, lay women are actively involved with all dimensions of church ministry, such as worship services, church activities, and programs.

Church fellowship after Sunday worship in particular is predominantly led by lay women. For example, in many Asian and Korean immigrant churches, sharing meal time after Sunday worship or in small-group gatherings in church programs is common. Particularly in smaller congregations, sharing meal time is the most critical and vital part of immigrant church ministry. This practice differs from the tea time of many white congregations. Sharing meals is one of the most distinctive phenomena in immigrant church ministry.[79] Not only many Asian immigrant churches but also other immigrant churches, such as African immigrant churches, also commonly practice meal sharing as a part of their ministry. Instead of standing and talking for five to ten minutes with tea or coffee, many immigrant church members sit and spend more time talking to the group who sits near them. It is not simply sharing meals but building a relationship. As they share meals, they share individual and communal immigrant lives together. Through the course of this weekly, repeated interaction, they develop an inner group within the church. Sharing meals counteracts the isolation of being immigrants. It is rooted in the colonial and postcolonial historical experience of sharing rice/food in Asian culture and, more specifically, in women's tradition. In this women's tradition, sharing food is often interpreted as providing hospitality and creating relationships of a deeper level. As they share meals, they welcome strangers, and simultaneously, they are more connected and build stronger bonds among themselves.[80] Therefore, sharing meal time is a necessary part of Asian immigrant Christian church lives, and it is impossible to have this fellowship without women's leadership. It is true that many immigrant women are aware and criticize this fellowship as exploiting women's labor under the influence of societal trends in the United States today. Because of this awareness, instead of making food, some women leaders create different ways to manage this fellowship, such as having the food catered and allocating different responsibilities to both men and women. Despite criticism, many Korean and Asian immigrant women continue this fellowship with or without pressure from the church, and women continue to play a vibrant part of this program.

Managing this fellowship is not the only prominent leadership role that women play in the church. There is another specific women's leadership position to introduce. It is called *Jeondosa* (전도사). Even though this position exists only in the Korean immigrant Protestant church, it is an interesting position to compare with other immigrant congregations as well as white congregations. It is a distinctive clergy leadership position for Korean women. It originates in Korean Christian congregations from Korea and has been continuously adopted by most Korean immigrant congregations in the United States. The position of *Jeondosa* is for both men and women who are in seminary or graduated from the seminary but not ordained. Many women who graduate from seminary stay in this position without ordination because after ordination, ordained clergy women rarely find positions in their ethnic churches. For men, it is more like a transitional position until ordination. However, for many women, *Jeondosa* is a permanent position until retirement. As mentioned earlier, the presence of ordained clergy women in the Korean immigrant church is very rare. Because of severe sexism in the Korean culture, ordained women are not welcomed in the Korean immigrant church. Like Asian immigrant clergy women, most ordained Korean women clergy work for other ethic churches as previously mentioned. However, the position of women *Jeondosa* is different. It exists in almost every Korean immigrant church. Women *Jeondosa* play a very crucial role in the church as *clergy*. The roles of women *Jeondosa* vary, from education directors for children to professional pastoral visitors for the elderly. This position is often regarded as a clergy position. Women *Jeondosa* often lead and preach many worship services, except Sunday worship service; teach Bible study classes from children to adults; lead pastoral visits especially for women church members and the elderly; and administer various church activities. Many Korean Protestant churches in Korea and in the United States have these women in the pulpit. From mega-churches to small congregations, the presence of women *Jeondosa* persists. In the mega-church, women *Jeondosa* often play the role of assistant pastors. In small congregations that cannot afford to hire full-time male pastors, women *Jeondosa* often play the role of associate pastors and sometimes senior pastors. When congregations grow, congregation members seek male clergy for senior pastor positions. However, women *Jeondosa* still remain in the same position under senior pastors in many cases. The position of women *Jeondosa* is not secular in terms of finance and job security. Most do not have proper salaries or pensions. However, despite these difficulties and recognitions, the position of women *Jeondosa* always exists and these women have exercised leadership in the pulpit as clergy.

In terms of the roles of ordained leadership and lay leadership, Asian immigrant women clearly suffer from both Western Christian patriarchal culture and Asian patriarchal culture. Their leadership is undermined and disdained by both Eastern and Western patriarchies. This doubly oppressive sexism is recognized as a constitutive feature of Asian immigrant lives against women's leadership. It results in the loss of women's full capacity in leadership. Fighting this doubly oppressive sexism, Asian women are tired and suffer much physical and psychological damage. However, at the same time, they have demonstrated leadership in the forms of relentlessness and resistance. Even though they suffer from the stereotypical images of submissiveness and obedience produced by both white and Asian immigrant patriarchal institutionalized cultures, Asian immigrant women demonstrate leadership against submissiveness and obedience throughout history in both the West and the East. Whether in ordained positions or in lay leaders' positions, Asian immigrant women perform leadership as a vital part of Christian ministry. Therefore, it is important to define leadership anew and recognize women's leadership from a different angle.

Difficulties of Developing Social Services

The second challenge of Asian immigrant Christian church leadership is developing social service for Asian immigrants. One of the main roles of the Asian immigrant church is helping Asian immigrants to adjust in a new land. The Asian immigrant church has to respond to the needs of church members and members of their ethnic community. Asian immigrant church leaders, including clergy and lay leaders, must address not only the needs of church members but also the needs of the immigrant community at large. Therefore, many immigrant churches, including Asian immigrant churches, are asked to provide social service to meet these needs. In this regard, one of the most important roles of clergy and lay leaders is providing social services for individual and communal needs and connecting resources between individual congregations and denominational and national linkages.

The research of Michael W. Foley and Dean R. Hoge shows that not only the Asian immigrant church but also other immigrant worship communities, both Protestant and Catholic, support more social service programs or community development programs and provide more financial support for them than the typical American Catholic or Protestant church.[81] In this study, the percentage that spent $10,000 or more on social service programs and the percentage that had congregation members volunteer are almost double in immigrant worship communities in comparison with American congregations.[82] Asian immigrant clergy and lay leaders understand church as a "mediator" between the white society and Asian immigrant communities and as "community builder" between Asian immigrant communities and other immigrant communities.[83] Based on this understanding, they have to know how to develop Asian immigrant identity with the church and at the same time, they have to learn how to introduce US culture and its values to their congregation members for their survival. Their leadership requires mediation between these two or more cultures in balance. Keeping this balance, Asian clergy and lay leaders navigate the church to offer various social services beyond spiritual worship services. The roles of clergy and lay leaders in this immigrant context are focused on how to mediate the process between individual immigrants and institutionalized systems and to protect individual immigrants from these systems.

In this process, the Asian immigrant church fosters "social capital," which "is not just the sum of the social networks and resources of its members" but reaches out to people and whole ethnic communities beyond church members.[84] Therefore, using human resources and finding institutional resources, Asian clergy and lay leaders in Asian immigrant churches are urged to develop more social service programs for both their church members and ethnic communities. However, the Asian immigrant church is not the only church that fosters social capital. Ammerman in *Congregation and Community* understands Christian congregations as particular spaces of sociability connecting communities and generating social capital.[85] In this research, she finds that "congregations and other voluntary organizations, then, generate the basic social capital of association, along with the civic capital of communication and organizational skills."[86] Many congregations and other voluntary organizations as social and civil capital assume the role of providing social services whether it is white, black, or Asian immigrant congregations. The question, then, is what are the distinctive needs of social service for Asian immigrants.

As Asian immigrant church channels social capital, Asia immigrant church leaders have difficulties learning how to support and develop social service in their Asian immigrant contexts. They try to address the immediate and unique needs of Asian immigrants and create a wide range of opportunities, such as English-language programs, educational programs for legal issues, health programs, shelter programs, and other educational programs for job-related training. At the same time, they also have to address the issues of Asian immigrants' longing to preserve their ethnic values in a new land. Therefore, clergy and lay leaders are asked to provide ethnic cultural programs such as Asian-language programs and ethnic music and art programs for children, youth, and the elderly. Each program requires many volunteers to participate. Tremendous effort by lay leadership is involved. Therefore, Asian immigrant Christian leadership is not just spiritual leadership. It is beyond worship-centered spiritual leadership because Asian immigrant clergy and lay leaders are always asked to participate more in social service to balance with spiritual leadership. From learning English to getting a driver's license, from providing a ride to finding a house, from giving legal advice to offering health care, and from being immigrants to being American citizens, the Asian immigrant church has to deliver various kinds of social service. To offer these services, it is important for immigrant church leaders to structure the church in connection to one another in settings such as small groups or organizing subgroup structures, because "bonding social capital is built largely through repeated face-to-face encounters."[87] Some programs like sharing meal time after Sunday worship or a small group/cell group meeting play a crucial role in providing the space for these repeated face-to-face encounters.

To build various social services for Asian immigrants, many Asian immigrant clergy and lay leaders have developed civic skills in leadership in different arenas. Foley and Hoge in their immigrant research introduce four areas in which church leaders, especially lay leaders, develop leadership. The first arena is "participation in worship service."[88] By leading worship service, many lay leaders develop leadership. In small congregations, many lay leaders, especially women and youth, are asked to share leadership roles in the worship service. By participating in the worship service, they learn how to be worship leaders. The second arena is "organizing the community's life."[89] By creating and managing small groups, and participating in subcommittees, many lay leaders learn how to organize and maintain community life. Strong women's leadership is present. The third arena is "governance."[90] Despite different levels of responsibility and power, many church leaders actively participate in the decision-making process, learn how to negotiate and develop coalition building, and take more responsibility for the life of the community. As members of governing committees, they are given the power to select pastors and the authority to control budgets. The fourth arena is "training in civil skills and civic engagement."[91] In this arena, they are more involved with civic engagement and thereby refine civic skills. In the previous three arenas, church leaders have already developed skills in public speaking through worship services, leading and organizing meetings through various church programs, and sociopolitical maneuvering through church outreach programs. Using these skills, they are now more connected with larger civic engagement and engaged with local community services. They know how to discuss political issues and provide more and better social service programs beyond congregation members. In each arena, the Asian immigrant church plays a significant role in training church leaders to develop civic skills. Out of necessity, Asian immigrant Christian leaders have to learn how to connect their church and ethnic community to the larger society. It is a sophisticated and delicate challenge for their leadership.

It is true that some white mega evangelical churches also emphasize this connectedness as the goal of their ministry. Clergy and lay leaders of these churches often claim to connect individual church members with marginalized people outside of church and society and to provide support and services for these people within and beyond the church. For example,

Timothy Keller indicates that the church leaders have to undertake four tasks in ministry. He proposes these takes as four "fronts": "1) Connecting people to God (through evangelism and worship); 2) Connecting people to one another (through community and discipleship); 3) Connecting people to the city (through mercy and justice); 4) Connecting people to the culture (through the integration of faith and work)."[92] His notion of the responsibilities of leaders seems similar to that of Asian immigrant clergy and church leaders, who work as mediators or community builders between people to God, other people, city, and culture.

However, there is a difference between these white church leaders and Asian immigrant church leaders. Many white mega church leaders do not envision these connections with actual immigrants, specifically in the intersections of race, sex and gender, and ethnicity, whereas Asian immigrant clergy and leaders daily encounter actual immigrants, and they remain at these intersections throughout their entire ministry. Many white mega church leaders emphasize connections without dealing with specific questions of immigration and its challenges, whereas Asian immigrant church leaders seek these connections with specific answers. The difficulties of developing social service and civil engagement for Asian immigrant leaders extend beyond finding financial resources. They have to know how to understand the concerns of actual people with real skin color, know what the intersections mean to them, fight with power at these intersections, make connections both inside and outside of communities, and create social services beyond their own communities. Developing social services is not an easy task, but every single immigrant church makes an effort to provide these services for their church members and immigrants in their ethnic communities.

Dis-communication between the First and the Second (and Third) Generations

The third challenge of Asian immigrant Christian church leadership is conflict or "dis-communication" between the first generation and the second (and third) generations. Many second and third generation members leave their ethnic church after they graduate from high school. They either stop going to church or go to a multiethnic church instead. In their research in the area of Asian religious leadership, Timothy Tseng and colleagues confirm this problem between the first and second generations with two issues. First, many younger pastors (and second-generation leaders) are critical of the immigrant churches and see them as "dysfunctional and hypocritical religious institutions."[93] Second, there are constant conflicts between the generations because of generational cultural differences such as different leadership styles and control issues.[94] As the second-generation pastors and leaders struggle, many of them choose a "silent exodus" and leave the immigrant church to develop Pan-Asian or multiethnic congregations.[95]

This chasm between the generations originates from different cultural social expectations. One of them is different expectations of family relations and life philosophy between Asian and US cultures. Grace Sangok Kim illustrates two different cultural values of family relations and life philosophy within the Asian immigrant church. Characteristics of traditional Asian cultural values are "family-oriented, interdependent, vertical, authoritarian, respect for parents and elders, family loyalty, filial piety, duty, and obedience" whereas characteristics of these values in North American culture are "individual-oriented, autonomous; independent; horizontal; democratic; variable depending on the family; value self-determination and personal happiness; freedom of choice, and independence."[96] Characteristics of life philosophy for the first generation are "family-kinship bonds; collectivism; success through self-discipline, will, and determination; sense of stoicism and fatalism; reciprocity and obligation; face-saving and status consciousness; and holistic living in harmony with nature," whereas characteristics of life philosophy for the second and third generations are "individualism, pragmatism, realizing one's talents and potentials, sense of opportunism and optimism, avoidance of obligation (for example, "going Dutch treat"), doing your own thing, self-satisfaction, control, and conquest of nature."[97]

The characteristics for first- and second-generation individuals are almost opposite. They do not show any similarities. However, they exist in every single immigrant family. It means that these are not just characteristics of individual church members and their family relations. As first-generation parents bring memories and experiences from their lives in Asia and move to the United States, they expect to have these values in their own family, for the most part. For first-generation immigrants, family is the first and last place to keep their values and beliefs. Many of them believe that it is their reason for existence in a new land. However, for second-generation immigrants, the values of family are not the same as the values of their parents. They give more value to their own individual selves. Whereas the first priority of first-generation immigrants is family, the first priority of second-generation immigrants is the individual self. It means that the more first-generation parents emphasize Asian values of family as the foundation of their existence, the more second-generation groups want to escape that pressure and find individual freedom from the culture of the first generation. These values and philosophy coexist within the church but are sharply separated between the first and the second (and third) generations.

What makes this problem deeper is dis-communication between these generations. Reflecting on the context of Asian immigrants and their working conditions, Ellen Tanouye explains communication problems between immigrant parents and their children with six points: "1) lack of opportunities to talk (because of parents' long hours of work), 2) language barriers and inadequate communication due to the poor command of English by the parents and the children's lack of Asian native-language capabilities, 3) lack of conversational topics, 4) ineffective communication styles, 5) ineffective listening, and 6) negative nonverbal communication."[98] After long hours of work, many immigrant parents have difficulty finding time to talk to their children. Their lack of confidence in English is the major problem for this dis-communication. Speaking English is one of the major stresses for first-generation immigrants. Especially for Asian immigrants, it is a harder task in comparison with other immigrants. The structure, characters, and usages of Asian languages are completely different from English, unlike other European rooted languages like French, German, and Spanish. Because first-generation parents do not have strong confidence in English at work and home and are tired of speaking English during the long hours at work, they prefer to speak ethnic languages at home. They speak to their children in ethnic languages or broken English with accents. As is discussed earlier, speaking with accents is disdained by white society. Some second-generation children are exposed to the strong influences of this discrimination. Even though they might not criticize their parents' poor English skills directly, they might have a similar white-dominated perception about English with Asian accents. This perception gives them dissatisfaction in communication with their parents. Therefore, first-generation immigrants are double bound by this complicity at home. Moreover, their authoritarian styles of one-way communication are not welcomed by their children. What first-generation immigrants know and practice is not appreciated by their children, the second generation. At the same time, what the second-generation immigrants say and do is not understood by their parents, the first generation. The chasm between the first generation and the second (and third) generations begins in the family and deepens at church.

Pastors and church leaders are bridging these two different values. Many immigrant church leaders try to find solutions to include the second generations in church structures and programs, such as providing translations in the main service or hiring English-speaking ministers for children and youth groups. They also provide educational programs such as ethnic language programs and ethnic cultural events. These are the most common model for youth ministry. However, these efforts are commonly unsatisfactory for the second generation. There are also other models that try to better meet the needs of the second generation, such as, a semi-independent youth ministry, "Pan-Asian American" church or the ministry sponsored by outside organizations.[99] All of these models coexist and serve the needs of the second generation, but not so perfectly. However, despite the mistakes and failures, leaders in the church still try to create a new model for the second generation.

Peter Yuen explains these existing models of immigrant ministry with a theory of the transformation process in six stages with five crises. He claims that many immigrant churches go though this process and it will take twenty-five to forty years to reach the final stage.[100] In stage one, Asian immigrant adults form the church and ask volunteers to help the children. Volunteers in this stage are the people who speak English well. The first crisis occurs: the church has difficulty finding these volunteers.[101] In stage two, volunteers will burn out and seek encouragement and mentoring. The second crisis occurs: the church tries to find leaders who not only speak English well but also understand both Asian and American culture. The solution is often found in hiring a part-time youth pastor.[102] In stage three, as children grow up, it is necessary to have youth ministry in English. The third crisis will follow: it is a language and cultural crisis. After youth graduate from high school, a young adult ministry is needed that is separate from the youth worship.[103] In stage four, an English department for young adults is created. The fourth crisis is a decision-making crisis: the English-speaking department wants to participate in the decision-making process.[104] In stage five, the first generation and the second, English speaking, generation work cooperatively. The fifth crisis is a power/focus crisis: conflicts between these two generations might occur.[105] In stage six, the English-speaking department becomes predominant but still needs a pastor for the non-English-speaking congregants.[106] Assumptions of this theory are, first, the congregation is static and there is no more immigration from outside, and second, members of English-speaking second and third generations will increase. However, most Asian immigrant church members are still dominated by the first generation because of continuous immigration and transnational exchanges from Asia. Many second- and third-generation church members left the church for several reasons, including the strong influence of capitalism and the cultural discrepancy between the first and second generations. Because of these two reasons, most current Asian immigrant churches stay between stages three and four. Very few Asian congregations reach stage five.

Various models are adopted and adapted to compensate for the distance between the first generation and the second generation. However, dis-communication continues within and beyond the church among immigrant societies. Both first-generation church leaders and second-generation church leaders confront the same dilemmas, but they have different approaches to find solutions.

In their study of Asian religious leadership, Timothy Tseng and colleagues claim that second-generation church leaders demonstrate hybrid spirituality and create different church models. Under strong influences from white evangelical mega churches such as Willow Creek Community Church in Illinois, Saddleback Community Church in Southern California, and Redeemer Presbyterian Church in New York, several second-generation churches adopt a seeker-sensitive model for their ministry. In this model, second-generation church leaders accept the formats of worship service that these mega churches offer. Their worship service structure is nontraditional and nonclassical. Several traditional classical liturgical elements are dismissed, and styles of sermons are open. Modern music in the form of contemporary gospel music is a prominent part of the worship service. Many parts of worship services and church structures are very similar to the white mega churches. However, these second-generation leaders distinguish themselves from white evangelical churches. They claim that their immigrant spirituality is not based on white individualistic evangelism but on community. They believe that "immigrants better understand and practice the key biblical concept of community because they come from a Confucian society that stresses the importance of the collective over the individual."[107] As they distinguish their Asian immigrant leadership from the white church leadership based on Confucian values, they also distinguish their leadership as different from the first-generation immigrant leadership on the issues of lay and clergy responsibilities. Second-generation church leaders emphasize nonhierarchal relationships and leadership between lay leaders and clergy. They encourage lay participation in the ministry and discourage hierarchal authoritarian leadership styles. They provide more educational programs to nurture lay leadership. However, despite the encouragement of nonhierarchal styles, they are not exempt from the criticism of patriarchal styles of leadership.[108] Their adaptation of the white evangelical church has not been completely free from patriarchal elements of church leadership structure. Their hybrid leadership stays in between the white evangelical church and the Asian immigrant church, even though they criticize immigrant churches as dysfunctional and hypocritical religious institutions.

Fighting with the Power of American Individualism

The fourth challenge of the Asian immigrant Christian church leadership is to fight with the power of American individualism. This is also another reason to explain the chasm between the first generation and second (and third) generations. As first-generation immigrants are oriented more toward communalism, second-generation immigrants are more exposed to American individualism. Under the strong impact of American individualism and white evangelism, not only Asian immigrant churches but also other churches, such as black churches, emphasize personal salvation and individual moral responsibility as core values of Christian teaching. Asian values of communalism and solidarity fade away under this impact, especially for second-generation immigrants. In close cooperation with racism, American individualism dismisses Asian communal identity and responsibility, displacing them with individual economic success. "The disruption of corporate identity and communal responsibility only increases amid the struggles for socioeconomic advancement by individualism in a systemically racist society."[109] American individualism co-opts Asian immigrants not only with racism and sexism but also with the colonial and postcolonial hegemony with which Asian immigrants struggle. American individualism creates unrealistic American dreams for Asian immigrants to pursue and terminates values of Asian communalism as primitive ancient forms of knowledge and disposition.

For first-generation immigrants, Asian communalism is used as a resistant ideology against Americanization to protect ethnic identity and roots. It gives them power to fight all discrimination as a group. However, for many second-generation immigrants, Asian communalism is seen as a hegemonic tool by which first-generation immigrants control them. This means that the second generation understands Asian communalism as a barrier to their individual socioeconomic advancement. In this understanding, the immigrant church is recognized as the ethnic ghetto to protect their ethnic communal identity.

Many scholars, such as Robert N. Bellah, Richard Madsen, William M. Sullivan, Ann Swidler, and Steven M. Tipton, claim that Protestantism has been formatively related to American individualism from the beginning of US history.[110] Before the Reformation, the church was the center of salvation. The role of the church was as a mediator between people and God. However, the Protestant Reformation rejected this role of the church and promoted salvation as attainable between an individual and God without mediation of the church:

> By the 1850s, "For religion to have emphasized the public order in the old sense of deference and obedience to external authorities would no longer have made sense. Religion did not cease to be concerned with moral order, but it operated with a new emphasis on the individual and the voluntary association. Moral teaching came to emphasize self-control rather than deference" and sermons became less doctrinal and "more emotional and sentimental." . . . Because American Protestant religion focuses strongly on personal relationship with God, Americans by and large do not resonate with religion that is based on community affiliations, social relationships, tradition and ritual.[111]

American Protestantism cultivates individual freedom and independence and opposes communal solidarity and interdependence in other religions. In the research of Adam B. Cohen and Peter C. Hill, American Protestant religious groups are identified as groups that are more religiously individualistic. They value personal feelings, faith, and the individual's relationship with God, whereas Judaism, Catholicism, Episcopalianism, and Hinduism value social connections and communal relation to one another.[112] The American Protestant religion promotes individual spirituality in a privatized, personalized, and experiential-expressive way, not only in religious spaces but also in secular spaces beyond the bounds of the Christian church. As American individualism is intrinsically connected with the Protestant church at its core, it is also deeply connected with white evangelical faith. Since many second-generation Asian immigrants are greatly influenced by Protestant white evangelism,

American individualism is inherently embedded in their psychological and social makeup.

Asian immigrant Christian leaders are keenly aware of this problem and fight American individualism as sin. When Protestant Christianity became the colonizer's religion under the power of colonialism and postcolonial influences in Asia, it introduced American individualism as freedom and justice to "examine" the communal cultures and religions that the colonized practiced. However, it could not break Asian communal cultures, even though serious damage resulted. Asian communalism is still one of the most dominant cultural aspects in many Asian countries. When Asian immigrants move to the United States and join the immigrant church, they reencounter this individualism in a more powerful way. They realize that American individualism is *the* dominant culture in the US. Because second- and third-generation Asian Americans are raised in this culture as their own culture, their great exposure to individualism is very common. Many second-generation church leaders are aware of this exposure and give more attention to criticizing the "a self-centered, cost/benefit calculation" behaviors that these second- and third-generation immigrants exhibit.[113] They claim "a God-centered worldview that expresses itself in a greater level of concern and commitment to the community of believers."[114] For first-generation Asian immigrants, this exposure to individualism is understood as a measure of acculturation. It is believed that to be American means to be individually independent. To be fully Americans, white society teaches immigrants to be independent of their ethnic enclaves. It encourages them to blend in with the white society and separate from their ethnic communities. First-generation immigrants are asked to exhibit individual independence from their ethnic community because, in the colonial/postcolonial institutional social construction, American individualism is equated with a measure of acculturation.

However, when first-generation immigrants try to assimilate into the white society, they find themselves in isolation and marginalization. Reuben Seguritan notes, "In our desire to assimilate into the mainstream of society, we isolated ourselves from one another. Lack of unity, the lack of interest and concern for each other's welfare, lack of compassion for the other's needs are just some of the pernicious effects bred by our colonial culture which have stalled our progress."[115] Individualism brings isolation to Asian immigrants. It creates a conflict between Asian immigrant congregations and communities. It attempts to destroy their communal mentality. As Asian immigrants become more individualistic, it is interpreted as the progress of assimilation. Despite the fact that they feel more isolated from white society, they are encouraged to stay away from their communities. The purpose of this assimilation is for immigrants to desire being white. Filipino American theologian Eleazar S. Fernandez argues that "desiring to be white" is an experience of alienation and a manifestation of internalized racism.[116] As Asian American immigrants internalize racism, they experience more isolation and alienation even within themselves. He warns that this will lead Asian immigrants as well as people of color to accept mistreatment and discrimination as a natural process of the immigrant experience. In the logic of individualism, isolation is not understood as alienation but as individual independence, whereas compassion is not understood as care but as an unnecessary emotion and a waste of time. Protestants view individualism as a natural and gradual part of the process of assimilation.[117]

"The real threat of the commodified notion of life embedded in the current economic individualism is its tendency to minimize the alienated state of people one from another."[118] The label "model minority" is often used for this minimization. As more Asian immigrants are exposed to individualism, individual success is more encouraged. On the one hand, when individuals break through the glass ceiling, their achievement is perceived as evidence of accomplishment for their entire community. It is one for all and all for one. The assumption is that if one person makes breakthroughs and joins the "mainline" society, others have the possibility of crossing over as well. It gives more hope for others who are in a similar condition. The people who achieve success become role models or are admired as leaders. However, on the other hand, it also serves as evidence of the openness of the "just" system. Using the designation of a model minority, society hides discriminatory practices of the social system, legal structure, and political games. It conceals the imperfection of the social construction. By intentionally allowing a few ethnic minorities to break the glass ceiling, racist social construction still controls the gates and exercises power to discriminate others in a new form of discrimination. By disguising the diabolic nature of this system, the model minority status minimizes the alienated state of immigrants one from another on individual and communal levels simultaneously.

Asian immigrant Christian leaders struggle against this minimization. Lifting up Asian communal values and cultures and reinterpreting Christian morals and responsibilities in an Asian immigrant context, they try to decentralize American individualism. Fernandez's de-centering and re-centering notions of "model" and "success" are good examples of this decentralization. By de-centering the notion of success as having "made it" to the top of the social ladder or "breaking the glass ceiling," he contests the criteria of success.[119] He challenges an undisputed allegiance to the American Dream and requests a new concept of success by re-centering success as "living with integrity."[120] He refuses to accept model minority as the synonym to describe people who are in upper class with sociopolitical influence. Rather, he re-defines "model minority" as those who challenge an unjust society and hold hope regardless of challenges.[121] Fernandez urges Christian leaders to reclaim Asians' great heritage and be proud of Asian traditions. His methodology of decentering and re-centering is one of the most important tactics employed by many Asian immigrant leaders to fight individualism. While American individualism encourages all people to define being on the top as success, many Asian immigrant Christian leaders encourage Asian immigrants to redefine success as living with others in love and care through their immigrant churches based on both Asian and Christian values.

To counteract the alienation of individualism, most Asian immigrant congregations and many other congregations adopt small group as one of the main congregational structures. Small-group ministry is the most popular form of ministry in both mainline and independent congregations. However, small groups that are formed in mainline churches do not nurture communal minds over individualism. Boyung Lee argues that the nature of small groups presented in current church structures does not cultivate communalism but "collectivism" that "lacks solidarity and kinship-like relationships."[122] These small groups are made of individuals who have similar needs and common interests as they develop personal, individual spirituality. "The notion of community in mainline small groups is more like a gathering of individuals in reciprocal relationships," and "if they find the group burdensome or unfulfilling, they frequently abandon it."[123] In a comparison with small groups in the mainline white church, Lee draws attention to a communal concept of the small group in Asian culture. In her understanding, communalists in small groups choose the goals of the group over individual interests and maintain good relationships with in-group members for harmony, whereas individualists in small groups choose their own needs and interests over the goal of the group. Communalists can sacrifice their personal lives if necessary for the group and its goals, whereas individualists abandon the group if the group goal does not match their own goals. Challenging both communalists' view and individualists' view, she suggests a model of community with a dual task: "first, acknowledgement that a communal worldview celebrates our group relatedness; and, second, this model needs to challenge notions of community that would sacrifice one's sacred calling as an individual to social hierarchy and nepotism."[124] Moving from multiculturality to interculturality, she requests that the church achieve liberating interdependence. She encourages theological educators and church leaders to work together for the liberation of the people who are most marginalized within their own ethnic communities and beyond.

Fighting American individualism is one of the hardest tasks Asian immigrant Christian church leaders undertake. The battle between Asian communality and American individuality continues within and outside of Asian immigrant congregations. The task for Asian immigrant Christian leaders is not simply to implant Asian communalism in their immigrant congregations. They are not about replacing individualism with communalism. It is more complicated. Individualism separates not just the first generation from the second generation. It separates every level and group of people from individual families and churches to communities and society. Asian immigrant Christian church leaders have to know, first, how to uncover the critical injuries that individualism has brought to families, churches, and society, and second, how to find resources and create the space for healing from these injuries. The responsibility to uncover the injuries and find solutions to heal those injuries lies with church leaders.

The challenges of Asian Christian immigrant leadership in this chapter are illustrated as the lack of ordained clergy women's leadership, developing social service, conflict or "dis-communication" between the first generation and the second (and third) generations, battling with American individualism, and so forth. However, these challenges are not the only challenges that Asian Christian immigrant leadership has faced. There are more challenges that Asian immigrants encounter in their daily lives. With a few of the challenges they face named, it is important to identify what Asian immigrant leadership is and how it needs to be defined to respond to these challenges.

Chapter 6

Critical Features of a Postcolonial Leadership

What is Asian immigrant leadership? How does it need to be defined? Naming and defining Asian immigrant leadership are not simple because there are countless Asian immigrant leaders who exercise different styles of leadership in various immigrant contexts and because Asian immigrants deal with multilayered situations. As is reviewed in previous chapters, there are multiple and distinctive forms of leadership that Asian immigrant leaders exhibit.

Rooted in Colonial Leadership and Colonial Internalization

One of the main challenges to understanding and naming Asian immigrant leadership is the variety of forms of leadership interacting with colonial and postcolonial institutional power. Many current theories in leadership studies give serious consideration to racism and sexism, but postcolonialism is rarely considered and discussed in past and current leadership study. However, the formidable influences of colonialism and postcolonialism have been experienced by many Asians and Asian immigrants. Many Asians have suffered under the power of colonialism and imperialism in their past and present, and many Asians in Asia and Asian immigrants in the United States still live under postcolonial influence.

The most powerful colonial leadership exercised under the history of colonialism and imperialism is dictatorial leadership. Dictatorial leadership is the most pervasive form of leadership exercised by colonizers. Common characteristics of this leadership are authoritarianism and narcissism.[1] Dictatorial leaders exhibit an "all-knowing" and "all-embracing" style of leadership that involves a particular intelligence and skills: "the ability to perceive the potential for dictatorial power, the skills to manipulate the followers and situations to help create the springboard to dictatorship, and the decisiveness to spring to power when the conditions are ripe."[2] Dictators recognize themselves as superiors to others. Their narcissism is often accompanied by grandiosity and arrogance.[3] These are the common characteristics that they exhibit in their authoritarian attitudes. These behaviors are often supported by the colonizer's colonial culture on both the individual and social levels. As they manipulate people to create the atmosphere of a dictatorship, they present their certain skills as universal, omnipotent ability. They firmly believe, and they make others absolutely believe, that they have the ability to know everything and understand everything. They claim to be chosen by God. Therefore, they believe they have to be in control of everything. There is nothing that they cannot decide and do.

Religions, especially Christianity, have frequently been used as powerful colonial implements in the service of dictatorships. "The church has greatly assisted the colonialist; backing his venture, helping his conscience, contributing to the acceptance of colonization—even by the colonized."[4] It operates in the function of cultural imperialism. These religions grant dictators authority and power. Ordained by God, dictators become God. Because of this firm misbelief, "all-knowing, all-embracing" dictators never allow criticism from others and communication with others.[5] Dictatorial leadership never considers the possibility of understanding others because dictators believe they do not have to know others, but others should recognize them. However, when the colonized refuse to recognize their "grandiose presumptions of superiority," dictators are compelled to demonstrate their power to maintain their grandiose self-images.[6] To keep their grandiose superiority, they impose a wrathful order on the colonized. The more the colonized suffer under the dictators' imperial megalomania, the more dictators feel unlimited power. Their narcissistic behaviors are cultivated by this pathological colonial hegemony. Colonial hegemony perceives the colonized as subjects to control. Leaders who accept this hegemony do not recognize others as equals. The colonial hegemony cultivates difference as inferiority. It never allows difference as difference in equality. In other words, it means equality is the most dangerous concept that colonizers work hard to suppress.

Fathali M. Moghaddam explains dictatorial leadership as "a mixture of transactional and transformative leadership; for example, a leader such as Hitler used both rewards and punishments to move people toward his desired goals and inspired change—albeit destructive change—at micro and macro levels."[7] Dictators reward the colonized who betray their own people and break their community, whereas they punish those who try to keep their own people and community together. This violent transactional leadership is often exercised in dictatorial leadership. Tactics of transactional leadership are the most common tool controlling the colonized. This model of leadership is exercised on both individual and communal levels to control the colonized. Using physical violence and provoking psychological fear, colonizers implant their colonial paradigm into the minds of the colonized. Furthermore, dictators form their own goal out of their own interests and inspire, or more precisely, manipulate, others to achieve these goals for them. Using psychological persuasion and spiritual inspiration, they fulfill the goal and move to a change beyond expectation. This fearful transformative leadership is commonly exercised by countless Western and Eastern dictators throughout colonial history. To achieve their toxic goals, it is necessary for dictators to inspire or control elite leaders among the colonized. Many of the colonized, especially these elite leaders among the colonized, participate in this dictatorial leadership directly and indirectly and mimic it consciously and unconsciously. The shadow of colonial leadership is unceasingly cast over them.

This dictator leadership was often exercised in the company of religious propaganda. European colonizers occupied many Asian countries and claimed colonization as civilizing or missionary work. Hiding the real agenda, desire of economic profits for their own countries, they violated Asian countries. Colonialism and imperialism have operated as two wheels of this capitalism. After World War II, imperialism signified "an ideology and a system of economic domination, identified with the USA"[8] and colonialism emphasized "the material condition of the political rule of subjugated people by the old European colonial powers."[9] Colonialism plundered, and imperialism was legitimated by constituting a global political system. Both imperialism and colonialism were directly involved with economic territorial domination and exploitation in colonized countries. By forcefully demanding physical and psychological subjugation, both accompanied violence and invented colonial internalization under it. Under imperial strategies of colonial internalization, many Asian traditions are condemned as barbaric and their traditional sociopolitical structures are disdained as primitive social constructions. The colonized internalize the image of the oppressors as superiors and want to assume their position.[10]

> But almost always, during the initial stage of the struggle, the oppressed, instead of striving for liberation, tend themselves to become oppressors, or "sub-oppressors." The very structure of their thought has been conditioned by the contradictions of the concrete, existential situation by which they were shaped. Their ideal is to be men; but for them, to be men is to be oppressors. This is their model of humanity. This phenomenon derives from the fact that the oppressed, at a certain moment of their existential experience, adopt an attitude of "adhesion" to the oppressor.... Their vision of the new man or woman is individualistic; because of their identification with the oppressor, they have no consciousness of themselves as persons or as members of an oppressed class. It is not to become free that they want agrarian reform, but in order to acquire land and thus become landowners—or, more precisely, bosses over other workers. It is a rare peasant who, once "promoted" to overseer, does not become more of a tyrant towards his former comrades than the owner himself. This is because the context of the peasant's situation, that is, oppression, remains unchanged.[11]

This embedded colonial internalization leads the colonized to accept the rules of the colonizer as the "advanced norm" of society as it presents the colonizer's economic power as a way for the colonized to eliminate poverty. The colonizer's economic power, often achieved through advanced technology, is presented as a tool to guarantee well-being for individuals. It is circulated as something that can be given for individuals for their advancement. It is publicized as something achievable and attainable for individuals who accept the rules of colonizers and obey their sovereignty and power. The hidden assumption is that it is accessible only for individuals, but not for community. It is encouraged for individuals to denounce their communal identity and work for their individual economic success. It replaces communal solidarity with individual success. It substitutes a communal survival with individual achievement. The colonizers are presented as the people who want to support these individuals and teach them how to make that advancement. It is believed that economic success can be guaranteed only by the support from the colonizers.

As the colonizer's economic and political power is desired by the colonized, the colonial internalization replaces colonization with the colonizer's propaganda, "helping the helpless." Colonization is translated in the words of the colonizer as an act of compassion for the colonized in the poor country. Colonized countries are identified as places that are exposed to poverty and dangerous illnesses, and the colonized are categorized as people who are ignorant and unprotected. Colonizers identify their own countries as aid donor countries. They claim to protect the unprotected from dangerous illnesses and poverty out of humanitarian concern. They believe they bring advancement for the colony. Many former colonizers still propagate their superiority and proclaim their colonial legacy as "capitalism and development" as a "gift to the world."[12] Unfortunately, this claim is often accepted by the elite leadership of the colonized. Internalizing colonial beliefs and practices, some elite leaders from the colonized admire the colonizer's country as an ideal model of modern advanced society. From this admiration, they accept the mentality of colonial dictator leadership as a necessary principle to build a better country. In the name of *development*, colonial dictator leadership is desired and legitimated, again. As these elite leaders adopt and exercise dictatorial leadership, Western colonial rules and social constructions remain to dominate the former Asian countries. The colonial internalization is perpetuated in a postcolonial Asia through colonial dictator leadership.

Without physical occupation, postcolonial domination occurs. The colonial system rules formerly colonized countries and controls economic welfare. Until or even after the condition of oppression is completely dissolved, this postcoloniality evokes the fear not to be oppressed again in the memory of the formally colonized. Under this fear, colonial infrastructure such as sociopolitical institutions, laws, and even religious lives in the postcolonial context are continuously recognized as necessary constructions for a global market. To not be oppressed, Asians feel compelled to develop their countries, and to develop their countries, they feel compelled to adopt the advanced modern systems created by colonizers. This conflictive circle confuses Asians concerning the images of ideal leaders under this colonial internalization and fear.

Colonial Imperial Racism

The mentality of colonial leadership is deeply formed and engaged with colonial imperial racism. Colonizers foster an atmosphere of colonial imperial racism for the colonized to accept an inferior existence. Racism, colonialism, and imperialism have been inseparable from the beginning of any colonial history. Colonialism and imperialism are always accompanied by racism in every colony. Albert Memmi describes three major ideological components that build this colonial racism: "one, the gulf between the culture of the colonialist and the colonized; two, the exploitation of these differences for the benefit of the colonialist; three, the use of these supposed differences as standards of absolute fact."[13] These components are spontaneously incorporated with difference between white and nonwhite skin color in every aspect of the colony to the degree that they permeate the minds of both the colonized and the colonizers.

In colonial imperial ideology, there were two ways to interpret this color difference in terms of racism. In the case of French colonialism, racism operated with the doctrine of assimilation. The basic assumption of this ideology starts from the concept of fundamental equality of all human beings. It claims that all people should benefit from "the uniform imposition of French culture in its most advanced contemporary manifestation."[14] As the French advancement became the standard for all races, this logic encouraged all to integrate their "primitive" practices into French culture. To achieve this integration, "an extreme degree of bureaucratic centralization" was both demanded and legitimated.[15] In the case of the British imperial system, this process was deeply related to the development of a cultural ideology of race. The assumption of British ideology was based on "racial superiority."[16] It emphasized the fundamental racial difference between colonizers and the colonized and criticized incapability of the natives to advance. This logic justifies "perpetual colonial rule" over the colonized in the name of a mission to civilize.[17] Both the French and British imperial ideologies foster white supremacy. Whether white supremacy is based on assimilating the colonized into the advanced form of culture or the perception of an innate existential difference, both cultivate strong racial discrimination against nonwhite races to legitimate colonial violence. These colonial imperial ideologies are a most toxic legacy, and they have been inherited as racism in the United States. Even after independence from Western colonization, many Asian countries have suffered from these postcolonial racist ideologies. Even while seeking the right leaders who can erase the toxic remnant of colonial inheritance in their society, they admire "powerful" leaders who present all-knowing, all-embracing characteristics.

Leaders from Asian countries have struggled to develop a leadership that overcomes these influences, even though many have failed and adopted the colonizer's oppressive leadership, as Freire has described. When Asians migrate to the United States, this colonial imperial racism is carried over and combines with classism and sexism/heterosexism, and, furthermore, is transfused with postcolonial ideology. These issues are intertwined and inseparable from each other in Asian immigrant context. Asian immigrants must deal with issues of both colonial imperial racism and US racism simultaneously in their immigrant context.

> It may be simplistic, but not groundless, to connect classism and racism with colonialism. This colonial spirit was operative in the West's expansion in Asia during the past three centuries. The history of the Asian peoples' struggle with the West's expansion in Asia is the history of the struggle for identity and dignity. Simply stated, the West's expansion in Asia has affected the formation, or the deformation, of the Asian North Americans' identity and our feelings about ourselves. The history of the West's encroachment affects our ways of being in, our wish to become integral and contributing members of, our newly adopted home.[18]

As colonialism and imperialism in an Asian colonialized context is undeniably connected with racism and classism, postcolonialism in an Asian immigrant US context is also deeply allied with racism and classism. As Asians struggled with colonial racism and white superiority in the past, as immigrants they doubly struggle with postcolonial racism and white superiority in the United States. *Asian immigrants were taught once to believe white superiority by European white colonizers in Asia and twice to believe white superiority by the white society in the United States.* This double internalization of colonial and postcolonial racism is inscribed in the minds of Asian immigrants. It is formed and refortified as the repository of colonial and postcolonial memory and history. This double internalization of colonial and postcolonial racism causes more harm to Asian immigrants and their identity formation. Without an awareness of the double complexities of postcolonial racism, it is impossible to understand the suffering of Asian immigrants. Consequently, it is important for Asian immigrant leaders to understand this double racial oppression process and to develop the strategies of deconstructing this toxic process. To develop these strategies, Asian immigrant leadership becomes the inevitable site of contestation to bring equality and justice for Asian immigrants. Furthermore, because most immigrant rights activities for Asian immigrants are very often initiated by religious communities, the church or religious organizations are the inevitable sites where progress toward equality and justice begin, and religious leaders are the main ones who carry out this task.

Unlike a colonial era, there is no clear distinction between colonized and colonizer in a postcolonial US context. Rather, postcolonialism is formed from the interactions between white and nonwhite groups along with the discourses of colonialism, imperialism, racism, gender and sex, and class. This creates various dynamics and complexities. It creates contradictions and ambiguities. In an earlier work, I explain the dynamics in the power of postcolonialism in two different approaches: the power of postcolonialism *within power structures and institutional ideologies* and the power of postcolonialism *within people*.[19] As strong colonial influences resurge in the postcolonial context, unlike in a colonial context, people interact with them in different ways. As immigrants who meet freedom in the present but still deal with the remnants of colonial history from the past and the double racism of the present, they recognize the difference in others as they find themselves as the other in US context. Under colonial context, their otherness is perceived as deviant difference. However, under postcolonial context, as they experience their achieved independence, they learn to recognize their otherness as equal difference. Many Asian immigrant leaders fight to create a shift from deviant difference in former colonial space to equal difference in current postcolonial space. Even though they recognize that they are treated as the marginalized other in their postcolonial immigrant context, they fight as, for, and with others who are put in similar situations and who make them *not* alone. In other words, they, as the others, see and create the possibilities of solidarity with and among others together in this postcolonial context.

In the process of this mutual recognition of otherness, many Asian immigrant leaders see others, not as essentially different others, but as *temporalizedly* different others in this transient transnational immigrant space.[20] Colonial structure requires essentially different others to make the colonized different in a deviant manner from the colonizer. It "invents" others as otherness of deviant difference.[21] However, Asian immigrant leaders try to challenge this colonial mentality and learn how to recognize difference, not as essential difference, but as temporalized difference. They work hard to reconstruct difference as difference in respect and equal existence to understand others in a postcolonial US immigrant context. As they re-collect the memories of their achieved independence over colonial violence, they see the possibility to create space to exercise their freedom in a mutual communication and equal power relationship with others. Within this possibility of hope, they try to transform their marginalized colonially experienced space into a postcolonial space of mutual recognition and peaceful harmonious co-existence. Even though they often discover more ambiguities and contradictions in this postcolonial immigrant space, they accept these challenges and create a leadership that helps their community know how to be different in an almost impossible, yet possible, vision of a peaceful harmonious co-existence. They dream that the power of postcolonialism within people transforms the space of ambiguities and contradictions into the space of resilient hope and unexpected expectations.

Definition of a Postcolonial Leadership

A postcolonial leadership is formed based on this almost impossible, yet possible, vision of a peaceful co-existence. It is a leadership of Asian immigrants and communities that challenges postcolonial institutional power and authority and embraces the power of postcolonialism within people. It is about how to navigate "the power of postcolonialism within people"[22] to nurture resilient hope and strengthen immigrants to battle various prejudices and discriminations, including race, class, sex and gender, and others. Out of survival, it is a leadership to recognize equal difference and honor it with respect and care. Postcolonial leadership develops a "consciousness of difference" to acknowledge the difference with authenticity in each person and community and simultaneously create a common ground to challenge the larger society in "solidarity of others" and with others.[23] The goal of a postcolonial leadership is to create better lives for Asian immigrants and their communities and for the whole society within and beyond the US postcolonial context. It expects to change physical realities as well as psychological and spiritual actualities for the immigrants, the powerless, the oppressed, and the marginalized. Therefore, a postcolonial leadership cannot have one specific style of leadership, such as transformative leadership, transactional leadership, or collaborative leadership, but can include them selectively and collectively depending on the context and groups of people with and without a consciousness of postcolonial dynamics. It is a leadership that requires and adopts various forms simultaneously. Forming a leadership in a postcolonial context is complicated because leaders must consider many complexities within which Asian immigrants live. Especially when encountering Christianity, this leadership becomes even complicated. To deal with these complexities in a postcolonial context in relation to Christianity, it is necessary to examine the different characteristics of postcolonial leadership of Asian immigrant Christian leaders in their immigrant churches.

One of the most distinctive features of a postcolonial leadership is the recognition of women's leadership. Women's struggle from extreme marginality in sociopolitical and religious leadership positions is the main narrative of a postcolonial leadership. Even though women play significant roles as leaders who support the movement, provide food for people, deliver resources for them, and take care of their families and communities in every single anticolonial struggle, campaign, freedom fight, and liberation movement, recognition of women's leadership is not treated equally in public discourse. The colonial construction often trivializes women's leadership and requires only subordination. Both colonial regimes and indigenous societies commonly exercise patriarchal power to exploit women and disdain their leadership. Women have perpetually struggled against "the double colonialization of patriarchal domination in its local as well as its imperial forms."[24] However, as a postcolonial discourse develops, women's experience is considered one of the most essential and conflictive experiences that postcolonial scholars needed to investigate. This postcolonial challenge by women requests a postcolonial discourse to reconfigure the struggle of women and their leadership that is often performed not by specifically named individuals, but by communal, nameless women. "It was the fact that women's resistance operated from below rather than from above, drawing on widespread popular support from ordinary women."[25] Because their leadership is performed from below, by ordinary women in many cases, communal involvement and participation are commonly embraced. This form of collaborative communal leadership has fallen outside of traditional patriarchal leadership. Women's collaborative communal leadership is often regarded as the nature of women's leadership that postcolonial scholars look into. In an Asian Christian immigrant context, this collaborative communal leadership is strongly practiced by both women clergy and lay women.

Critical Features of a Postcolonial Leadership

Therefore, in the next section, recognizing Asian Christian leaders, especially women clergy and lay leaders, and their immigrant churches, I examine two pairs of features that a postcolonial leadership includes: 1) hybridity and authenticity, and 2) communality and individuality. Even though each pair seems contradictive to each other, they coexist simultaneously in postcolonial leadership. Simultaneity is the important key for these features. Each characteristic exists as pair. One cannot exist without the other in postcolonial leadership. For example, hybridity cannot exist without authenticity and communality cannot exist without individuality in the postcolonial leadership. Moreover, hybridity and authenticity cannot exist in an Asian immigrant context without communality and individuality. These features are critical parts of a postcolonial leadership that many Asian immigrant leaders need to be aware of. There are limits and possibilities of a postcolonial leadership. While illustrating a postcolonial immigrant Christian context and reinterpreting the problems of inequality and injustice that Asian immigrants face, it is critical to observe how Asian Christian leaders engage these features and use them in their theological practice.

Hybridity and Authenticity

Hybridity

Hybridity is the most common and distinctive leadership feature of Asian immigrant leaders. What is hybridity? Homi K. Bhabha describes hybridity as follows:

> Hybridity is the sign of the productivity of colonial power, its shifting forces and fixities; it is the name for the strategic reversal of the process of domination through disavowal (that is, the production of discriminatory identities that secure the 'pure' and original identity of authority). Hybridity is the revaluation of the assumption of colonial identity through the repetition of discriminatory identity effects. It displays the necessary deformation and displacement of all sites of discrimination and domination. It unsettles the mimetic or narcissistic demands of colonial power but reimplicates its identifications in strategies of subversion that turn the gaze of the discriminated back upon the eye of power.[26]

> Hybridity is a problematic of colonial representation and individuation that reverses the effects of the colonialist disavowal, so that other "denied" knowledges enter upon the dominant discourse and estrange the basis of its authority—its rules of recognition. Again, it must be stressed, it is not simply the content of disavowed knowledges—be they forms of cultural otherness or traditions of colonialist treachery—that return to be acknowledged as counter-authorities.[27]

Bhabha defines the meaning of hybridity as a "process of disavowal" of colonial power and its representation by recognizing marginalized denied knowledge in postcolonial movement.[28] Act of hybridity requires a shift from colonial unchanging order, fixity, rigidity, and dominant knowledge to postcolonial disorder, fluctuation, flexibility, and marginalized denied knowledge. This shift constantly exists and disappears in interstitial space. It is a repeated reconstructing process to re-evaluate the current existing structure and normativity.

Kwok explains hybridity as the concept to deal with "colonial authority and power of representation."[29] It displaces simplistic, binary, unitary, and monological understandings of cultural purity and dismantles colonial beliefs and authority. Criticizing the connotation of mere mixing or simple pluralism, Kwok defines hybridity as a power that invades the dominant discourse and exposes the colonial reality.[30] In a similar manner, Joh understands the concept of hybridity as it relates to three basic trajectories: 1) "The product of oppression"; 2) "undermine authority and (to) displace the binary thinking"; and 3) "thick description" of historical and geographical situations."[31] As she emphasizes these trajectories, she underlines the importance of mutuality and "a space of negotiation where "power is unequal but its articulation may be equivocal."[32] Both Kwok and Joh agree with Bhabha that hybridity allows marginalized knowledge to make a dialogue with the dominant discourse and challenges that discourse with voices of the oppressed. As these scholars demonstrate, hybridity is a pertinent concept through which to understand that postcolonial Asian immigrant context. It creates an old and new co-existing space to intersect and interact past and present. At the same time, it renews and expands this space to future. The concept of hybridity legitimates difference as equal difference because as it touches difference, otherness becomes a part of "we." By creating the third space, not as a melting pot of multiple cultures, but as a possibility of multi-intercultural movement, it encourages multi-intercultural interactiveness and nurtures multi-intercultural dialogues and analysis.

Even though hybridity is never included as a leadership feature in current leadership studies, Asian immigrant Christian leaders perform it daily both deliberately and unconsciously because the need for hybridity exists in every dimension of Asian immigrant lives. By creating a third space and hybridizing their ethnic cultures with the dominant cultures, they try to find a way to fight prejudice and discrimination against Asian immigrants and acquire access to justice and equality for immigrant lives. As they meet an ever-changing hybrid reality, immigrants have to hybridize a new space for a new negotiation and convergence.

Immigrant church is a good example of this hybrid space. Hybridity starts from Asian immigrant worship experience. As many Asian immigrants see the first-generation and second-generation church members, religious leaders know that they cannot have a worship service in one language. They try to create a new space that includes both generations by conducting bilingual worship service or translating their sermons in English for each Sunday worship service. As they listen to the difficulties of communication between first-generation immigrant parents and second-generation immigrant children, they know that they cannot communicate with parents and children in the same way. They must hybridize the issue of language communication problems, multi-intercultural family dynamics, cultural generational gaps, the dynamics of society at large, and more. Intentionally and instinctively, they handle the situation. Living in the Asian immigrant church, they must make an effort to hybridize not only two languages and two cultures but also multi-intercultural interactions and intersections.

As the Asian immigrant church is the most complex hybrid space in immigrants' lives, Asian immigrant Christian leaders perform hybridity as an essential part of their leadership. It is not just demonstrating the sum of their abilities of flexibility, adaptation, adjustment, openness, negotiation, creativity, and so forth. Hybridity in leadership is a selective and collective performance that creates interstitial spaces for integration of these abilities and non-binary dialogical conversations in-between and beyond. They have to know how to hybridize the understandings of Jesus to the understandings of the church in an Asian immigrant context, from living in binary Asian and American cultures to living in nonbinary but entangled Asian immigrant culture, from the center to the periphery, from deconstructing colonial power to reconstructing postcolonial power, from dealing with Asian communalism and American individualism to dealing with in-between and from a mono-stream of thinking to plural streams of thinking, and vice versa. Asian immigrant life is hybridity itself. It is both and multiple ways of flows and beyond. Asian immigrant leaders learn how to avoid a binary way of thinking from their personal and social communal experiences. They have learned complex multiple skills in simultaneous multi-intercultural communications. Living in a hybrid space makes them practice hybridity as unequivocally the most important feature of their leadership. Hybridity has been always an undeniable part of Asian immigrant leadership.

However, hybridity can often be confused with the concept of assimilation as is discussed in the previous section. Assimilation is a process that starts with "acculturation, the acquiring of the distinctive cultural patterns of the white society," and ends with an exclusively white American national identity.[33] It insinuates immigrants join the white dominant society as second-class citizens. The goal of this process is the impossibility of becoming white. However, the process of hybridity is different. It is a process that starts with what is called authentic, the acquiring of difference, and ends with a permanent irregular connection between authentic beings and things. It disrupts established colonial structures and destabilizes them with suspicion. It intervenes in its own and other spaces and mediates with and without the presence of questionable power and authority. It challenges the dominant discourse with creativity and ambiguity. It requests a reinterpretation of knowledge and tradition. It refuses to be in the space of categorization and classifications. By establishing the Asian immigrant church, by creating various styles of worship service, and by developing social service and civil engagement, Asian immigrant leaders constantly challenge the dominant discourse, request reinterpretation of knowledge and tradition, and refuse to stay in the space of categorization. They resist, negotiate, and seek change. It is impossible for Asian immigrants to survive in the postcolonial US without the power to hybridize.

Understanding the importance of hybridity for Asian immigrants and their postcolonial contexts, it is necessary for Asian immigrant leaders to exercise hybridity as their transforming power. As is shown in colonial dictatorships, colonial leadership requires "production of differentiation, individuations, and discriminatory practices" against the oppressed and "modes of discrimination cultural, racial, administrative . . . that disallow a stable unitary assumption of collectivity."[34] In other words, this type of leadership emphasizes differentiation and individuation in the form of colonial hierarchy. This colonial hierarchy is fortified by discriminatory practices. However, hybridity destabilizes this hierarchy and sets up a movement against cultural purity. In a postcolonial immigrant context, this movement is the effort of "de-transcendentalizing" the ruse of various immigrant ethnic communal identities adopting an individual white identity.[35] Asian immigrant leadership in this movement challenges and deconstructs the white colonial hierarchy that is deeply ingrained in the United States. It questions the production of differentiation and individuation as the subject of investigation and revisits discriminatory practices with suspicion and inquiries.

In an Asian immigrant Christian context, hybridity exposes the assumptions of authority and power from colonial and postcolonial constructions within and beyond religious institutions. It contests not only the divine images and authority but also clergy images and authority. Differentiation between clergy and lay leaders is cast in doubt. Hybridity as a feature of postcolonial leadership revisits the boundaries of right or wrong and creates more fluid boundaries to seek various possible answers in God's vision. It requests equality including but not limited to economic restructuring and sociopolitical redistributive justice based on the Christian faith. Even though negative impacts and remnants of colonial and postcolonial constructions exist as the indispensable conditions of Asian immigrant reality, in the process of hybridization, immigrant leaders recognize the consequences of these impacts and try to transform them into a new form of production. In this sense, hybridity can be a will of people who exercise transforming power with God who transforms.

Through the process of hybridity, Asian immigrant Christian leaders try to adapt, challenge, and transform. They constantly mimic and analyze the current structures and negotiate changes simultaneously. To this negotiation process, they serious engage with creativity. Creativity is another side of hybridity. It opens the possibilities of the unknown and hopes for impossible vision into reality. Power of creativity is embedded within the people who transform the negativity of colonial/postcolonial oppression into the power of liberation. It is used and exercised by those people with power of resistance and resilience. In the space of creativity, resistance and resilience are the continuous effort to hybridize. In this sense, hybridity becomes an important trait of resistant and resilient leadership against colonial and imperial hierarchy in a postcolonial space. It stays between resistance and acceptance and between resilience and contentment.

However, the concepts of resistance and resilience are seldom described as characteristics of leaders but merely as dangerous features of followers, the marginalized, subalterns, the oppressed, subordinates, workers, and women. The power of postcolonialism within institutional structures and ideologies teaches acceptance and contentment in the current construction as the standard model of leadership. When this power is exercised in a white postcolonial managerial context, resistance is mainly seen as a dangerous power to eliminate.[36] The goal of management in a white-dominated leadership context is to manage and sustain the current colonial/postcolonial structure and social order. And embracing innovation and vision is the role of white leaders in power, not the followers who are often immigrants and marginalized ethnic groups. In this sense, resistance is understood as a threat to the current leadership because it is the nature and innate power of followers, the grass roots, subalterns, subordinates, workers, and women, but not leaders. Therefore, power embedded in resistance is perceived as something dangerous, unsafe, uncontrollable, irrepressible, oppositional, and illegitimate.

Resistant and resilient leadership has always been treated as a nonconventional and rebellious form of the current leadership. However, the existence of this leadership is undeniable throughout colonial and postcolonial history. It always exists as one indisputable form of leadership. It has been the main power to fight colonial violence. Even though resistance is often described as the main resource in the studies of politics, history, sociology, theology, and other human sciences, resistant and resilient leadership has not been discussed as the dominant discourse of leadership studies. However, in recent years, a few scholars have begun to develop resistance leadership as a part of leadership study.

Brigid Carroll and Helen Nicholson demonstrate in their research that resistance and power in leadership dynamics are crucial elements for leadership development. The first step of this research is the retheorization of resistance. Recognizing the traditional meaning of resistance in current leadership studies, they introduce resistance in the relationship with power such as "mutually implicated, co-constructed, interdependent, multiple, ambiguous and contradictory,"[37] and as a "chiaroscuro," in which the "two play off each other through mixture, contrast and blurring."[38] From this relationship between resistance and power, they agree with Robyn Thomas and Annette Davies that resistance is "a constant process of adaptation, subversion and reinscription."[39] In this definition, resistance is not merely rejecting something. It includes the process of hybridity. It struggles with adaptation but, at the same time, it creates subversion in the dialectical process. In this hybridized movement between adaptation and subversion, reinscription is formed. It is the product of hybrid movement between adaptation and subversion. As this process is repeated, resistant leadership is developed. Carroll and Nicholson conclude that resistance is "an act of live leadership within a programme" and leadership development is "a site of 'resisting work.'"[40] They assert that resistance plays a powerful force to develop leadership and productive learning. By analyzing three interactions (dampening resistance, firing resistance, and resistance indecision), they find resistance from the participants when the power of certain discourses "attempt to shape one's identity, the power of expertise, and the disciplinary power of peers and 'hierarchy' who monitor and try to regulate one's conduct."[41] As people experience the power of certain discourses, it is natural to resist. Through resistance, they develop leadership. Even though the scope of this research is limited to individuals, it gives a glimpse of how resistance can be a force of development for the community.

Allen and Barbara Isaacman categorize resistance into five concepts in anticolonial movements: "day-to-day forms of resistance (including cultural practices, crime, and a wide variety of forms of insubordination), resistance through withdrawal and migration, maroonage, social banditry, and peasant revolts."[42] From day-to-day occurrences to revolutionary anticolonial movements, resistance has been carried out by ordinary people, especially by women and the grass roots.

> The history of women's activism in the liberation movements in many respects operates in a comparable way to the history of resistance by peasants, tribals, nomads and those of low caste (which were themselves often initiated by women). . . . Such local, small-scale forms require an acknowledgement of the long history of indigenous resistance which often, as in the case of women's struggles or guerrilla wars, for example in the Philippines, continued scarcely without interruption from the colonial to the independence period. Recognition of the value of small-scale movements and acts of opposition has produced an emphasis on resistance rather than larger forms of emancipation and liberation. This suits the women's movements

for whom there can be no single revolutionary moment, but rather apparently unending sequences of battles that have to be fought.[43]

Women's leadership is predominately recognized in small-scale movements. (Even though they always work together with men in larger movements, their leadership is often denied or invisible in these movements.) Women have led countless movements toward liberation throughout history in the form of resistant and resilient leadership. Their presence is a historical fact, but their leadership is not recognized as leadership in history. Often, no names are given in history because their leadership is generally performed in a collaborative, communal, resilient, resistant form. They resiliently resist together for the survival of the community. Resistance, along with resilience, has been presented as the unceasing tenacious power of women, the oppressed, the powerless, and the marginalized. In a postcolonial immigrant context, their collaborative, communal, resilient, resistant leadership opens up possibilities of different ways to define leadership. Instead of measuring leadership in large-scale movements, it highlights leadership at various scales in movements and organizations. Postcolonial leadership in the form of resistance and resilience denies the ownership of leadership by the privileged class, sex and gender, and race. Rather, it creates a leadership of otherness. It attends voices of the unheard and values leadership by the underprivileged. It brings a new understanding of leadership in an Asian immigrant context. It is communal, nameless, and collaborative. As colonial leadership tries to maintain the current colonial structure by acceptance and contentment with an individual leader at top, postcolonial leadership tries to dismantle the current structure by resistance and resilience with countless nameless mass leaders.

In an Asian immigrant postcolonial context, especially in an Asian immigrant Christian context, resistant and resilient leadership is very frequently demonstrated among women clergy and lay leaders. It attempts to shift the position of leadership from privileged male clergy to women clergy and local lay leaders. Struggling with existing current colonial and postcolonial constructions and social order, resistant and resilient leadership embraces Asian immigrant leaders, women clergy, and lay leaders to nurture the resistant and resilient ability to hybridize between various cultures and discern colonial and postcolonial challenges. In the postcolonial space of creativity, this leadership challenges Asian immigrant leaders to learn how to hybridize communities and individuals, individuals and individuals, and communities and other communities in the complex postcolonial context. Asian immigrant leaders resist both individualism and communalism but hybridize them in their own situations. Resistant and resilient leadership requires Asian immigrant leaders to legitimate their power of resistance as the creative force to establish postcolonial leadership. Resistant and resilient leadership becomes an actual practice of performing hybridity in a postcolonial context as a critical part of postcolonial leadership.

The purpose of Asian immigrant leadership is to help Asian immigrants to live in the United States without losing their self. Survival is the main purpose for Asian immigrant leadership, and hybridity in the form of resistance and resilience is the main skill for this survival. In the case of Asian immigrant Christian leadership, survival is also an important goal of leadership. However, it aims beyond survival. Along with this purpose, Asian immigrant Christian leaders emphasize transformation in the process of resistance and resilience and use hybridity to create the bridge between Asian immigrant earthly context and God's kin-dom. They encourage Asian immigrant Christians to move from a survival mode to abundant living and well-being as people of faith through and beyond their church and community. Fighting and struggling against the white dominant discourse, Asian immigrant leaders must recognize how to negotiate but resist the white dominant discourse in dialogue with their own ethnic, religious, cultural discourses as well as other multi-intercultural discourses. Transforming leadership from otherness to togetherness, Asian immigrant Christian leaders in particular have to learn how to resiliently adapt, examine, adjust, resist, challenge, negotiate, and transform to live better lives and create their own space in harmony with others in God's abundance.

Hybridity for Asian immigrants includes not only resistance and resilience but also authenticities of difference in openness and flexibility. Hybridity is not the opposite of purity of authenticities. Rather, it recognizes each position's authenticity and hybridizes those in one's own way. Hybridity for Asian Christian immigrant leadership requires a process of recognizing authenticity in connections. It connects each being and thing in openness without losing authenticity. It recognizes them in flexible forms and practices. Therefore, hybridity and authenticity cannot be separated in an Asian immigrant context. In fact, they are deeply connected to each other.

Authenticity

Authenticity is commonly described as an important leadership feature, and authentic leadership is one of the newest areas of leadership study. Northouse introduces that authentic leadership is found in these three perspectives: intrapersonal (within the leaders themselves), interpersonal (relational), and developmental (nurtured, not fixed).[44] Knowing who I am (within the leaders themselves), being genuine to others (relational), and nurturing the relationship with others (developmental) are common features of authentic leadership. Authentic leadership is something about authentic to themselves and others.

However, authenticity is often confused with purity in the opposite sense of hybridity, especially in a white Christian context. It is something neither contagious nor mixed. It is something pure and original. In individual sense, authenticity is understood as a personal original self, which is misinterpreted as a mono or singular identity. In communal sense, it is understood as cultural distinctiveness, cultural purity. Both individual and communal senses perceive authenticity as something distinctively originary. It does not allow any tainted characters. It emphasizes purity, which leads to essential difference. In order to be authentic, it should be purely different. In this understanding, authenticity requests difference. In the context of the dominant US culture, authenticity requires "the unspoiled African, Asian, or Native American, who remains more preoccupied with her/his images of the *real* native—the *truly different*—than with the issues of hegemony, racism, feminism, and social change."[45] To be authentic means to be distinctively different. Distinctive Asianness is insisted and ordered. It demands absolute otherness in difference. When authenticity is equated with difference under colonial/postcolonial immigrant context, this can be used as another mode of "apparatus of colonial power" to discriminate Asian immigrants.[46] Because of this confusion and colonial misinterpretation, authenticity is often dismissed and misused. Therefore, understanding and defining authenticity is an important part of this discussion.

The concept of authenticity in Asian immigrant context should not be defined as purity, cultural distinctiveness, or essential difference, but as the sense of identity process such as who I/we were as Asians in the past, who I/we are as Asian immigrants in the present, and who I/we want to be in the future in relation to individual others and communal others. It is about how Asian immigrants authentically relate to one's own self and community in different times (past, present, and future) and spaces (native lands, immigrant shores, and transnational spaces). It is about embracing this individual and communal identity formation in the openness to local truths and temporal similarities/differences that they experience. Therefore, the concept of authenticity in Asian immigrant leadership needs to be also defined in-between this individual and communal identity formation process. Defining the concept of authenticity in Asian immigrant leadership in-between these formation processes requires Asian immigrant leaders to have a deep understanding of these processes in multi-intercultural immigrant contexts beyond their own ethnic contexts and a keen awareness of cultivating openness in relation to individual and communal others.

This requirement challenges Asian immigrant leaders to demonstrate how open and perceptible they are as leaders within multi-intercultural immigrant contexts, how they empower their own ethnic immigrant groups, and what capacities they have to nurture the relationship with other immigrant groups in relation to society at large. However, their authentic leadership goes beyond these relations. They also must understand their authenticity as Asians to their native countries while being Americans to the United States at the same time. They have to be authentic to multiple national and transnational communities in global and transnational contexts. Being authentic does not mean having one identity or showing loyalty to one specific ethnic group in an Asian immigrant context, even though this loyalty is required in some Asian contexts. For Asian immigrant leaders, being authentic means being hybrid. Being an authentic leader in an Asian immigrant context means how to hybridize difference of times and spaces in these relationships. They need to learn how to be faithful to themselves and others in a part of multiple hybrid communities with their own creative hybridized authenticity. Without being hybrid, they cannot be authentic leaders in their immigrant context.

However, most authentic leadership studies do not include the concept of authenticity in relation to hybridity in connection to communities. Rather, the field tends to focus on individual fulfillment and the individual characteristics of authentic leaders. Robert W. Terry develops an authentic action wheel with six components: "Around the top of the wheel are Meaning (guiding values, principles, and ethics), Mission (goals, objectives and desires), and Power (energy, motivation, morale, and control); clockwise around the bottom are Structure (system, policies, and procedures), Resources (people, capital, information, equipment, and time), and Existence (history and identity)."[47] The center of the wheel is Fulfillment. It shows how leaders are *authentic to their goals* by analyzing productivity and its problems. As Terry designs this leadership to focus on problem areas, Bill George designs another form of authentic leadership to focus on characteristics of authentic leaders. Researching 125 successful leaders, George illustrates five dimensions of authentic leadership (purpose, values, relationships, self-discipline, and heart) and relates these dimensions to "passion, behavior, connectedness, consistency, and compassion" as the characteristics that individuals need to develop to become authentic leaders.[48] Both these studies focus on authentic leadership as independent individual achievement.

Unlike these two studies, Haina Zhang, André M. Everett, Graham Elkin, and Malcolm H. Cone have a different understanding of authentic leadership. Reflecting Chinese perspectives on authenticity, they show how authentic leadership can be performed in a Chinese context. They illustrate how Chinese authentic leaders achieve authentic identity and form authentic relationships with others for communal harmony. Analyzing a dilemma between individual independent attitudes and communal harmony, they warn that "the shortage of institutional support and resources induces ordinary people to distort their authentic attitudes and behaviors in interactions with others to pursue their goals."[49]

This dilemma is also a critical challenge that Asian immigrant leaders face in the complexities of a long tradition of Asian communal culture and history, American individualism, colonial hierarchy, and postcolonial hybridization. From the perspective of US individualism, communal harmony is criticized as a premodern paradigm to oppress individual excellence. From the perspective of Asian communal history and culture, an individual independent attitude is evaluated as a harmful to communal harmony. At the same time, communal harmony is encouraged by Asian communal culture and an individual independent attitude is empowered by the spirit of US independent liberation and individualism. The ability to solve this complexity is most important for Asian immigrant leaders as a demonstration of authentic leadership. They need to be authentically relational to these multi-intercultural power dynamics. As every Asian immigrant family and immigrant church between the first and the second (and third) generations deals with this complexity in their daily lives, Asian immigrant Christian leaders need to show the balance to achieve harmony between individual independent attitudes and authentic communal demands for their church members, ethnic communities and a larger society. To understand this complexity, hybridity is required as a critical feature of this authentic leadership.

An understanding of authenticity in this complexity is a common but difficult issue that many Asian immigrant leaders face. It is particularly complicated to understand this complexity for Asian immigrant Christian leaders because the concepts of authenticity are greatly influenced by a combination of Christianity along with various Asian religions. Deeply related to self-awareness, including self-evaluation, self-reflection, self-control, self-completion, and emptiness of self based on Asian religions, authenticity is essential for Asian immigrant Christian leaders—not only with oneself but also with others before God.

In a Christian context, knowing who I am is understood on an individual level. Being authentic to oneself in Christian belief means recognizing one's sin, renouncing oneself, and following Jesus on a personal level. It is, in fact, akin to the concept of emptiness of self in Asian religions. By confessing sin, people know who they are and what they have done. Without complete repentance of one's sin within oneself, it is impossible to be authentic to oneself in a Christian context. Many Christians, including evangelicals, fundamentalists, and liberal Christians, emphasize confession of sin as the first step to becoming a Christian, both with and without acute awareness of communal sins. In an Asian immigrant Christian context, knowing oneself is deeply related to individual and communal immigrants' identity in the sinful context of racism, sexism, heterosexism, classism, and postcolonialism. This question is always asked on the individual and communal levels simultaneously. They concern the authentic immigrant identity, immigrants' capacity to know who they really are and how authentic they can be in the United States. At the same time, they question what they should do and how authentic they can act in the action of sinful violence against them and within them at the intersections of various discriminations that they face in their daily lives.

These questions naturally lead to the next question. What is meant by the request to be genuine and/or authentic to others, then? In Christian belief, the request to be authentic to others requires restoration of justice and love with others. It is answered with Jesus's commandment. The request to be authentic to others is greatly connected with the Christian's greatest commandment: "Love your neighbor as yourself."[50] This is the most important Christian teaching and the goal of Christian leadership. In an Asian immigrant context, the requirement involves Asian immigrants' knowledge of who their neighbors are and how best to relate to them.

Namsoon Kang asks, "If the core message of Christianity, loving one's neighbor as oneself, is merely a spiritualized or romanticized rhetoric that people just chant in the church without rigorously wrestling with the hard questions such as who one's neighbors are, to whom I/we are neighbors, and what constitutes loving oneself and neighbors, then the significant value of loving one's neighbor as oneself entirely loses its profound meaning and sociogeopolitical implication for daily reality."[51] She indicates that in the attempt to hold on to its meaning and subversive hope, it is important for Christians to practice this commandment with firm knowledge of the difference between *what-is* and *what-ought-to-be*. Kang challenges the status quo, *reality-as-it-is*, and seeks "an alternative *reality-as-it-ought-to-be, the world-to-come,* the *kindom of God.*"[52] Tracing the history of revolutionary movement such as the women's movement and various liberation movements, she finds new possibilities to transform existing reality and creates visions of the kin-dom of God. In these possibilities, Kang understands Jesus as "a primary reference for Christians, as a prophetic utopian, whose eschatological hope and vision for the Kindom of God is the passion for the impossible, the witness to the subversive hope against hope."[53] Like Kang, many Asian immigrant theologians and church leaders identify Jesus as the primordial model of the authentic leader who transforms impossible hope to possible reality.

To be authentic to oneself and to others as Jesus has, Asian immigrant Christian leaders try to solve the dilemma between an individual independent attitude and communal harmony by listening to others individually as the voice of God and finding communal needs by consensus as God's need as they understand themselves as immigrants and know what they have to do with others. They hybridize these two levels of communication simultaneously with this double conscious authenticity. In this process, the meaning of authenticity in an Asian immigrant context is not separable from the meaning of hybridity.

In summary, authenticity and hybridity are not contradictory but complementary concepts in Asian immigrant postcolonial leadership. The distinctiveness of the Asian immigrant colonial and postcolonial context demands specific forms and actions of hybridity and authenticity as the essential features of Asian immigrant postcolonial leadership. These features support Asian immigrant leaders, including Asian immigrant Christian leaders, in their efforts not only toward survival of Asian individual immigrants but the well-being of the community in relation to others.

Communality and Individuality

Coexistence between communality and individuality is another distinctive feature of postcolonial leadership for Asian immigrant leaders. Many Asian immigrant leaders are put in the position of navigating between a strong Asian cultural communality and a powerful US individuality. Conflicts between Asian communal culture and US individual culture are profound. As is discussed in the previous section, these complications cause problems of dis-communications between first-generation immigrants and second-/third-generation immigrants, creating a bridge between Asian immigrant culture and the dominant white culture and locating Asian immigrant experience between colonial and postcolonial discourses. Under the pressure of these complications, Asian immigrant leaders struggle to find balance between communality and individuality as they maintain authenticity.

However, the meaning of communality and individuality in postcolonial leadership is more complicated than these binary concepts of communality and individuality. Even though community has been emphasized as the most important concept of Asian immigrant leadership, individual leadership is assumed as the typical leadership style in Asian immigrant culture, like that of the US culture. As it is discussed throughout this book, the assumption of leadership is that one person is the leader and the others are followers. This individual leadership in the form of hierarchy has been commonly practiced in any community, whether Asian immigrant or the white. Especially in Confucian Asian cultures, as the Global Leadership and Organizational Behavior Effectiveness research program (GLOBE) shows, this leadership is often exercised by a leader "who works and cares about others but who uses status and position to make independent decisions without the input of others" in an autocratic manner.[54] Under a patriarchal culture, Asian and Asian American leaders exercise their positions as the power to lead without collaboration with others.

Communal Leadership in Current Leadership Studies

While this individual leadership is generally practiced, it is interesting to observe that the communal leadership is also commonly practiced in Asian immigrant communities. As the GLOBE study also indicates, in-group collectivism is a common feature of leadership both in Confucian Asian and Southern Asian cultures.[55] Even though an intergenerational perpetuation of community in an Asian sense is discontinued in an Asian immigrant US context, in-group collectivism is strongly exercised to sustain ethnic communalities. It has formed a complex network of religious communities, social ethnic institutions, and historical, political, colonial, and postcolonial constructions for communal survival. In this formation, communal leadership is exercised.

This communal leadership is slightly different from the communal leadership that current leadership study discusses, because that type of leadership is typically identified as a form of women's leadership. It is not about communal leadership performed by the community or multiple leaders within the community, but about the communal characteristics of a female leader. Feminized leadership characteristics such as "sharing responsibility, developing others' skills and abilities, helping others, building and maintaining connections and relationships" are often performed by many women leaders in a style that opposes autocratic styles of leadership.[56] Unlike these features, the "agentic, assertive and independent" approaches of management and leadership are more associated with male leadership in the form of traditional hierarchal leadership.[57] In these studies, many theories deal with undervaluation of women's effectiveness as leaders and their communal characteristics. Women leaders' undervaluation is explained with theories such as lack of fit theory,[58] role congruity theory,[59] expectation states theory,[60] and think manager–think male paradigm.[61] However, there is an opposite theory, such as a female gender advantage theory. As this theory tries to prove that women are better leaders than men in our era, women's leadership is increasingly identified with communal leadership.[62] It demonstrates female approaches to communal leadership as the better-quality leadership skills for current society.

In a study of top women leaders, Ashleigh Shelby Rosette and Leigh Plunkett Tost collect both agentic and communal characteristics and use them to compare female and male leaders. Measuring agentic characteristics with five qualities (confidence, skillfulness, competitiveness, power, and capability) and communal characteristics with six qualities (warmth, good nature, friendliness, consideration, caring and understanding), they claim that top women leaders are more agentic and communal than top men leaders and are evaluated more favorably than top men leaders in terms of leadership effectiveness.[63] In this research, the communal characteristics performed by top women leaders are regarded as communal leadership.

These characteristics are perceived as producing more effective leadership when performed by top women leaders.

However, this study also shows that female leaders in middle manager positions are not rated as more effective than male leaders in middle manager positions or top women leaders.[64] Even if women leaders in middle manager positions demonstrate the same communal or agentic characteristics, their leadership is not perceived to be more effective leadership like leadership that is performed by top women leaders. In other words, when these characteristics are exercised by women leaders who are not at top organizational levels, they are not equally recognized as factors of effective leadership. Therefore, neither communal characteristics nor agentic characteristics are factors that necessarily enhance effectiveness of leadership. These characteristics are evaluated as more effective only when top women leaders exercise them. Only people on the top in hierarchy can choose either of these characteristics, or both. If they decide to forgo communal characteristics, communal leadership does not exist. In this sense, communal leadership is dependent on leaders, specifically leaders at the top organization level who demonstrate communal characteristics in relationships and facilitate communal participation.

Current communal leadership is developed on the basis of individual leadership in the form of hierarchy. It is still based on individual leaders' ability and will to perform communal leadership characteristics. Decisions to share responsibility, develop others' skills and abilities, help others, and build and maintain connections and relationships are expected by only one individual who has authority at the top. The hidden assumption of communal leadership in current Western leadership studies is that the center of communal leadership lies with one independent individual. It stays in the concept of individuality. The question, then, is what differences are performed by Asian immigrant collaborative communal leadership?

Asian Immigrant Collaborative Communal Leadership

Even though the meaning of communal leadership in an Asian immigrant context also includes the current definition of communal leadership, which is based on individuality and encourages Asian immigrant top leaders to develop these communal characteristics, it surpasses this definition with three differences. First, the existence of communal leadership in an Asian immigrant context does not depend on communal features of individual leaders at the top only because communal leadership in an Asian immigrant context includes not only developing communal characteristics for individual leaders, but also leadership by the community itself and by multiple communal leaders. Decisions to share responsibility, develop others' skills and abilities, help others, and build and maintain connections and relationships are not dependent on one individual at the top organizational level, but on community and multiple communal leaders.

The authority of Asian immigrant communal leadership is led by the community from the web of relationships with others and connections with their communal culture and history. The church is often the main institution to play this role. The community and the Asian traditional values nurtured there preclude a strong communication code of how to share responsibility and to develop relationships. The "individualized consideration of organizational members, the idealized influence of their behavior and intellectual stimulation,"[65] are not only committed by individual leaders but also by the community and its strong social values to a greater extent.

Second, whereas communal leadership in current leadership studies assumes authority in a fixed position, Asian immigrant communal leadership does not assume authority in a fixed position. It does not give authority to communal leaders merely at the top of the hierarchy. In fact, most Asian immigrant communal leaders are not those who hold power at the top of the hierarchy. In reality, "the legitimacy of communal representative and umbrella bodies is constantly in question."[66] Communal leaders hold a certain degree of legitimacy derived from small sectors of the community. However, in many cases, it is hard for all communal leaders to be accepted and recognized as legitimate leaders with equal voices. Because of this ambiguity, communal consensus is important. Furthermore, as many Asian immigrant communities work mostly through religious institutions, communal consensus is more important and strongly encouraged.

From the perspective of current leadership studies, leadership in religious institutions can be understood as based on a form of nonprofit organizational leadership that emphasizes communal consensus. Like leaders from nonprofit organizations, church leaders demonstrate "different informational, interpersonal and decisional roles" from for-profit organizational leaders.[67] In a comparison between nonprofit and for-profit organizational leaders, Lynn Taliento and Lee Silverman find that "the complexity of the nonprofit management challenge is not appreciated by business executives."[68] As many leadership studies are drawn from for-profit organizations, the complexity of the nonprofit organization has not been recognized. Analyzing this complexity, Taliento and Silverman identify five problem are as:

> 1. the lesser authority and control possessed by the typical nonprofit CEO; 2. the wider range of stakeholders most nonprofits have, and the premium this places on consensus-building; 3. the challenge of monitoring performance using innovative metrics; 4. the requirement that successful nonprofit leaders must pay more attention to communications; and 5. the difficulty of building highly effective organizations when resources are scarce and training is limited.[69]

Based on this research, it is assumed that the authority of nonprofit organizational leaders is less centralized. Because of less authority, the roles of nonprofit organizational leaders are focused more on consensus. Using innovative metrics and creating more open communication, it is essential for nonprofit organization leaders to supply motivation (instead of a reward system) for consensus despite limited resources.

Based on this research, Kelly A. Phipps and Mark E. Burbach develop six propositions for nonprofit leaders: 1) "Effective nonprofit strategic leaders increase the organization's learning capacity"; 2) "Effective nonprofit strategic leaders increase the organization's capacity for change"; 3) "Effective nonprofit strategic leaders improve organizational performance through the exercise of managerial wisdom"; 4) "The organizational context influences the behaviors of an effective nonprofit strategic leader"; 5) "Effective strategic leaders contribute to improved organizational innovation in nonprofits"; and 6) "Effective nonprofit strategic leaders contribute to 'mission trajectory.'"[70] As nonprofit organizations, Asian immigrant religious congregations do not seek financial gain or profit for individuals but religious vision and fulfillment for communal well-being. As these studies indicate, many Asian immigrant Christian leaders, especially women clergy and lay leaders who have less authority with limited resources, face similar challenges and are expected to develop these propositions. As the legitimacy of both women clergy and lay leaders as communal representatives is constantly in question, they seek communal consensus as their legitimated authority. To gain consensus, they invite more participants and nurture open communication. Despite limited resources and training opportunities, they try to improve immigrant congregations' capacity to learn a new context, change the current environment, and contribute to improved church innovation and mission trajectory. Therefore, seeking consensus and creating open communication are necessary to their leadership.

In this process, it is natural for women clergy and lay leaders to exercise collaborative leadership. This is the third difference. The concept of communal leadership in current leadership studies does not necessarily include collaborative leadership by multiple leaders as a part of communal leadership. However, Asian immigrant communal leadership includes collaborative leadership with multiple leaders as an essential part of this leadership. Especially in Asian immigrant Christian congregations, collaborative leadership with multiple leaders is a necessary practice of women clergy and lay leaders' leadership. As is discussed previously in chapter 1, collaborative leadership is performed by many women leaders who demonstrate skills such as interdependence, trust, agreement, reciprocity, and partnership. Many Asian women clergy and lay leaders exercise these leadership skills as they serve congregations. They "promote broad and active participation" by church members and their ethnic community and "facilitate group dynamics" between church members and between the church and community.[71] They invite others not only as participants but also as co-leaders of the group. Women clergy and lay leaders usually assume the roles of "facilitators or mediators."[72] They hesitate to call themselves leaders but become "influencers, collaborators, or contributors."[73] They often start the leadership process with face-to-face dialogue in conversations through small-group gatherings or prayer-group gatherings. Through these intimate conversations, they try to build trust. As they build trust, they invite others to be part of the group and share ownership of the group. They commit themselves to a process of mutual recognition and open themselves to reciprocal gain.[74]

Based on these three differences, the basic principle of Asian immigrant collaborative communal leadership can be summarized as "leading together in solidarity." It includes two components. First, "leading together in solidarity" means Asian immigrant leaders, including many Asian women clergy and lay leaders, commit themselves to lead together in the form of strong solidarity with God and others. Solidarity is an important part of Asian immigrant postcolonial leadership in a Christian context. Anselm Min explains the meaning of solidarity with four points.

> It is, first of all, an ontological category referring to the constitutive interdependence of all reality, both the fundamental solidarity of human existence and the metaphysical interconnectedness of all things, including human beings, in nature. Second, it refers to the historical process in which all nations and all aspects of life are becoming interdependent, spectacularly and painfully so in our day. Third, it is also an ethical concept, the challenge to recognize our metaphysical and historical interdependence as an intrinsic definition of our own being, as our common destiny, and to transform such interdependence into self-conscious *acts* of ethnical, political solidarity. Fourth, solidarity is a theological concept referring to koinonia, "the communion of saints," the fellowship of those reborn in Christ by the power of the Holy Spirit as children of God, the Father and Mother of us all, an eschatological vocation and destiny to which all are called.[75]

His concept of solidarity is not just solidarity with others, but of others. He claims that without decentering the privileged position of one's own group, solidarity is not solidarity but a tool to use others for one's own liberation. Therefore, to place others as truly equal others, he rejects the centrality of any one group. He understands solidarity from the perspectives of interdependence and interconnectedness of others in the body of Christ and describes it in the sense of communion that implies "a state of union already achieved and an interpersonal, face-to-face relationship."[76] As Asian immigrant Christian leaders lead together with others, they lead as others, not as the center. They denounce their centrality. Many women clergy and lay leaders, in particular, often take their positions as the other, not as the center. At the same time, when they have to be the center of leadership, they acknowledge their privileges and try to release them in a collaborative way. As equal others, they want to share leadership roles and take turns to be leaders. They want to lead together simultaneously, so they often co-lead.

Next, "leading together in solidarity" means that these leaders invite many participants as co-leaders. They are happy to give this role to others and exchange roles with followers. They often practice the exchange of roles in this leadership. Exchanging roles is a difficult but crucial principle in communal leadership that women clergy and lay leaders attempt to practice in Asian immigrant congregational lives. As they try to lead together, this principle becomes a necessary concept of their communal leadership. This concept was explained by Burns as the leader-follower paradox within transformational leadership. Burns calls it the "Burns Paradox—a designation that would be immodest but for its being not a solution or formula but a problem."[77]

> With such a dynamic and mutually empowering interaction between leader and follower, a crucial change occurs. The process is so complex and multidimensional, so fluid and transforming, that persons initially labeled "leaders" or "followers" come to succeed each other, merge with each other, substitute for each other. Leader and follower roles become ephemeral, transient, and even indistinct. This view of empowerment does not diminish the role of leadership itself but rather enhances it. Leadership electrifies the system as followers become leaders and vice versa. . . . we see the whole process as a *system* in which the function of leadership is palpable and central but the actors move in and out of leader and follower roles. At this crucial point we are no longer seeing individual leaders; rather we see *leadership* as the basic process of social change, of causation in a community, an organization, a nation—perhaps even the globe.[78]

An exchange of role between leaders and followers is not an easy concept to understand because it is a radical transforming paradigm shift of leadership roles. In Asian immigrant congregations, in fact, there are several prerequisites in this transforming paradigm that women clergy and lay leaders exercise. First, this transforming paradigm assumes that all people can be leaders and followers in the presence of God. It is possible for anyone to be a leader working with God. However, it does not necessarily mean everyone is a leader. It means that people have equal access to become leaders. Many women clergy and lay leaders attempt to give people equal access to take the role of a leadership position. They recognize roles of leadership not as given by God, but as possibilities of nurturing and training with God.

Second, it assumes leadership as a role to be played, not as a given position. Instead of seeing leadership as a binary relationship between leaders who are in power and followers who are not in power, people as actors in God's play can play roles of leaders and followers in flexibility, depending on the situation. Understanding human finitude, many women clergy and lay leaders try to approach their roles as more transient positions than permanent positions and play these roles with a great degree of flexibility.

Third, this paradigm assumes that people want to share leadership roles in different forms. Sometimes, many women clergy and lay leaders take turns being leaders. Other times, they play the role of leader and follower at the same time. Depending on time and space, they take leadership roles in different manners.

Fourth, it assumes that leaders can follow followers and followers can lead leaders. It changes the paradigm from "being leaders to lead and being followers to follow" to "being leaders to follow and being followers to lead." The roles of leaders are becoming followers as the roles of followers are becoming leaders. Women are often in charge of children's education in many Christian congregations. Their greatest hope and challenge is how to transform their children, youth, and young adults into leaders so that they become followers of them. They are willing to be followers when the next generation can lead. This is the main hope of their education.

Fifth, it assumes that this paradigm focuses on the function of leadership, but not on the people in positions of power. Leadership does not depend on individual leaders, but on the function of leadership as a communal system. Women clergy and lay leaders often focus not on individual leaders' ability to lead but on the function of leadership that God leads through community. They try to see an exchange of the roles between leaders and followers as "an ever-reconstituting system" that God creates and changes.[79]

Exchanging roles of leaders and followers is a radical but not uncommon paradigm that many women clergy and lay leaders exercise in Asian immigrant congregations both deliberately and instinctively. It is a conflictive but necessary part of Asian immigrant communal leadership. For survival of immigrant lives, many women clergy and lay leaders choose to lead together in the form of collaborative communal leadership. They use their less given authority as a way to perform this leadership. They create this collaborative communal leadership in solidarity with others and of others through hybridity, authenticity, ambiguity, and flexibility. As this communal leadership is performed by multiple leaders collaboratively, including both clergy and lay leaders in Asian immigrant congregations, women clergy and lay leaders transform their less given authority into this collaborative communal leadership to claim legitimacy as leaders.

Eunjoo Mary Kim suggests this shared communal leadership, "leading together in solidarity," in the Asian immigrant church through preaching. She claims preaching as an art of shared leadership.[80] Seeing the current challenges to church leadership, she denounces official clergy leadership and embraces a leadership shared between pastors and lay leaders.[81] Preaching has been traditionally recognized as the preserve of clergy alone, a service lay people cannot provide. It has been considered the exclusive domain of leadership by the clergy. However, in *Women Preaching: Theology and Practice Through the Ages*, Kim claims that "preaching is no longer a clergy-only ministry; the pulpit is no longer exclusively the place for professionally trained preachers."[82] From the Early Church to the colonial and postcolonial eras, she illustrates how many women preachers fight for peace, the gift of the wholeness of God, and show their leadership as partnership, working with members of the church and especially the marginalized in society.[83] She describes Asian women preachers as "true partners of God, fulfilling the politics of God on earth" during the colonial and postcolonial eras.[84]

Observing Asian women preachers as well as other women preachers who demonstrate their shared leadership in preaching, Kim uses the relationality of God in the Trinitarian structure as the foundation of shared leadership to rethink the nature and practice of preaching in the form of solidarity of others and with others.[85] This suggestion challenges a traditional paradigm of preaching as clergy leadership. Instead of clergy leadership in preaching, an exchange between hearers and preachers occurs in this shared ministerial preaching context and creates a bond between them. This bonding creates the common identity of co-preacher, which formulates solidarity between them. Her concept of "the sensibilities of interpathy," which means "the capacity to join others in their worlds,"[86] implies the possibility to perform an exchange of roles between preachers and hearers and creates solidarity of others beyond these performers. In order to practice preaching as a shared leadership, she proposes four prerequisites for both clergy and the lay leaders: 1) reconstructing "the understanding of authority"[87]; 2) having "a humble mind or humility"[88]; 3) the pastors' responsibility "to train and work with preaching partners"[89]; 4) the pastors' skills to "build up relationships with others."[90] These prerequisites can open the possibilities to deliberate various forms of preaching in collaborative communal leadership such as storytelling, co-preaching, music, dance, audiovisual technology, sermon reflection/feedback, and others, based on each person's gift. It invites many participants not only to participate but also to turn into leaders in solidarity.

These various forms of preaching as leadership can be a good example to open up possibilities of Asian immigrant communal leadership in the church beyond preaching itself.

There is another great example in this Asian immigrant collaborative communal leadership led by lay women. That is a fellowship after Sunday worship. Preparing weekly fellowship is a very sensitive, difficult but important task. It is one of the most important parts of lay immigrant leadership and its practice. This weekly fellowship is usually led by not only women clergy and lay leaders but also many women (and men) participants.[91] Space of this fellowship is a space of exchange leaders and participants. This is the space that many participants can easily participate and relate with other church members. After they get involved with this fellowship, many participants are invited to be leaders in this weekly event. In fact, they often become leaders of not only this fellowship but also other parts of ministry. Preparing weekly fellowship entails skills of careful communication and allocation for equal workload. It requires a sensitivity to organize not only the task but also the relationship among and beyond church members. Both the leaders and participants of this fellowship take a turn for leadership roles or change the roles regularly. They want to make sure that no one is abused on this task, shared equal responsibility and exercise leadership together. The function of this task is always carried by multiple leaders and participants simultaneously. Sometimes, this space becomes a springboard of people's voices and influences decisions of church leadership. Without a leader at top, many Asian women leaders and participants in their immigrant churches exercise powerful collaborative communal leadership through this fellowship.

In summary, the coexistence of communality and individuality and of hybridity and authenticity is a prominent phenomenon in Asian immigrant communities because it leads naturally to a practice of Asian immigrant leadership. Without the coexistence of hybridity, authenticity, community, and individuality between Asian and US cultures, between colonial and postcolonial discourses, and between individual and communal leadership, it is impossible to understand a postcolonial leadership that Asian immigrant leaders, including Asian religious leaders, exercise. Asian immigrant communal leadership often performed by women clergy and lay leaders, in particular, is the most distinctive feature of a postcolonial leadership. A postcolonial leadership and its challenges cannot be discussed outside the context of the collaborative communal leadership that is performed daily in Asian immigrant lives.

Conclusion

In the complex discourses of race, sex and gender, class, age, disability, colonialism, and postcolonialism, Asian immigrant leadership has seldom been recognized even though it has been performed from the beginning of US immigrant lives. In fact, it has been rigorously performed and sustained through Asian immigrant religious institutions and communities. However, this leadership is commonly understood only as followership, being resistant and resilient. It has been in a constant battle with Eurocentric colonial individualism, white Christian evangelical ideology, US imperialism, global capitalism, and Asian hierarchal, patriarchal culture. Struggling with these forces in every aspect of Asian immigrant lives, Asian immigrant leadership is challenged and conflicted. Sometimes, it mimics and accepts models of white dominated individual leadership without any critical thought or adaptation, causing intensive conflict between Asian immigrant community and the dominant society. Other times, it shows a complete rejection of white leadership without considering any benefits and effective skills. This is, then, marked as a failure of immigrant adjustment.

As the existence of Asian immigrants is condemned as that of a forever-foreigner in the United States, their leadership is deemed to be the production of inept social skills. However, Asian immigrant leadership has persisted in the form of postcolonial leadership despite constant challenges. It resists the model of Eurocentric individual leadership and creates its own model. It exists in the hybrid forms of individual/communal faith, individual/communal demands, individual/communal morality and ethics, and in the space between. It is continuously performed in both individual and communal culture, history, and society. And in its own existence of authenticity, it still repeats a hybrid process of acceptance/rejection, adaptation/resistance, and transformation/transforming in ever-changing Asian immigrant multi-intercultural multi-religious contexts.

Leadership is real only in community with others. Asian immigrant leadership is real only when it is engaged with the individual and communal lives of Asian immigrants. And it has been real in everyday Asian immigrant lives with and without recognition. In fact, Asian immigrant collaborative communal leadership has been greatly demonstrated in its daily performance in an Asian immigrant Christian church context by many women clergy and lay leaders. They have performed their collaborative communal leadership in the service of Asian immigrant communities. The ultimate concerns of this leadership are the well-being of Asian immigrants and the betterment of lives in communities of faith beyond their own ethnic boundaries. Encountering a lack of authority and scarce resources, Asian immigrant leaders, especially many Asian immigrant women clergy and lay leaders, struggle and challenge the current cultural structures and social system. They experience the tremendous weight of prejudice and discrimination. They are abused and brutalized. They are asked to sacrifice their personal lives without recognition. However, many clergy and lay leaders still have the faith to resist. They have the strength to be resilient. They continue to seek human rights and God's justice as they provide hospitality as a radical form of love for and with others. They have not lost hope yet. They have created a postcolonial leadership that simultaneously includes outstanding individual transformational leadership, powerful collaborative communal leadership, resistant and resilient leadership, authentic leadership, hybrid leadership, and many other forms of diverse leadership.

This postcolonial leadership is a leadership that has existed and been performed in the space of immigrants, the oppressed, the marginalized, and the voiceless. Because their presence is dismissed as that of the forever-foreigner in the United States, Asian immigrant leaders, including Asian immigrant Christian leaders, are on a mission to show who they are not only as immigrants, the oppressed, the marginalized, and the voiceless but also as equal citizens and free human beings. With countless sacrifices and tears, their resilient movement for a better life creates this postcolonial leadership. Without recognition, without legitimated authority, and without institutional power, they exercise leadership and gain authority and power by mediating communal consensus and being in solidarity with and of others. They exercise this leadership out of survival and beyond.

This postcolonial leadership is also a leadership that these Asian immigrant leaders want to learn and create. It exists in the process of creating. They have been taught by society to follow white individual leadership. They have often failed to recognize the value of their collaborative communal leadership because this leadership has not been recognized as leadership but followership. However, as they live in-between hybrid cultures, they know that they have to understand an ever-changing culture and want to learn a new leadership to meet the needs of people in this culture. They have to learn how to continuously create and recreate their leadership based on their own characteristics, abilities, relationships, needs, and their external and internal environment. Therefore, their postcolonial leadership cannot be contained in one form of leadership. It is selectively and collectively performed and dismissed. It is evolving. It is developing. It is an ever-learning leadership that implants a hope for Asian immigrants to live as free human beings and be treated as equal citizens.

Notes

Chapter 1

1. Joseph C. Rost, *Leadership for the Twenty-First Century* (New York: Praeger, 1991), 40.
2. Ibid., 40–42.
3. Ibid., 42.
4. Ibid., 43.
5. Ibid., 69.
6. Jean Lau Chin, "Overview: Women and Leadership: Transforming Visions and Diverse Voices," in *Women and Leadership: Transforming Visions and Diverse Voices*, ed. Jean Lau Chin, Bernice Lott, Joy K. Rice, and Janis Sanchez-Hucles (Malden, MA: Blackwell, 2007), 5–11.
7. Victor Dulewicz and Malcolm Higgs, "Leadership at the Top: The Need for Emotional Intelligence in Organizations," *International Journal of Organizational Analysis* 11, 3 (1993): 193–210.
8. Rost, *Leadership for the Twenty-First Century*, 70–88.
9. Peter G. Northouse, *Leadership: Theory and Practice*, 6th ed. (Thousand Oaks, CA: Sage, 2013), 5.
10. Ibid., 19–452.
11. Joanne B. Ciulla, "Trust and the Future of Leadership," in *The Blackwell Guide to Business Ethics*, ed. Norman E. Bowie (Oxford: Blackwell, 2002), 340.
12. John Antonakis, Anne T. Cianciolo, and Robert J. Sternberg, "Leadership: Past, Present, and Future," in *The Nature of Leadership*, ed. John Antonakis, Anne T. Cianciolo, and Robert J. Sternberg (Thousand Oaks, CA: Sage, 2004), 5.
13. Chin, "Overview: Women and Leadership: Transforming Visions and Diverse Voices," 5.
14. David Shriberg, "Psychology," in *Practicing Leadership: Principles and Applications*, 2nd ed., ed. Arthur Shriberg, David Shriberg, and Carol Lloyd (New York: John Wiley & Sons, 2002), 16–17.

15. Ralph M. Stogdill, *Handbook of Leadership: A Survey of Theory and Research* (New York: Free Press, 1974), 17.

16. Frank Dumont, *A History of Personality Psychology: Theory, Science, and Research from Hellenism to the Twenty-First Century* (Cambridge: Cambridge University Press, 2010), 160.

17. Ibid., 161.

18. Ibid., 171–74.

19. Ibid., 175.

20. Ibid., 174–75.

21. Ibid., 176.

22. Paul T. Costa Jr. and Robert R. McCrae, *The NEO Personality Inventory Manual* (Odessa, FL: Psychological Assessment Resources, 1985), 2; Paul T. Costa Jr. and Robert R. McCrae, *NEO-PI-P-R, Professional Manual* (Odessa, FL: Psychological Assessment Resources, 1992), 3; Dumont, *A History of Personality Psychology: Theory, Science and Research from Hellenism to the Twenty-First Century*, 178.

23. Stogdill, *Handbook of Leadership: A Survey of Theory and Research*, 8.

24. Ibid., 62.

25. Ibid., 62.

26. Ibid., 62–81.

27. John W. Gardner, *On Leadership* (New York: Free Press, 1990), 48–53.

28. Susan E. Rivers, Marc A. Brackett, Peter Salovey, and John D. Mayer, "Measuring Emotional Intelligence as a Set of Mental Abilities," in *The Science of Emotional Intelligence: Knowns and Unknowns*, ed. Gerald Matthews, Moshe Zeidner, and Richard D. Roberts (Oxford Scholarship Online, 2012), DOI:10.1093/acprof:oso/9780195181890.003.0009.

29. John D. Mayer, Peter Salovey, and David R. Caruso, "Models of Emotional Intelligence," in *Handbook of Intelligence*, ed. Robert J. Sternberg (Cambridge: Cambridge University Press, 2000), 396–420.

30. Stephen J. Zaccaro, Cary Kemp, and Paige Bader, "Leader Traits and Attributes," in *The Nature of Leadership*, ed. John Antonakis, Anne T. Cianciolo, and Robert J. Sternberg (Thousand Oaks, CA: Sage, 2004), 101–24.

31. Arthur Shriberg, Gordon Barnhart, and David Shriberg, "Modern Leadership Theories," in *Practicing Leadership: Principles and Applications*, 2nd ed., ed. Arthur Shriberg, David Shriberg, and Carol Lloyd (New York: John Wiley & Sons, 2002), 182–83.

32. Ibid., 188.

33. Peter Y.T. Sun and Marc H. Anderson, "The Importance of Attributional Complexity for Transformational Leadership Studies," *Journal of Management Studies* 49, 6 (September 2012): 1001.

34. James MacGregor Burns, *Leadership* (New York: Harper and Row, 1978), 3.

35. Bernard M. Bass, *Leadership and Performance Beyond Expectations* (New York: Free Press, 1985), 11.
36. Ibid., 121–34.
37. Ibid.
38. Ibid., 135–49.
39. Ibid.
40. Bernard M. Bass, *Transformational Leadership: Industry, Military, and Educational Impact* (Mahwah, NJ: Lawrence Erlbaum Associates, 1998), 5–6.
41. Ibid., 5.
42. Bass, *Leadership and Performance Beyond Expectations*, 20.
43. James MacGregor Burns, *Transforming Leadership: A New Pursuit of Happiness* (New York: Grove Press, 2003), 170–85.
44. Bass, *Leadership and Performance Beyond Expectations*, 45–48.
45. Ibid., 49–51.
46. Robert. J. House, "A 1976 Theory of Charismatic Leadership," in *Leadership: The Cutting Edge*, ed. J.G. Hunt and L.L. Larson (Carbondale: Southern Illinois University, 1977), 189–207.
47. Gary A. Yukl and David D. Van Fleet, "Cross-Situational, Multimethod Research on Military Leader Effectiveness," *Organizational Behavior and Human Performance* 30 (1982): 87–108.
48. Arthur Larson, *The President Nobody Knew* (New York: Popular Library, 1968), 21; Bass, *Leadership and Performance Beyond Expectations*, 17.
49. Harry S. Truman, *Memoirs* (New York: Doubleday, 1958), 139; Bass, *Leadership and Performance Beyond Expectations*, 17.
50. See Robert E. Quinn and Richard H. Hall, *Organizational Theory and Public Policy* (Beverly Hills: Sage, 1983).
51. Bass, *Leadership and Performance Beyond Expectations*, 112.
52. Bass, *Transformational Leadership: Industry, Military, and Educational Impact*, 18–27.
53. Burns, *Transforming Leadership: A New Pursuit of Happiness*, 211–13.
54. Tom Burns and G.M. Stalker, *The Management of Innovation*, 2nd ed. (London: Social Science Paperbacks, 1966).
55. Rosabeth Moss Kanter, *Men and Women of the Corporation* (New York: Basic Books, 1977).
56. Beth J. Haslett, Florence L. Geis, and Mae R. Carter, *The Organizational Woman: Power and Paradox* (Norwood, NJ: Ablex, 1992), 41.
57. Karen L. Suyemoto and Mary B. Ballou, "Conducted Monotones to Coacted Harmonies: A Feminist (Re)conceptualization of Leadership Addressing Race, Cass, and Gender," in *Women and Leadership: Transforming Visions and Diverse Voices*, ed. Jean Lau Chin, Bernice Lott, Joy K. Rice, and Janis Sanchez-Hucles (Malden, MA: Blackwell, 2007), 41.

58. Roz D. Lasker and Elisa S. Weiss, "Broadening Participation in Community Problem-solving: A Multidisciplinary Model to Support Collaborative Practice and Research," *Journal of Urban Health* 80, 1 (2003): 14–60.

59. Chris Ansell and Alison Gash, "Collaborative Governance in Theory and Practice," *Journal of Public Administration Research and Theory* 18, 4 (2007): 554.

60. Suyemoto and Ballou, "Conducted Monotones to Coacted Harmonies: A Feminist (Re)conceptualization of Leadership Addressing Race, Cass, and Gender," 41.

61. Paul 't Hart, *Understanding Public Leadership* (New York: Palgrave Macmillan, 2014), 90.

62. Lawrence Susskind and Jeffrey Cruikshank, *Breaking the Impasse: Consensual Approaches to Resolving Public Disputes* (New York: Basic Books, 1987), 95.

63. Barbara Gray, *Collaborating: Finding Common Ground for Multi-Party Problems* (San Francisco, CA: Jossey-Bass, 1989).

64. Ansell and Gash, "Collaborative Governance in Theory and Practice," 550; Hart, *Understanding Public Leadership*, 92.

65. Hart, *Understanding Public Leadership*, 89–96.

66. Craig L. Pearce and Jay A. Conger, eds., *Shared Leadership: Reframing the Hows and Whys of Leadership* (Thousand Oaks, CA: Sage, 2003), 1; Marceline M. Lazzari, Lisa Colarossi, and Kathryn S. Collins, "Feminists in Social Work: Where Have All the Leaders Gone?" *Journal of Woman and Social Work* 24, 4 (2009): 348.

67. Chin, "Overview: Women and Leadership: Transforming Visions and Diverse Voices," 10.

68. Ibid., 15.

69. Hart, *Understanding Public Leadership*, 72–99.

70. Judy B. Rosener, "Ways Women Lead," *Harvard Business Review* 68, 6 (Nov./Dec. 1990): 124–25.

Chapter 2

1. Arthur J. Wolak, *Religions and Contemporary Management: Moses as a Model for Effective Leadership* (London, UK: Anthem Press, 2016), 100.

2. Burns, *Leadership*, 241–42; Wolak, *Religions and Contemporary Management: Moses as a Model for Effective Leadership*, 37; Lorin Woolfe, *The Bible on Leadership: From Moses to Matthew: Management Lessons for Contemporary Leaders* (New York: Amacom, 2002); Paul J. Herskovitz and Esther E. Klein, "The Biblical Study of Moses: Lessons in Leadership for Business," *The Journal of Leadership Studies* 6, 3/4 (1999): 84–95; Sigmund Freud, *Moses and Monotheism*, trans. Katherine Jones (New York: Vintage Books, 1939).

3. Harvey Minkoff, "Moses and Samuel: Israel's Era of Charismatic Leadership," *Jewish Bible Quarterly* 30, 4 (2002): 257–61; Wolak, *Religions and Contemporary Management: Moses as a Model for Effective Leadership*, 40.

4. Wolak, *Religions and Contemporary Management: Moses as a Model for Effective Leadership*, 18.

5. Evangeline Anderson, "Engendering Leadership: A Christian Feminist Perspective from India," in *Responsible Leadership: Global and Contextual Ethical Perspectives*, ed. Christoph Stückelberger and J.N.K. Mugambi (Geneva, Switzerland: WCC Publications, 2007), 14; Wolak, *Religions and Contemporary Management: Moses as a Model for Effective Leadership*, 18.

6. Lorin Woolfe, *The Bible on Leadership: From Moses to Matthew: Management Lessons for Contemporary Leaders* (New York: Amacom, 2002), 33.

7. Ibid., 33.

8. Martien A. Halvorson-Taylor, "Secrets and Lies: Secrecy Notices (Esther 2:10, 20) and Diasporic Identity in the Book of Esther" in *Journal of Biblical Literature* 131, 3 (2012): 467–85.

9. Anne-Mareike Wetter, "In Unexpected Places: Ritual and Religious Belonging in the Book of Ester," in *Journal for the Study of the Old Testament* 36, 3 (2012): 329–30.

10. Ibid., 329–30.

11. Ibid., 329–30.

12. Ibid., 329–30.

13. E. Paul Colella, "How We Got There: Premodern Thoughts on Leadership," in *Practicing Leadership: Principles and Applications*, 2nd ed., ed. Arthur Shriberg, David Shriberg, and Carol Lloyd (New York: John Wiley & Sons, 2002), 231–32.

14. Thad Williamson, "The Good Society and the Good Soul: Plato's *Republic* on Leadership," *The Leadership Quarterly* 19, 4 (2008): 399.

15. Colella, "How We Got There: Premodern Thoughts on Leadership," 232–33.

16. Williamson, "The Good Society and the Good Soul: Plato's *Republic* on Leadership," 402.

17. Colella, "How We Got There: Premodern Thoughts on Leadership," 232–33.

18. Ibid., 234.

19. Leonhard Goppelt, "Church Government and the Office of the Bishop in the First Three Centuries," in *Episcopacy in the Lutheran Church? Studies in the Development and Definition of the Office of Church Leadership*, ed. Ivar Asheim and Victor R. Gold (Philadelphia: Fortress Press, 1970), 3.

20. Ibid., 8.

21. Corinthians 12:28, New Revised Standard Version.

22. Goppelt, "Church Government and the Office of the Bishop in the First Three Centuries," 9.

23. Ibid., 10.

24. Ibid., 16.

25. Ibid., 22–23.

26. Frances Young, "Hermeneutical Questions: The Ordination of Women in the Light of Biblical and Patristic Typology," in *Women and Ordination in the Christian Churches: International Perspectives*, ed. Ian Jones, Janet Wootton, and Kirsty Thorpe (New York: T&T Clark International, 2008), 22.

27. Erich Beyreuther, "Church Government and the Office of Bishop from the Fourth Century to the Reformation," in *Episcopacy in the Lutheran Church? Studies in the Development and Definition of the Office of Church Leadership*, ed. Ivar Asheim and Victor R. Gold (Philadelphia: Fortress Press, 1970), 35; "Only Where the Bishop Is, There Is the Church" is originally cited from Hans E. Feine, *Kirchliche Rechtsgeschichte: Die Katholische Kirche*, 4th ed. (Cologne: Böhlau Verlag, 1964), 39ff.

28. Ibid., 48.

29. Bernhard Lohse, "The Development of the Offices of Leadership in the German Lutheran Churches: 1517–1918," in *Episcopacy in the Lutheran Church? Studies in the Development and Definition of the Office of Church Leadership*, ed. Ivar Asheim and Victor R. Gold (Philadelphia: Fortress Press, 1970), 51.

30. Ibid., 51–53.

31. Ibid., 63.

32. Robert K. Greenleaf, *Servant Leadership: A Journey into the Nature of Legitimate Power & Greatness* (New York: Paulist Press, 1997), Kindle Location 2758, 2893 of 4357.

33. Ibid., Kindle Location 3046 of 4357.

34. Ibid., Kindle Location 3026 of 4357.

35. Ibid., Kindle Location 3026–101 of 4357.

36. Larry C. Spears, "Tracing the Past, Present, and Future of Servant-Leadership," in *Focus on Leadership: Servant-Leadership for the 21st Century*, ed. Larry C. Spears and Michele Lawrence (New York: John Wiley & Sons, 2002), 1–16.

37. A. Gregory Stone, Robert F. Russell, and Kathleen Patterson, "Transformational versus Servant Leadership: A Difference in Leader Focus," *Leadership & Organization Development Journal* 25, 3/4 (2004): 354.

38. Ibid., 354.

39. Ibid., 356–57.

40. Louis W. Fry, "Toward a Theory of Spiritual Leadership," *The Leadership Quarterly* 14, 6 (2003): 695.

41. Chin-Yi Chen, Chun-Hsi Vivian Chen, and Chun-l Li, "The Influence of Leader's Spiritual Values on Servant Leadership on Employee Motivational

Autonomy and Eudaemonic Well-Being," *Journal of Religion and Health* 52, 2 (2013): 423.

42. Fry, "Toward a Theory of Spiritual Leadership," 694.

43. Andrey V. Shirin, "Is Servant Leadership Inherently Christian?," *Religion and Business Ethics* 3, 1 (2015): 1–27.

44. Chen, Chen, and Li, "The Influence of Leader's Spiritual Values on Servant Leadership on Employee Motivational Autonomy and Eudaemonic Well-Being," 421.

45. Don Page and Paul T.P. Wong, "A Conceptual Framework for Measuring Servant Leadership," in *The Human Factor in Shaping the Course of History and Development*, ed. Senyo B-S. K. Adjibolosoo (Lanham, MD: University Press of America, 2000).

46. James M. Kouzes, "Finding Your Voice," in *Insights on Leadership: Service, Stewardship, Spirit, and Servant-leadership*, ed. Larry C. Spears (New York: John Wiley, 1998), 322–25.

47. John W. Stewart, *Envisioning the Congregation Practicing the Gospel: A Guide for Pastors and Lay Leaders* (Grand Rapids, MI: Wm. B. Eerdmans, 2015), 138.

48. Ibid., 140.

49. Ibid., 144.

50. James Martin, *Jesus: A Pilgrimage* (New York: HarperOne, 1989), 351.

51. Stewart, *Envisioning the Congregation Practicing the Gospel*, 143.

52. Robert Wuthnow and John Evans, eds., *The Quiet Hand of God: Faith-Based Activism and the Public Role of Mainline Protestants* (Berkeley: University of California Press, 2002), 131; Stewart, *Envisioning the Congregation Practicing the Gospel*, 142.

53. Mark Lau Branson, "Leading Change," in Mark Lau Branson and Juan F. Martínez, *Churches, Cultures & Leadership: A Practical Theology of Congregations and Ethnicities* (Downers Grove, IL: InterVarsity Press, 2011), 211.

54. Ibid., 210–11; George Hunsburger and Craig Van Gelder, eds., *The Church Between Gospel and Culture* (Grand Rapids, MI: Wm. B. Eerdmans, 1996), 337.

55. Mark Lau Branson, "Practical Theology and Multicultural Initiatives," in Mark Lau Branson and Juan F. Martínez, *Churches, Cultures & Leadership: A Practical Theology of Congregations and Ethnicities*, 55.

56. See http://www.vatican.va/roman_curia/congregations/cfaith/documents/rc_con_cfaith_doc_19761015_inter-insigniores_en.html and Jérôme Hamer, *Declaration on the Question of Admission of Women to the Ministerial Priesthood*, Vatican, Rome, 1976.

57. *Declaration on the Question of Admission of Women to the Ministerial Priesthood*, Vatican, Rome, 1976.

58. Paul VI, *Declaration on the Ordination of Women* (Inter Insigniores), AAS69, 1977.

59. *Declaration on the Question of Admission of Women to the Ministerial Priesthood*, Vatican, Rome, 1976.

60. Paul VI, *Declaration on the Ordination of Women* (Inter Insigniores), AAS69, 1977.

61. *Declaration on the Question of Admission of Women to the Ministerial Priesthood*, Vatican, Rome, 1976.

62. Paul VI, *Declaration on the Ordination of Women* (Inter Insigniores), AAS69, 1977.

63. *Declaration on the Question of Admission of Women to the Ministerial Priesthood*, Vatican, Rome, 1976.

64. *Declaration on the Question of Admission of Women to the Ministerial Priesthood*, Vatican, Rome, 1976.

65. Paul VI, *Declaration on the Ordination of Women* (Inter Insigniores), AAS69, 1977.

66. *Declaration on the Question of Admission of Women to the Ministerial Priesthood*, Vatican, Rome, 1976.

67. John Paul II, *Apostolic Letter Mulieris Dignitatem of the Supreme Pontiff John Paul II on the Dignity and Vocation of Women on the Occasion of the Marian Year*, AAS80, 1988.

68. Joseph Ratzinger, *Letter to the Bishops of the Catholic Church on the Collaboration of Men and Women in the Church and in the World*, Congregation for the Doctrine of the Faith, 2004. http://www.vatican.va/roman_curia/congregations/cfaith/documents/rc_con_cfaith_ doc_20040731_collaboration_en.html.

69. Catherine Gyarmathy-Amherd, "The Ordination of Women in the Roman Catholic Church," in *Women and Ordination in the Christian Churches: International Perspectives*, 43.

70. Ratzinger, *Letter to the Bishops of the Catholic Church on the Collaboration of Men and Women in the Church and in the World*.

71. Gyarmathy-Amherd, "The Ordination of Women in the Roman Catholic Church," 43.

72. Karen Jo Torjesen, *When Women Were Priests: Women's Leadership in the Early Church and the Scandal of Their Subordination in the Rise of Christianity* (San Francisco, CA: HarperCollins, 1993), 9–52.

73. Ibid., 53–178; Young, "Hermeneutical Questions," 25.

74. Torjesen, *When Women Priests*, 155–202.

75. Ruth Edwards, *The Case of Women's Ordination* (London: SPCK, 1989), 182; Young, "Hermeneutical Questions," 29.

76. Young, "Hermeneutical Questions," 29.

77. Ibid., 30.

78. Elisabeth Behr-Sigel, *The Ministry of Women in the Church*, trans. Stephen Bigham (Crestwood, NY: St. Vladimir's Seminary Press, 1999), 116; Young, "Hermeneutical Questions," 31.

79. Young, "Hermeneutical Questions," 32.

80. Behr-Sigel, *The Ministry of Women in the Church*, 207; Young, "Hermeneutical Questions," 35.

81. Ibid., 194; Young, "Hermeneutical Questions," 35.

82. Katheryn Pfisterer Darr, *Far More Precious than Jewels: Perspectives on Biblical Women* (Louisville, KY: Westminster John Knox Press, 1991).

83. Delores S. Williams, *Sisters in the Wilderness: The Challenges of Womanist God-Talk* (New York: Orbis Books, 1993).

84. Elisabeth Schüssler Fiorenza, *In Memory of Her: A Feminist Theological Reconstruction of Christian Origins* (New York: Crossroad, 1998).

85. Barbara Brown Zikmund, "Ordination," in *Dictionary of Feminist Theologies*, ed. Letty M. Russell and J. Shannon Clarkson (Louisville, KY: Westminster John Knox Press, 1996), 197.

86. Ibid., 197.

87. Rhashell Hunter, "PC(USA) Celebrates 60 years of Women Clergy: Remembering Six Decades of Pioneering Pastors," May 24, 2016, http://www.pcusa.org/news/2016/ 5/24/pcusa-celebrates-60-years-womens-ordination/.

88. Daniel Burke, "Survey: Number of Female Senor Pastors Doubles in 10 years," *USA Today*, September 17, 2009, http://usatoday30.usatoday.com/news/religion/2009-09-17-female-pastors_N.htm.

89. Barna Group, "Number of Female Senior Pastors in Protestant Churches Doubles in Past Decade," *Leaders & Pastors*, September 14, 2009, http://www.barna.com/research/number-of-female-senior-pastors-in-protestant-churches-doubles-in-past-decade/#.V8LtDTV1woI.

90. https://www.gbhem.org/sites/default/files/documents/clergywomen/CW_LWPP2009essay.pdf.

91. Barna Group, "Number of Female Senior Pastors in Protestant Churches Doubles in Past Decade."

92. Eunjoo Mary Kim and Deborah Beth Creamer, "Introduction," in *Women, Church, and Leadership: New Paradigms*, ed. Eunjoo Mary Kim and Deborah Beth Creamer (Eugene, OR: Wipf and Stock, 2012), xx.

93. Hart, *Understanding Public Leadership*, 72–99.

94. Susan Willhauck and Jacqulyn Thorpe, *The Web of Women's Leadership: Recasting Congregation Ministry* (Nashville: Abingdon Press, 2001), 24.

95. Eunjoo Mary Kim, "Preaching as an Art of Shared Leadership," in *Women, Church, and Leadership*, 83.

96. Ibid., 69–86.

97. Willhauck and Thorpe, *The Web of Women's Leadership: Recasting Congregation Ministry*, 31.

98. Karen L. Suyemoto and Mary B. Ballou, "Conducted Monotones to Coacted Harmonies: A Feminist (Re)conceptualization of Leadership Addressing Race, Class, and Gender," in *Women and Leadership: Transforming Visions and Diverse*

Voices, ed. Jean Lau Chin, Bernice Lott, Joy K. Rice, and Janis Sanchez-Hucles (Malden, MA: Blackwell, 2007), 41.

Chapter 3

1. Jim Collins, *Good to Great: Why Some Companies Make the Leap . . . and Others Don't*, Kindle ed. (New York: HarperCollins, 2001), Kindle Location 2123 of 5730.
2. Michael Maccoby, *The Leaders We Need and What Makes Us Follow* (Boston, MA: Harvard Business School Press, 2007), 8.
3. Ibid., 10.
4. Refer to Bernard M. Bass, *Transformational Leadership: Industry, Military, and Educational Impact* (Mahwah, NJ: Lawrence Erlbaum Associates, 1998).
5. Collins, *Good to Great: Why Some Companies Make the Leap . . . and Others Don't*, Kindle Location 339 of 5730.
6. Ibid., 339 of 5730.
7. Ibid., 339 of 5730.
8. Ibid., Kindle Location 350–54 of 5730.
9. Ibid., Kindle Location 638 of 5730.
10. Ibid., Kindle Location 2409 of 5730.
11. Maccoby, *The Leaders We Need and What Makes Us Follow*, 14.
12. Ibid., 65.
13. Ibid., 10.
14. Ibid., 65.
15. Linda Akutagawa, "Breaking Stereotype: An Asian American's View of Leadership Development," *Asian American Journal of Psychology* 4, 4 (2013): 280, Doi:10.1037/a0035390.
16. Maccoby, *The Leaders We Need and What Makes Us Follow*, 65.
17. David Collinson, "Prozac Leadership and the Limits of Positive Thinking," *Leadership* 8, 2 (2012): 78–107; Barbara Ehrenreich, *Bright-Sided: How the Relentless Promotion of Positive Thinking Has Undermined America* (New York: Metropolitan Books, 2009).
18. Walter Earl Fluker, *Ethical Leadership: The Quest for Character, Civility, and Community* (Minneapolis: Fortress Press, 2009), vii–viii.
19. David A. Frank, "Obama's Rhetorical Signature: Cosmopolitan Civil Religion in the Presidential Inaugural Address January 20, 2009," *Rhetoric and Public Affairs* 14, 4 (2011): 605–30.
20. Leroy Dorsey, "The President as Rhetorical Leader," in *The Presidency and Rhetorical Leadership*, ed. Leroy Dorsey (College Station: Texas A&M University Press, 2002), 9.

21. Adam J. Gaffey, "Obama's Change: Republicanism, Remembrance, and Rhetorical Leadership in the 2007 Presidential Announcement Speech," *Southern Communication Journal* 79, 5 (2014): 407–26.

22. Mahzarin R. Banaji and Anthony G. Greenwald, *Blindspot: Hidden Biases of Good People* (New York: Delacorte Press, 2013), 32–120.

23. Paul Rosenkrantz, Susan Vogel, Helen Bee, Inge Broverman, and Donald M. Broverman, "Sex-Role Stereotypes and Self-Concepts in College Students," *Journal of Consulting and Clinical Psychology* 32, 3 (1968): 291.

24. Rosenkrantz et al., "Sex-Role Stereotypes and Self-Concepts in College Students," 287–95.

25. Inge K. Broverman, Donald M. Broverman, Frank E. Clarkson, Paul S. Rosenkrantz, and Susan R. Vogel, "Sex-Role Stereotypes and Clinical Judgements of Mental Health," *Journal of Consulting and Clinical Psychology* 34, 1 (1970): 1–7.

26. Muriel N. Nesbitt and Nolan E. Penn, "Gender Stereotypes After Thirty Years: A Replication of Rosenkrantz et al. (1968)," *Psychological Reports* 87, 2 (2000): 493–511.

27. Thomas A. Widiger and Shirley A. Settle, "Broverman et al. Revisited: An Artifactual Sex Bias," *Journal of Personality and Social Psychology* 53, 3 (1987): 463–69.

28. Alice H. Eagly and Steven J. Karau, "Role Congruity Theory of Prejudice Toward Female Leaders," *Psychological Review* 109, 3 (2002): 573.

29. Madeline E. Heilman and Alice H. Eagly, "Gender Stereotypes Are Alive, Well, and Busy Producing Workplace Discrimination," *Industrial and Organizational Psychology* 1, 4 (2008): 393–98.

30. Madeline E. Heilman, Caryn J. Block, Richard F. Martell, and Michael C. Simon, "Has Anything Changed? Current Characteristics of Men, Women, and Managers," *Journal of Applied Psychology* 74, 6 (1989): 935–42.

31. Alice H. Eagly and Steven J. Karau, "Role Congruity Theory of Prejudice Toward Female Leaders," 573–98.

32. Laurie A. Rudman, "Self-promotion as a Risk Factor for Women: The Cost and Benefits of Counterstereotypical impression management," *Journal of Personality and Social Psychology* 74, 3 (1998): 629–45.

33. Anne M. Koenig, Alice H. Eagly, Abigail A. Mitchell, and Tiina Ristikari, "Are Leader Stereotypes Masculine? A Meta-Analysis of Three Research Paradigms," *Psychological Bulletin* 137, 4 (2011): 619.

34. http://www.catalyst.org/knowledge/statistical-overview-women-workforce, accessed on January 19, 2017.

35. Koenig, Eagly, Mitchell, and Ristikari, "Are Leader Stereotypes Masculine? A Meta-Analysis of Three Research Paradigms," 617–18.

36. Koenig et al., "Are Leader Stereotypes Masculine? A Meta-Analysis of Three Research Paradigms," 619.

37. William T.L. Cox and Patricia G. Devine, "Stereotypes Possess Heterogeneous Directionality: A Theoretical and Empirical Exploration of Stereotype Structure and Content," *PLOS ONE* 10, 3 (2015): 9, e122292, DOI:10.1371/journal.pone.0122292.

38. Maylon Hanold, "(De/Re) Constructing Leading Bodies: Developing Critical Attributes and Somaesthetic Practices," in Lois Ruskai Melina, Gloria J. Burgess, Lena Lid Falkman, and Antonio Marturano, eds., *The Embodiment of Leadership* (San Francisco, CA: Jossey-Bass, 2013), 90.

39. Michel Foucault, *Discipline and Punish: The Birth of the Prison*, 2nd ed. (London, UK: Penguin Books, 1977).

40. Madeline E. Heilman, "Description and Prescription: How Gender Stereotypes Prevent Women's Ascent Up the Organizational Ladder," *Journal of Social Issues* 57, 4 (Winter 2001): 660.

41. Daniel Katz and Kenneth Braly, "Racial Stereotypes in One Hundred College Students," *Journal of Abnormal and Social Psychology* 28, 3 (1933): 280–90.

42. He illustrated nine traits: superstitious, musical, lazy, ignorant, pleasure-loving, happy-go-lucky, very religious, ostentatious, and stupid. See G.M. Gilbert, "Stereotype Persistence and Change among College Students," *Journal of Abnormal and Social Psychology* 46, 2 (1951): 247–49.

43. Traits of African Americans in this study include being musical, pleasure-loving, happy-go-lucky, lazy, ostentatious, sensitive, gregarious, talkative, imitative, superstitious, ignorant, very religious, unreliable, slovenly, stupid, naïve, and physically dirty. See Marvin Karlins, Thomas L. Coffman, and Gary Walters, "On the Fading of Social Stereotypes: Studies in Three Generations of College Students," *Journal of Personality and Social Psychology* 13, 1 (1969): 1–16.

44. The top 20 percent of synonyms used for African American males are "athletic," followed by "antagonistic, dark skin, muscular, criminal, and speak loudly." See Yolanda Niemann, Leilani Jennings, Richard Rozelle, James Baxter, and Elroy Sullivan, "Use of Free Responses and Cluster Analysis to Determine Stereotypes of Eight Groups," *Personality and Social Psychology Bulletin* 24, 4 (1994): 379–90.

45. The top 20 percent of synonyms used for African American females are "speak loudly," followed by "dark skin, antagonistic, athletic, pleasant, unmannerly, and sociable." See Ibid., 379–90.

46. They listed other traits such as "being athletic, rhythmic, low in intelligence, poor, criminal, and loud." See Patricia G. Devine and Andrew J. Elliot, "Are Racial Stereotypes Really Fading? The Princeton Trilogy Revisited," *Personality and Social Psychology Bulletin* 21, 11 (1995): 1139–150.

47. Cox and Devine, "Stereotypes Possess Heterogeneous Directionality: A Theoretical and Empirical Exploration of Stereotype Structure and Content," 9.

48. Patricia S. Parker, "Gender, Culture, and Leadership: Toward a Culturally Distinct Model of African-American Women Executives' Leadership Strategies," *The Leadership Quarterly* 7, 2 (1996): 189–214.

49. Traits of female Anglo-Americans are supportive, cooperative and nurturing and of male Anglo-Americans are self-confident, independent and autonomous. Ibid., 193.

50. Ibid., 193.

51. Ibid., 195–97.

52. Ibid., 192, 202–6.

53. G.M. Gilbert, "Stereotype Persistence and Change among College Students," *Journal of Abnormal and Social Psychology* 46, 2 (1951): 250.

54. Niemann et al., "Use of Free Responses and Cluster Analysis to Determine Stereotypes of Eight Groups," 383.

55. Ibid., 384.

56. Gilbert, "Stereotype Persistence and Change among College Students," 248.

57. Niemann et al., "Use of Free Responses and Cluster Analysis to Determine Stereotypes of Eight Groups," 383.

58. Alice H. Eagly and Jean Lau Chin, "Diversity and Leadership in a Changing World," *American Psychologist* 65, 3 (2010): 217.

59. Ibid., 219–20.

60. Lee H. Butler Jr., *Liberating Our Dignity, Saving Our Souls: A New Theory of African American Identity Formation* (St. Louis, MO: Chalice Press, 2006), 11.

61. Peter J. Paris, "Moral Development for African-American Leadership," in *The Stones that the Builders Rejected: The Development of Ethical Leadership from the Black Church Tradition*, ed. Walter Earl Fluker (Harrisburg, PA: Trinity Press International, 1998), 24.

62. Ibid., 25.

63. Ibid., 30.

64. Bass, *Transformational Leadership: Industry, Military, and Educational Impact*, 5.

65. Bass, *Leadership and Performance Beyond Expectations*, 20.

66. Paris, "Moral Development for African-American Leadership" 31.

67. Ibid.

68. Walter Earl Fluker, *Ethical Leadership: The Quest for Character, Civility, and Community* (Minneapolis: Fortress Press, 2009), 33.

69. Ibid., 57–84.

70. Ibid., 85–120.

71. Ibid., 131–56.

72. Ibid., 167–74.

73. Peter J. Paris, *Black Religious Leaders: Conflict in Unity* (Louisville, KY: Westminster John Knox Press, 1991), 100–10.

74. Martin Luther King Jr., *Why We Can't Wait* (New York: Harper & Row, 1963), 85–86; quoted in Paris, *Black Religious Leaders: Conflict in Unity*, 120–21.

75. Walter Earl Fluker, *Ethical Leadership: The Quest for Character, Civility, and Community*, 27.

76. Martin Luther King Jr., *Strength to Love*, 1st ed. (Philadelphia, PA: Fortress Press, 1981), 28.

77. Martin Luther King Jr., "The Dimensions of a Complete Life," in *Tongues of Angels, Tongues of Men*, ed. John F. Thornton and Katharine Washburn (New York: Doubleday, 1999), 641.

78. King, *Strength to Love*, 146–54.

79. Thandeka, *Learning to Be White: Money, Race, and God in America* (New York: Continuum, 2001), 82.

80. Ibid., 82.

81. Ibid.

82. Ibid., 83.

83. Dale P. Andrews, *Practical Theology for Black Churches: Bridging Black Theology and African American Folk Religion* (Louisville, KY: Westminster John Knox Press, 2002), 52–66.

84. Ibid., 60–61.

85. Ibid., 72–82.

86. Ibid., 52–66.

87. Ibid., 50–88.

88. Lee H. Butler Jr., *A Loving Home: Caring for African American Marriage and Families* (Cleveland, OH: Pilgrim Press, 2000), 66.

89. Butler, *Liberating Our Dignity, Saving Our Souls*, 11.

90. Ibid.

91. Thandeka, *Learning to Be White*.

92. Michael Omi and Howard Winant, *Racial Formation in the United States: From the 1960s to the 1990s*, 2nd ed. (New York: Routledge, 1994), 88.

93. Butler, *Liberating Our Dignity, Saving Our Souls: A New Theory of African American Identity Formation*, 158.

94. Ibid., 162.

95. Ibid., 165.

96. Ibid., 166–70.

97. Ibid.

98. Ruth L. Hall, BraVada Garrett-Akinsanya, and Michael Hucles, "Voices of Black Feminist Leaders: Making Spaces for Ourselves," in *Women and Leadership: Transforming Visions and Diverse Voices*, ed. Jean Lau Chin et al. (Malden, MA: Blackwell, 2007), 282.

99. Ibid., 282.

100. Ibid., 283.

101. Ibid., 283–86.

102. Ibid., 286–88.

103. Ibid., 288.

104. Ibid., 288–91.

105. Ibid., 292.

106. Marcia Y. Riggs, *Awake, Arise and Act: A Womanist Call for Liberation* (Cleveland: Pilgrim Press, 1994), 47–98.

107. Ibid., 47–98.

108. Marcia Y. Riggs, "Living into the Bonds of Justice: A Challenge for Ethical Leadership into the Twenty-First Century," in *The Stones That the Builders Rejected: The Development of Ethical Leadership from the Black Church Tradition*, ed. Walter Earl Fluker (Harrisburg, PA: Trinity Press International, 1998), 39.

109. Ibid.

110. Ibid.

111. Ibid.

112. Riggs, *Awake, Arise and Act: A Womanist Call for Liberation*, 90–91.

113. Ibid., 77.

114. Riggs, "Living into the Bonds of Justice: A Challenge for Ethical Leadership into the Twenty-First Century," 43.

115. Toni C. King and S. Alease Ferguson, "Introduction: Looking to the Motherline," in *Black Womanist Leadership: Tracing the Motherline*, ed. Toni C. King and S. Alease Ferguson (Albany: State University of New York Press, 2011), 10.

116. Ibid., 11.

117. Ibid., 231–48.

118. Susan C. Pearce, Elizabeth J. Clifford, and Reena Tandon, *Immigration and Women: Understanding the American Experience—Finding Agency, Negotiating, and Bridging Cultures* (New York: New York University Press, 2011), 2.

119. "Herman Cain Proposes an Electrified Fence as Immigration Reform, Says He Was Joking," *Huffington Post*, October 18, 2011, https://www.huffingtonpost.com/2011/10/ 16/herman-cain-electrified-border-fence-immigration_n_1013872.html; Ediberto Román, *Those Damned Immigrants: Americas Hysteria over Undocumented Immigration* (New York: New York University Press, 2013), 19.

120. "Herman Cain's Electrified Border Fence 'Joke': Bad Taste?" *The Weeks*, October 17, 2011, http://theweek.com/articles/480948/herman-cains-electrified-border-fence-joke-bad-taste; Ediberto Román, *Those Damned Immigrants: Americas Hysteria over Undocumented Immigration* (New York: New York University Press, 2013), 19.

121. Gregory Korte and Alan Gomez, "Trump Ramps Up Rhetoric on Undocumented Immigrants: 'These are not people. These are animals,'" *USA Today*, May 16, 2018, https://www.usatoday.com/story/news/politics/2018/05/16/trump-immigrants-animals-mexico-democrats-sanctuary-cities/617252002/.

122. Ibid.

123. Julie Hirschfeld Davis, "Trump Calls Some Unauthorized Immigrants 'Animals' in Rant," *The New York Times*, May 16, 2018, https://www.nytimes.com/2018/05/16/ us/politics/trump-undocumented-immigrants-animals.html.

124. Pearce, Clifford, and Tandon, *Immigration and Women: Understanding the American Experience*, 6.

125. Omi and Winant, *Racial Formation in the United States: From the 1960s to the 1990s*, 36–47.

126. Ibid.

127. Ibid., 45.

128. Sarah L. Buckingham, Lindsay Emery, Surbhi Godsay, Anne E. Brodsky, Jill E. Scheibler, "'You opened my mind:' Latinx immigrant and receiving community interactional dynamics in the United States," *Journal of Community Psychology*, 46 (2018): 172. https://onlinelibrary-wiley-com.ezproxy.bu.edu/doi/epdf/10.1002/jcop.21931.

129. Grace Yukich, *One Family Under God: Immigration Politics and Progressive Religion in America* (New York: Oxford University Press, 2013).

130. Ruth Milkman, "L.A. Past, American's Future? The 2006 Immigrant Rights Protest and Their Antecedents," in *Rallying for Immigrant Rights: The Fight for Inclusion in the 21st Century America*, 1st ed., ed. Kim Voss and Irene Bloemraad (Berkeley: University of California Press, 2011), 201–14; Randy Shaw, "Building the Labor-Clergy-Immigrant Alliance," in *Rallying for Immigrant Rights*, 82–100.

131. Sasha Costanza-Chock, *Out of the Shadows, into the Streets! Transmedia Organizing and the Immigrant Rights Movement* (Boston, MA: MIT Press, 2014), 22.

132. Ibid., 23.

133. Ibid.

134. Shaw, "Building the Labor-Clergy-Immigrant Alliance," in *Rallying for Immigrant Rights*, 87.

135. Costanza-Chock, *Out of the Shadows, into the Streets*, 23.

136. Manuel Pastor and John Mollenkopf, "The Cases in Context: Data and Destinies in Seven Metropolitan Areas," in *Unsettled Americans: Metropolitan Context and Civic Leadership for Immigrant Integration*, ed. Manuel Pastor and John Mollenkopf (Ithaca, NY: Cornell University Press, 2016), Location 725–28 of 7844.

137. Ruth Milkman and Veronica Terriquez, "'We are the ones who are out in Front:' Women's Leadership in the Immigrant Rights Movement," *Feminist Studies* 38, 3 (Fall 2012): 724.

138. Lisa M. Martinez, "The Immigrant Rights Movement: Then and Now," *Mobilizing Ideas*, December 2, 2015, https://mobilizingideas.wordpress.com/2015/12/03/the-immigrant-rights-movement-then-and-now/, accessed January 27, 2017.

139. Yukich, *One Family Under God: Immigration Politics and Progressive Religion in America*; Monisha Das Gupta, *Unruly Immigrants: Rights, Activism, and Transnational South Asian Politics in the United States* (Durham, NC: Duke University Press, 2006); Randy Shaw, *Beyond the Fields: Cesar Chavez, the UFW,*

and the Struggle for Justice in the 21st Century (Berkeley: University of California Press, 2008).

140. http://www.migrationpolicy.org/programs/data-hub/charts/largest-immigrant-groups-over-time, accessed on November 21, 2018.

141. Deborah G. Felder, *The 100 Most Influential Women of All Time* (New York: Citadel, 2001), 48–49; https://www.u-s-history.com/pages/h1050.html.

142. Nina Asher, "Dorothy Jacobs Bellanca: Women Clothing Workers and Runaway Shops," in *A Needle, A Bobbin, a Strike*, ed. Joan M. Jensen and Sue Davidson (Philadelphia: Temple University Press, 1984).

143. Milkman and Terriquez, "We Are the Ones Who Are Out in Front': Women's Leadership in the Immigrant Rights Movement," 724.

144. Ibid., 748.

145. Ibid., 724.

146. Ibid.

147. Ibid.

148. Pearce, Clifford, and Tandon, *Immigration and Women: Understanding the American Experience*, 210.

149. Bass, *Transformational Leadership: Industrial, Military, and Educational Impact*, 5.

150. Pearce, Clifford, and Tandon, *Immigration and Women: Understanding the American Experience*, 215.

151. Milkman and Terriquez, "We Are the Ones Who Are Out in Front': Women's Leadership in the Immigrant Rights Movement," 739.

152. Maria Elena Durazo, "Making Movement: Communities of Color and New Models of Organizing Labor-Afternoon Keynote Address," *Berkeley Journal of Employment & Labor Law* 27, 1 (2006): 235–36.

153. Ibid., 236.

154. Jorge Morales Almada, *La Opinión*, Los Angeles, CA. May 07, 2006. Translated by LEC.

155. Ibid.

156. James Rainey, "Rusty Hickes Chosen to run L.A. County Federation of Labor," *Los Angeles Times*, November 18, 2014.

157. Niki T. Dickerson, "'We are a Force to be Reckoned With': Black and Latina Women's Leadership in the Contemporary U.S. Labor Movement," *Journal of Labor and Society* 1089–7011, 9 (September 2006): 300.

158. Hilary Cunningham, *God and Caesar at the Rio Grande: Sanctuary and the Politics of Religion* (Minneapolis: University of Minnesota Press, 1995) xiii; Gregory Freeland, "Negotiating Place, Space, and Boarders: The New Sanctuary Movement," *Latino Studies* 8, 4 (2011): 488.

159. Kara L. Wild, "The New Sanctuary Movement: When Moral Mission Means Breaking the Law, and the Consequences for Churches and Illegal

Immigrants," *Santa Clare Law Review* 50, 3 (2010): 987; Michele Altemus, "The Sanctuary Movement," *Whittier Law Review* 9 (1988): 687–88.

160. Freeland, "Negotiating Place, Space, and Boarders: The New Sanctuary Movement," 488.

161. Wild, "The New Sanctuary Movement: When Moral Mission Means Breaking the Law, and the Consequences for Churches and Illegal Immigrants," 989; Altemus, "The Sanctuary Movement," 710–11.

162. Ibid., 989.

163. Ibid., 990.

164. Freeland, "Negotiating Place, Space, and Boarders: The New Sanctuary Movement," 490.

165. Ibid., 490.

166. Yukich, "New Sanctuary Movement," *One Family Under God: Immigration Politics and Progressive Religion in America*, 4 of 40; http://www.oxfordscholarship.com.ezproxy.bu. edu/view/10.1093/acprof:oso/9780199988662.001.0001/acprof-9780199988662-chapter-2?print=pdf.

167. Ibid., 4.

168. Ibid.

169. Freeland, "Negotiating Place, Space, and Boarders: The New Sanctuary Movement," 491.

170. Ibid., 494.

171. Grace Yukich, "Constructing the Model Immigrants: Movement Strategy and Immigrant Deservingness in the New Sanctuary Movement," *Social Problems* 60, 3 (2013): 309.

172. Ibid., 302–20.

173. Ibid.

174. Ibid.

175. Ibid.

176. Ibid.

177. Costanza-Chock, *Out of the Shadows, into the Streets! Transmedia Organizing and the Immigrant Rights Movement*, 130; Arely M. Zimmerman, "Documenting Dream: New Media, Undocumented You and the Immigrant Rights Movement," University of Southern California Annenberg School for Communication & Journalism, Civic Paths' Media, Activism, and Participatory Politics Project, Los Angeles, June 6, 2012, http://ypp.dmlcentral.net/sites/ default/files/publications/Documenting_DREAMs.pdf, accessed April 11, 2014).

178. Prerna Lai, "How Queer Undocumented Youth Built the Immigrant Rights Movement," *Huffington Post*, March 28, 2013, http://archive.is/5ULwu, accessed October 12, 2013; Costanza-Chock, *Out of the Shadows, into the Streets! Transmedia Organizing and the Immigrant Rights Movement*, 130.

179. Costanza-Chock, *Out of the Shadows, into the Streets! Transmedia Organizing and the Immigrant Rights Movement*, 131.

Chapter 4

1. Peter G. Northouse, *Leadership: Theory and Practice*, 6th ed. (Thousand Oaks, CA: Sage, 2013), 404; Robert J. House, Paul. J. Hanges, Mansour Javidan, Peter W. Dorfman, and Vipin Gupta, eds., *Culture, Leadership and Organizations: The GLOBE Study of 62 Societies* (Thousand Oaks, CA: Sage, 2004).

2. Ibid.

3. Twenty-two positive leadership attributes are trustworthy, just, honest, has foresight, plans ahead, encouraging, positive, dynamic, motive arouser, confidence builder, motivational, dependable, intelligent, decisive, effective bargainer, win-win problem solver, communicative, informed, administratively skilled, coordinative, team builder, and excellence oriented. Eight negative leadership attributes are loner, asocial, noncooperative, irritable, nonexplicit, egocentric, ruthless, and dictatorial. Ibid., 383–404.

4. Northouse, *Leadership: Theory and Practice*, 391.

5. Ibid., 398–99.

6. Ibid.

7. Ibid., 394.

8. Ibid., 400.

9. Ibid., 401.

10. Ibid., 400.

11. Michael A. Witt and Günter K. Stahl, "Foundations of Responsible Leadership: Asian versus Western Executive Responsibility Orientations toward Key Stakeholders," *Journal of Business Ethics* 136, 3 (2016): 628, DOI 10.1007/s10551-014-2534-8.

12. Even though each Asian country has its own indigenous religious practices and principles that influence each nation's leadership styles, it is hard to discuss them in each national context. Therefore, in this chapter, I limit the discussion of Asian leadership to the concepts of Confucian virtues and Buddhist practices that are typically exercised in many Asian countries as an example.

13. LingLing Lang, Beverly J. Irby, and Genevieve Brown, "An Emergent Leadership Model Based on Confucian Virtues and East Asian Leadership Practices," *International Journal of Education Leadership Preparation* 7, 2 (Summer 2012): 6.

14. Ibid., 2.

15. Jae Myung Su, "*Rén, Yì, Lǐ, Zhì*, Four Virtues for People to Practice," *GoSungMiRae Newspaper*, February 10, 2017, from http://www.gofnews.com/news/ articleView.html?idxno=2831.

16. Lang, Irby, and Brown, "An Emergent Leadership Model Based on Confucian Virtues and East Asian Leadership Practices," 3.

17. Su, "*Rén, Yì, Lǐ, Zhì*, Four Virtues for People to Practice."

18. Lang, Irby, and Brown, "An Emergent Leadership Model Based on Confucian Virtues and East Asian Leadership Practices," 4.

19. Paul Williams, *Mahāyāna Buddhism: The Doctrinal Foundations* (New York: Routledge, 1989), 42.

20. Grace Ji-Sun Kim, *The Grace of Sophia: A Korean North American Women's Christology* (Cleveland: The Pilgrim Press, 2002), 85.

21. Lang, Irby, and Brown, "An Emergent Leadership Model Based on Confucian Virtues and East Asian Leadership Practices," 4.

22. Ibid., 5.

23. Eddie C.Y. Kuo, "Confucianism and the Chinese Family in Singapore: Continuities and Changes," in *Confucianism and the Family*, ed. Walter H. Slote and George A. DeVos (Albany: State University of New York Press, 1998), 238.

24. Lang, Irby, and Brown, "An Emergent Leadership Model Based on Confucian Virtues and East Asian Leadership Practices," 5.

25. Lao-Tzu, *Te-Tao Ching: A New Translation Based on the Recently Discovered Ma-wang-tui Texts*, trans. Robert G. Henricks, with an introduction and commentary (New York: Ballantine Books, 1989), 56.

26. Ibid., 56.

27. The Four Noble Truths have to do with suffering, what it is, why it happens, how it can be eliminated, and what practices are needed. The First Noble Truth is suffering (*dukkha*) itself. It concerns the suffering of *Sang* (birth), *No* (aging), *Byung* (sickness), *Sa* (death) from the circles of human life. It explains what suffering is from the experience of pain, dissatisfaction, loss, among other experiences, from life itself. It manifests all dimensions of suffering. The Second Noble Truth explains "the origin, roots, nature, creation, or arising (*samudaya*) of suffering" (208 of 4060). It explains the roots of suffering in terms of thirst, desire, greed, or craving. It illustrates the contingence of suffering and existence of suffering. "The Third Noble Truth is cessation (*nirodha*) of creating suffering by refraining from doing the things that make us suffer" (219 of 4060). It explains how to end suffering. It introduces the existence of emancipation from suffering. "The Fourth Noble Truth is the path (*marga*) that leads to refraining from doing the things that cause us to suffer" (224 of 4060). The Fourth Noble Truth will lead to the Noble Eightfold Path. Refer to Thich Nhat Hanh, *The Heart of the Buddha's Teaching–Transforming Suffering into Peace, Joy, and Liberation: The Four Noble Truths, the Noble Eightfold Path, and Other Basic Buddhist Teachings*, Kindle ed. (New York: Harmony Books, 2015), Location 208–24 of 4060.

28. The Noble Eightfold Path is a practice to overcome suffering. It has eight conceptual paths. However, the boundary of each path is not clear. It is not in a sequence. It is not a step of development. It is not divisible but intertwined. Each path is interdependent on each other. To end suffering, we are asked to understand and practice the Noble Eightfold Path: *sammādiṭṭhi* (right views), *sammāsankappo* (right thinking/right intention/right aim), *sammāvacā* (right speech), *sammākammanto* (right action/right conduct), *sammā ājīvo* (right livelihood), *sammā vāyāmo* (right effort/right exertion/right diligence), *sammā sati* (right mindfulness/

right keeping in mind), *sammāsamādhi* (right concentration/right meditation). Refer to Oscar Frankfurter, "Buddhist Nirvāna, and the Noble Eightfold Path," *The Journal of the Royal Asiatic Society of Great Britain and Ireland* New Series 12, 4 (1880): 555–57. http://www.jstor.org.ezproxy.bu.edu/stable/25196863.

29. Thich Nhat Hanh perceives these practices as interconnected and requiring nourishment from each other. He explains right view as the foundation of creating a path to understand the Four Noble Truths. It starts with Buddha's belief that there are people who can overcome and end suffering. It is the eye to discern wholesome roots from unwholesome roots. It means right view requires good consciousness to understand things as they really are. Right thinking is the foundation of right view. It is always in the company of right view in pursuit of a way to transform suffering. Right mindfulness is the energy that brings us back to the present moment by remembering. It brings us all to the present, it nourishes others, and relieves us from suffering by deep looking and understanding. The precondition of right speech is listening to others with compassion and true presence with right mindfulness. Without this precondition, speech will cause suffering to others. Right action is a nonviolent practice of loving others and preventing harm. Every act should reflect the five mindfulness trainings, reverence for life, generosity, sexual responsibility, right speech, and mindful eating, drinking, and consuming. Right diligence or right effort is where to put energy to touch the present. It needs a practice of preventing unwholesome seeds and nurturing wholesome seeds in the mind. Right concentration cultivates a mind to pursue happiness, leading to right action. The purpose of right concentration is to live deeply each moment. To practice right liveliness is to live life without transgressing the ideals of love and compassion. It is not a mere personal matter but a collective task. Refer to Nhat Hanh, *The Heart of the Buddha's Teaching*, Location 802–1725 of 4060.

30. Williams, *Mahāyāna Buddhism: The Doctrinal Foundations*, 46.

31. Ibid., 48.

32. Nhat Hanh, *The Heart of the Buddha's Teaching*, Location 2212 of 4060.

33. Ibid., Location 2215, 2225 of 4060.

34. Williams, *Mahāyāna Buddhism: The Doctrinal Foundations*, 51.

35. Ibid., 52.

36. Joan Marques, Satinder Dhiman, and Jerry Biberman, "Moral Crossroads: Contemplating Formal and Informal Economy through the Noble Eightfold Path," *Journal of Applied Business and Economics* 14, 1 (2013): 99–109.

37. Chau-kiu Cheung and Andrew Chi-fai Chan, "Benefits of Hong Kong Chinese CEOs' Confucian and Daoist Leadership Styles," *Leadership & Organization Development Journal* 29, 6 (2008): 474.

38. Ibid., 474–503.

39. Lang, Irby, and Brown, "An Emergent Leadership Model Based on Confucian Virtues and East Asian Leadership Practices," 6–11.

40. Ibid., 6.
41. Ibid., 6–7.
42. Ibid., 7.
43. Ibid., 8.
44. Ibid., 7–8.
45. Bass, *Leadership and Performance Beyond Expectations.*
46. Burns, *Leadership.*
47. Lang, Irby, and Brown, "An Emergent Leadership Model Based on Confucian Virtues and East Asian Leadership Practices," 9–10.
48. Ibid., 10.
49. Ibid., 10–11.
50. William Theodore De Bary, *Nobility and Civility: Asian Ideals of Leadership and the Common Good*, Kindle ed. (Cambridge, MA: Harvard University Press, 2004), Locations 93–95 of 2509.
51. Burns, *Transforming Leadership*, 213.
52. Jean Lau Chin, "Introduction: Special Section on Asian American Leadership," *Asian American Journal of Psychology* 4, 4 (2013): 235.
53. Pyong Gap Min, "Major Issues Related to Asian American Experiences," in *Asian Americans: Contemporary Trends and Issues*, 2nd ed., ed. Pyong Gap Min (Thousand Oaks, CA: Pine Forge Press, 2006), 83.
54. Stefanie K. Johnson and Thomas Sy, "Why Aren't There More Asian Americans in Leadership Positions?" *Harvard Business Review*, December 19, 2016, https://hbr.org/2016/12/why-arent-there-more-asian-americans-in-leadership-positions?
55. Kimberly Burris, Roya Ayman, Yi Che, and Hanyi Min, "Asian Americans' and Caucasians' Implicit Leadership Theories: Asian Stereotypes, Transformational, and Authentic Leadership," *Asian American Journal of Psychology* 4, 4 (2013): 258; Katarina, H. *Why are so few highly qualified and ambitious Asians making it to the top? 2011*, Retrieved from www.worklifepolicy.org; Eagly, A. H., & Chin, J. L. Diversity and leadership in a changing world. *American Psychologist*, 65 (2010), 216–24. doi:10.1037/a0018957.
56. Beth G. Chung-Herrera and Melenie J. Lankau, "Are We There Yet? An Assessment Fit Between Stereotypes of Minority Managers and the Successful-Manager Prototype," *Journal of Applied Social Psychology* 35, 10 (2005): 2047, DOI: 10.1111/j.1559-1816.2005.tb02208.x.
57. Katherine R. Xin, "Asian American Managers: An Impression Gap? An Investigation of Impression Management and Supervisor-Subordinate Relationships," *Journal Applied Behavior Science* 40, 2 (2004): 168–91, DOI:10.1177/0021886304263853.
58. Johnson and Sy, "Why Aren't There More Asian Americans in Leadership Positions?"
59. Ibid.

60. Ron Heifetz and Donald Laurie, "The Work of Leadership," *Harvard Business Review* 79, 11 (2001): 137.

61. Parker, "Gender, Culture, and Leadership: Toward a Culturally Distinct Model of African-American Women Executives' Leadership Strategies," 193.

62. George P. Hollenbeck and Douglas T. Hall, "Self-Confidence and Leader Performance," *Organizational Dynamics* 33, 3 (2004): 257–58.

63. Ibid., 261.

64. Heifetz and Laurie, "The Work of Leadership," 137.

65. Collinson, "Prozac Leadership and the Limits of Positive Thinking," 78–107; Ehrenreich, *Bright-Sided: How the Relentless Promotion of Positive Thinking Has Undermined America*.

66. Hollenbeck and Hall, "Self-Confidence and Leader Performance," 256.

67. Stephen Fineman, "On Being Positive," *Academy of Management Review* 31, 2 (2006): 270–91.

68. Chung-Herrera and Lankau, "Are We There Yet? An Assessment Fit between Stereotypes of Minority Managers and the Successful-Manager Prototype."

69. Norman Vincent Peale, *The Power of Positive Thinking* (New York: Prentice-Hall, 1952), 1–218.

70. Ibid., 5.

71. Collinson, "Prozac Leadership and the Limits of Positive Thinking," 94.

72. Dong Min Kim, Jang Wan Ko, and Seon-Joo Kim, "Exploring the Ethical Aspects of Leadership: From a Korean Perspective," *Asian Philosophy* 25, 2 (2015): 118, http://dxdoi.org/10.1080/09552367.2015.1013732.

73. Ibid., 121.

74. Ibid., 123.

75. Lao-Tzu, *Te-Tao Ching*, 35.

76. Ibid., 43.

77. Ibid., 59.

78. F. Luthans and B.J. Avolio, "Authentic Leadership: A Positive Developmental Approach," in *Positive Organizational Scholarship*, ed. Kim S. Cameron, Jane E. Dutton, and Robert E. Quinn (San Francisco, CA: Barrett-Koehler, 2003), 241–61; Haina Zhang, André M. Everett, Graham Elkin, and Malcolm H. Cone, "Authentic Leadership Theory Development: Theorizing on Chinese Philosophy," *Asian Pacific Business Review* 18, 4 (2012): 587–605.

79. Lao-*Te-Tao Ching*, 54.

80. Linda Akutagawa, "Breaking Stereotypes: An Asian American's View of Leadership Development," *Asian American Journal of Psychology* 4, 4 (2013): 282–83, DOI:10.1037/a0035390.

81. Hollenbeck and Hall, "Self-Confidence and Leader Performance," 254.

82. Akutagawa, "Breaking Stereotypes: An Asian American's View of Leadership Development," 280.

83. Ibid., 280.

84. Ibid.

85. Jean Lau Chin, "Introduction: Special Section on Asian American Leadership," 238.

86. Zhang, Everett, Elkin, and Cone, "Authentic Leadership Theory Development: Theorizing on Chinese Philosophy," 587–605; Luthans and Avolio, "Authentic Leadership: A Positive Developmental Approach," 241–61.

87. Hollenbeck and Hall, "Self-Confidence and Leader Performance," 254.

88. Chung-Herrera and Lankau, "Are We There Yet? An Assessment Fit between Stereotypes of Minority Managers and the Successful-Manager Prototype," 2029–56.

89. See Pyong Gap Min, "Korean Americans," in *Asian Americans: Contemporary Trends and Issues*, ed. Pyong Gap Min (Thousand Oaks, CA: Pine Forge Press, 2006), 230–59.

90. Karthick Ramakrishnan and Celia Viramontes, *Civil Inequalities: Immigrant Volunteerism and Community Organizations in California* (San Francisco: Public Policy Institutes of California, 2006).

91. Min, "Major Issues Related to Asian American Experiences," in *Asian Americans: Contemporary Trends and Issues*, 84.

92. Rosina Lippi-Green, *English with an Accent: Language, Ideology and Discrimination in the United States*, 2nd ed. Kindle ed. (New York: Routledge, 2012), 290 of 355, 9202 of 12055.

93. Ibid., 291 of 355, 9214 of 12055.

94. Ibid., 299 of 355, 9470 of 12055.

95. Megumi Hosoda, "The Effects of Foreign Accents on Employment-Related Decisions," *Journal of Managerial Psychology* 25, 2 (2010): 113–32. Doi 10.1108/02683941011019339.

96. Helen Rose Ebaugh and Janet Saltzman Chafetz, *Religion and the New Immigrants: Continuities and Adaptations in Immigrant Congregations* (New York: AltaMira, 2000), 118.

97. Akutagawa, "Breaking Stereotypes: An Asian American's View of Leadership Development," 279–81.

98. Ibid., 282–83.

99. Ibid., 283.

100. Jean Lau Chin, "Introduction: Special Section on Asian American Leadership," 238.

101. Thomas Sy, Lynn M. Shore, Judy Strauss, Ted H. Shore, Susanna Tram, Paul Whiteley, Kristine Ikeda-Muromachi, "Leadership Perceptions on a Function of Race-Occupation Fit: The Case of Asian Americans," *Journal of Applied Psychology* 95, 5 (2010): 902–19, DOI:10.1037/a0019501.

Chapter 5

1. Peter C. Phan, "Introduction: Asian Christianity/Christianities," in *Christianities in Asia*, ed. Peter C. Phan (Malden, MA: Wiley-Blackwell, 2011), 2.
2. Ibid., 3.
3. Peter C. Phan, *Christianity with an Asian Face: Asian American Theology in the Making* (New York: Orbis Books, 2003), 3–26.
4. James MacGregor Burns, *Transforming Leadership: A New Pursuit of Happiness* (New York: Grove Press, 2003), 10.
5. Mark Allan Powell, *Jesus as a Figure in History: How Modern Historians View the Man from Galilee* (Louisville, KY: Westminster John Knox Press, 1998), 51–65.
6. Ibid., 83–166.
7. Andrew Sung Park, "The Bible and Han," in *The Other Side of Sin: Woundedness from the Perspective of the Sinned-Against*, ed. Andrew Sung Park and Susan L. Nelson (Albany: State University of New York Press, 2001), 47–48.
8. Andrew Sung Park, *The Wounded Heart of God: The Asian Concept of Han and the Christian Doctrine of Sin* (Nashville, TN: Abingdon Press, 1993), 31.
9. Ibid., 124–26.
10. Ibid., 9–178.
11. Chung Hyun Kyung, *Struggle to Be the Sun Again: Introducing Asian Women's Theology* (New York: Orbis Books, 1990), 53.
12. Ibid., 53–73; Chung Hyun Kyung, "Who Is Jesus for Asian Women?" in *Asian Faces of Jesus*, ed. R.S. Sugirtharajah (New York: Orbis Books, 1993), 223–46.
13. Pyong Gap Min, "Major Issues Related to Asian American Experiences," 88–90.
14. Rita Nakashima Brock, *Journeys by Heart: A Christology of Erotic Power* (New York: Crossroad, 1992), 69.
15. Ibid., xvii.
16. Kwok Pui-lan, *Chinese Women and Christianity, 1860–1927* (Atlanta, GA: Scholars Press, 1992), 177.
17. Ibid., 29–57.
18. Kwok Pui-lan, *Introducing Asian Feminist Theology* (Sheffield, England: Sheffield Academic Press, 2000), 79–97.
19. Kwok Pui-lan, *Postcolonial Imagination and Feminist Theology* (Louisville, KY: Westminster John Knox Press, 2005), 168–85.
20. Ibid., 182–85.
21. Harry H.L. Kitano and Roger Daniels, *Asian Americans: Emerging Minorities*, 3rd ed. (Upper Saddle River, NJ: Prentice Hall, 2001), 6–8.

22. Linda Akutagawa, "Breaking Stereotypes: An Asian American's View of Leadership Development," in *Asian American Journal of Psychology* 4, 4 (2013): 282, DOI:10.1037/a0035390.

23. Grace Ji-Sun Kim, *The Grace of Sophia: A Korean North American Women's Christology*, 80–130.

24. Ibid.

25. Wonhee Anne Joh, *Heart of the Cross: A Postcolonial Christology* (Louisville, KY: Westminster John Knox Press, 2006), xxi.

26. Ibid., xxvi.

27. C.S. Song, *Jesus and the Reign of God* (Minneapolis: Augsburg Fortress, 1993).

28. Phan, *Christianity with an Asian Face*, 146–70.

29. C.S. Song, *Jesus, the Crucified People* (Minneapolis: Fortress Press, 1996).

30. C.S. Song, *The Compassionate God: An Exercise in the Theology of Transposition* (New York: Orbis Books, 1982), quoted in Phan, *Christianity with an Asian Face*, 153.

31. Song, *Jesus, the Crucified People*, 223.

32. Phan, *Christianity with an Asian Face*, 125–45.

33. Ibid., 245.

34. Peter C. Phan, *Being Religious Interreligiously: Asian Perspectives on Interfaith Dialogue* (New York: Orbis Books, 2004), 128–46.

35. See Sugirtharajah, *Asian Faces of Jesus*.

36. M. Thomas Thangaraj, *The Crucified Guru: An Experiment in Cross-Cultural Christology* (Nashville: Abingdon Press, 1994), 89–106.

37. Ibid., 107–128.

38. Ibid., 129–152.

39. Kosuke Koyama, *Water Buffalo Theology* (New York: Orbis Books, 1999), 87.

40. Ibid., 150–70.

41. Kosuke Koyama, *No Handle on the Cross: An Asian Meditation on the Crucified Mind* (New York: Orbis Books, 1977), 61.

42. Jung Young Lee, *Marginality: The Key to Multicultural Theology* (Minneapolis: Fortress Press, 1995).

43. Anselm Kyongsuk Min, "The Political Economy of Marginality: Comments on Jung Young Lee, *Marginality: The Key to Multicultural Theology*," *Journal of Asian and Asian American Theology* 1 (1996): 84.

44. Ibid., 94.

45. Anselm Kyongsuk Min, *The Solidarity of Others in a Divided World: A Postmodern Theology after Postmodernism* (New York: T & T Clark International, 2004), 1.

46. Patrick S. Cheng, *Radical Love: An Introduction to Queer Theology* (New York: Seabury Books, 2011), 69–98.

47. Ibid., 85.

48. Patrick S. Cheng, *Rainbow Theology: Bridging Race, Sexuality, and Spirit* (New York: Seabury Books, 2013), 145.

49. Ibid., 145–57.

50. John Ford, "Ministries in the Church," in *The Gift of the Church: A Textbook on Ecclesiology in Honor of Patrick Granfield, O.S.B.*, ed. Peter C. Phan (Collegeville, MN: The Liturgical Press, 2000), 293–94.

51. Ibid., 293.

52. James E. Dittes, *When the People Say No: Conflict and the Call to Ministry* (New York: Harper & Row, 1979), 1, quoted in Michael Jinkins, "Religious Leadership," in *The Wiley Blackwell Companion to Practical Theology*, ed. Bonnie J. Miller-McLemore (Malden, MA: Wiley-Blackwell, 2014), 314.

53. Seward Hiltner, *Preface to Pastoral Theology: The Ministry and Theory of Shepherding* (Nashville, KY: Abingdon Press, 1958), 199–201.

54. William H. Willimon, *Pastor: The Theology and Practice of Ordained Ministry* (Nashville, KY: Abingdon Press, 2002).

55. Timothy Keller, *Center Church: Doing Balanced Gospel-Centered Ministry in Your City* (Grand Rapids, MI: Zondervan, 2012), 288.

56. Lisa R. Berlinger, "The Behavioral Competency Approach to Effective Ecclesial Leadership," *Journal of Religious Leadership* 2, 2 (Spring 2003): 96.

57. Collinson, "Prozac Leadership and the Limits of Positive Thinking," 94.

58. Martha Ellen Stortz, *PastorPower* (Nashville, KY: Abingdon Press, 1993), 65–67.

59. Ibid., 43–68.

60. Ibid., 65–67.

61. Ford, "Ministries in the Church," 299.

62. Scott Cormode, "Multi-Layered Leadership: The Christian Leader as Builder, Shepherd, and Gardener," *Journey of Religious Leadership* 1, 2 (Fall 2002).

63. Ford, "Ministries in the Church," 302–5.

64. Ibid.

65. LingLing Lang, Beverly J. Irby, and Genevieve Brown, "An Emergent Leadership Model Based on Confucian Virtues and East Asian Leadership Practices," *International Journal of Education Leadership Preparation* 7, 2 (Summer 2012): 10–11.

66. Helen Rose Ebaugh and Jane Saltzman Chafetz, *Religion and the New Immigrants: Continuities and Adaptations in Immigrant Congregations* (New York: AltaMira, 2000), 50–52.

67. Michael W. Foley and Dean R. Hoge, *Religion and the New Immigrants: How Faith Communities Form Our Newest Citizens* (New York: Oxford University Press, 2007), 154.

68. Ibid., 23–55.

69. Ebaugh and Chafetz, *Religion and the New Immigrants: Continuities and Adaptations in Immigrant Congregations*, 55.

70. Su Yon Pak, "Women Leaders in Asian American Protestant Churches," in *Religious Leadership: A Reference Handbook (1)*, ed. Sharon Callahan (Thousand Oaks, CA: Sage, 2013), 298.

71. HiRho Y. Park, *Develop Intercultural Competence: How to Lead Cross-Racial and Cross-Cultural Churches* (Nashville, TN: General Board of Higher Education & Ministry, 2018).

72. Su Yon Pak, "Women Leaders in Asian American Protestant Churches," 298.

73. Ibid., 298–99.

74. Ibid., 299.

75. Ibid.

76. Ibid., 299–300.

77. Helen Lee, "Silent Exodus: Can the East Asian Church in America Reverse the Flight of Its Next Generation?" *Christianity Today*, August 12, 1996, quoted in Pak, "Women Leaders in Asian American Protestant Churches," 299.

78. Foley and Hoge, *Religion and the New Immigrants*, 75.

79. I have conducted numerous research projects focused on the immigrant church and women at Anna Howard Shaw Center from 2006 to 2015. One of the most distinctive immigrant church ministries that differs from the ministry of white congregations is sharing meal time after Sunday worship or in small-group gatherings. Various immigrant congregations practice this fellowship as the most vital and crucial church activity. Centered on this fellowship, church members share their personal immigrant lives and understand communal difficulties. The function of this fellowship is to provide a social network as well as psychological and spiritual support for immigrants. See Choi Hee An, *A Postcolonial Self: Korean Immigrant Theology and Church* (Albany: State University of New York Press, 2015), 36–152.

80. Ibid., 136–52.

81. Foley and Hoge, *Religion and the New Immigrants*, 128.

82. Ibid., 128.

83. Ellen Tanouye, "The Church as Mediator between Cultures," in *People on the Way: Asian North Americans Discovering Christ, Culture, and Community*, ed. David Ng (Valley Forge, PA: Judson Press, 1996), 189–99.

84. Foley and Hoge, *Religion and the New Immigrants*, 108–13.

85. Nancy Tatom Ammerman, *Congregation and Community* (New Brunswick, NJ: Rutgers University Press, 1997), 355–67.

86. Ibid., 365.
87. Foley and Hoge, *Religion and the New Immigrants*, 112.
88. Ibid., 153.
89. Ibid., 155.
90. Ibid., 156.
91. Ibid., 158.
92. Keller, *Center Church: Doing Balanced Gospel-Centered Ministry in Your City*, 293.
93. Timothy Tseng et al., "Asian Religious Leadership Today: A Preliminary Inquiry," in *Pulpit and Pew Research on Pastoral Leadership* (Durham, NC: Duke Divinity School, 2005), 24.
94. Ibid.
95. Russell Jeung, "Asian-American Pan-Ethnic Formation and Congregational Culture," in *Religions in Asian America: Building Faith Communities*, ed. Pyong Gap Min and Jung Ha Kim (Walnut Creek, CA: AltaMira Press, 2002), 215–43.
96. Grace Sangok Kim, "Asian North American Immigrant Parents and Youth: Parenting and Growing Up in a Cultural Gap," in *People on the Way: Asian North Americans Discovering Christ, Culture, and Community*, ed. David Ng (Valley Forge, PA: Judson Press, 1996), 137.
97. Ibid., 138.
98. Ellen Tanouye, "Learning Parental Skills Together in an Asian American Context," Japanese Presbyterian Conference, 1991, quoted in Kim, "Asian North American Immigrant Parents and Youth: Parenting and Growing Up in a Cultural Gap," 143.
99. Kim, "Asian North American Youth: A Ministry of Self-Identity and Pastoral Care," 224.
100. Robert D. Goette, "The Transformation of a First-Generation Church into a Bilingual Second-Generation Church," in Ho-Youn Kwon, Kwang Chung Kim, and R. Stephen Warner, eds., *Korean Americans and Their Religions: Pilgrims and Missionaries from a Different Shore* (University Park: The Pennsylvania State University Press, 2001), 125.
101. Ibid., 129.
102. Ibid., 129–30.
103. Ibid., 131–32.
104. Ibid., 132–35.
105. Ibid., 135.
106. Ibid.
107. Tseng et al., "Asian Religious Leadership Today: A Preliminary Inquiry," 24.
108. Ibid., 24.
109. Andrews, *Practical Theology for Black Churches: Bridging Black Theology and African American Folk Religion*, 58.

110. Robert N. Bellah, Richard Madsen, William M. Sullivan, Ann Swidler, and Steven M. Tipton, *Habits of the Heart: Individualism and Commitment in American Life* (Berkeley: University of California Press, 1985).

111. Ibid., 222–23, quoted in Adam B. Cohen and Peter C. Hill, "Religion as Culture: Religious Individualism and Collectivism among American Catholics, Jews, and Protestants," *Journal of Personality* 75, 4 (2007): 711, DOI:10.1111/j.1467-6494.2007.00454.x.

112. Cohen and Hill, "Religion as Culture: Religious Individualism and Collectivism among American Catholics, Jews, and Protestants," 712–13.

113. Tseng et al., "Asian Religious Leadership Today: A Preliminary Inquiry," 25.

114. Ibid., 25.

115. Reuben S. Seguritan, *We Didn't Pass through the Golden Door: The Filipino American Experience* (Institute for Filipino American Research, 1997), 117–18; Eleazar S. Fernandez, "Postcolonial Exorcism and Reconstruction: Filipino Americans' Search for Postcolonial Subjecthood," in *Realizing the America of Our Hearts: Theological Voices of Asian Americans*, ed. Fumitaka Matsuoka and Eleazar S. Fernandez (St. Louis, MI: Chalice Press, 2003), 84.

116. Fernandez, "Postcolonial Exorcism and Reconstruction: Filipino Americans' Search for Postcolonial Subjecthood," 85.

117. Tseng, "Beyond Orientalism and Assimilation: The Asian American as Historical Subject," in *Realizing the American of Our Hearts: Theological Voices of Asian Americans*, 68.

118. Fumitaka Matsuoka, "Creating Community Amidst the Memories of Historic Injuries," in *Realizing the America of Our Hearts: Theological Voices of Asian Americans*, 37.

119. Eleazar S. Fernandez, "Postcolonial Exorcism and Reconstruction: Filipino Americans' Search for Postcolonial Subjecthood," 88–89.

120. Ibid.

121. Ibid.

122. Boyung Lee, *Transforming Congregations through Community: Faith Formation from the Seminary to the Church* (Louisville, KY: Westminster John Knox Press, 2013), 5.

123. Ibid.

124. Ibid., 17.

Chapter 6

1. Fathali M. Moghaddam, *The Psychology of Dictatorship* (Washington, DC: American Psychological Association 2013), 183–95.

2. Ibid., 160.

3. William E. Wycislo, "Narcissism and Tyranny," *The Classical Bulletin* 76, 1 (2000): 76.

4. Albert Memmi, *The Colonizer and the Colonized*, expanded ed. (Boston: Beacon Press, 1991), 72.

5. Moghaddam, *The Psychology of Dictatorship*, 175.

6. Wycislo, "Narcissism and Tyranny," 77.

7. Moghaddam, *The Psychology of Dictatorship*, 160.

8. Robert J. C. Young, *Postcolonialism: An Historical Introduction* (Malden, MA: Blackwell, 2001), 26.

9. Ibid., 27.

10. See Paulo Freire, *Pedagogy of the Oppressed*, 30th anniversary ed. (New York: Continuum, 2009).

11. Ibid., 45–46.

12. Pat Noxolo, "Postcolonial Leadership: A Discursive Analysis of the Conservative Green Paper 'A Conservative Agenda for International Development'" *Area* 43, 4 (2011): 509–10.

13. Memmi, *The Colonizer and the Colonized*, 71.

14. Young, *Postcolonialism*, 32.

15. Ibid., 33.

16. Ibid.

17. Ibid.

18. Stephen S. Kim, "Seeking Home in North America: Colonialism in Asia; Confrontation in North America," in *People on the Way: Asian North Americans Discovering Christ, Culture, and Community*, 5.

19. Choi Hee An, *A Postcolonial Self: Korean Immigrant Theology and Church* (Albany: State University of New York Press, 2015), 2–3.

20. The concept of temporalizedly difference can be understood from the concept of temporization, described by Jacques Derrida in his explanation of différance. See Jacques Derrida, *Margins of Philosophy*, trans. Alan Bass (Chicago: The University of Chicago Press, 1982), 1–28.

21. Jacques Derrida, *Psyche: Inventions of the Other*, ed. Peggy Kamuf and Elizabeth Rottenberg, vol. 1 (Stanford, CA: Stanford University Press, 2007), 1–47.

22. Choi, *A Postcolonial Self*, 3.

23. Min, *The Solidarity of Others in a Divided World*, 2.

24. Young, *Postcolonialism*, 379.

25. Ibid., 368.

26. Homi K. Bhabha, *The Location of Culture* Taylor and Francis. Kindle Edition. (London: Routledge, 1994), 159.

27. Ibid., 162.

28. Ibid., 163.

29. Kwok Pui-lan, *Postcolonial Imagination and Feminist Theology*, 170.

30. Ibid., 170–71.

31. Joh, *Heart of the Cross: A Postcolonial Christology*, 53.
32. Ibid., 54.
33. Foley and Hoge, *Religion and the New Immigrants*, 25.
34. Homi K. Bhabha, "Signs Taken for Wonders," in *The Postcolonial Studies Reader*, ed. Bill Ashcroft, Gareth Griffiths, and Helen Tiffin (New York: Routledge, 1995), 33–34.
35. Gayatri Chakravorty Spivak, *Nationalism and the Imagination* (New York: Seagull Books, 2015), 54.
36. Brigid Carroll and Helen Nicholson, "Resistance and Struggle in Leadership Development," *Human Relations* 67, 11 (2014): 1416, DOI: 10.1177/0018726714521644.
37. David Collinson, "Dialectics of Leadership," *Human Relations*, 58, 11 (2005): 1427, quoted in Carroll and Nicholson, "Resistance and Struggle in Leadership Development," 1416.
38. Peter Fleming and Andre Spicer, "Beyond Power and Resistance: New Approaches to Organizational Politics," *Management Communication Quarterly* 21, 3 (2008): 305, quoted in Carroll and Nicholson, "Resistance and Struggle in Leadership Development," 1416.
39. Robyn Thomas and Annette Davies, "Theorizing the Micro-Politics of Resistance: New Public Management and Managerial Identities in the UK Public Services," *Organization Studies* 26, 5 (2005): 687, quoted in Carroll and Nicholson, "Resistance and Struggle in Leadership Development," 1416.
40. Carroll and Nicholson, "Resistance and Struggle in Leadership Development," 1433.
41. Ibid., 1428.
42. Young, *Postcolonialism*, 358; Allen F. Isaacman and Barbara Isaacman, *The Tradition of Resistance in Mozambique: Anti-Colonial Activity in the Zambesi Valley 1850–1921* (London: Heinemann, 1976).
43. Young, *Postcolonialism*, 357.
44. Northouse, *Leadership: Theory and Practice*, 254.
45. Trinh T. Minh-Ha, "Writing Postcoloniality and Feminism," in *The Postcolonial Studies Reader*, 267.
46. Bhabha, *The Location of Culture*, 106.
47. Robert W. Terry, *Authentic Leadership: Courage in Action* (San Francisco: Jossey-Bass, 1993), 84; quoted in Northouse, *Leadership: Theory and Practice*, 255.
48. Bill George, *Authentic Leadership: Rediscovering the Secrets to Creating Lasting Value* (San Francisco, CA: Jossey-Bass, 2003).
49. Haina Zhang, André M. Everett, Graham Elkin, and Malcolm H. Cone, "Authentic Leadership Theory Development: Theorizing on Chinese Philosophy," *Asian Pacific Business Review* 18, 4 (2012): 601.
50. Mark 12:31, New International Version.

51. Namsoon Kang, *Cosmopolitan Theology: Reconstituting Planetary Hospitality, Neighbor-Love, and Solidarity in an Uneven World*, Kindle ed. (Atlanta, GA: Chalice Press, 2013), Kindle Locations 4334–38 of 7631.

52. Ibid., Kindle Locations 4356–57 of 7631.

53. Ibid., Kindle Locations 4396–99 of 7631.

54. Northouse, *Leadership: Theory and Practice*, 398.

55. Ibid., 391–94.

56. Nanette Fondas, "Femininization Unveiled: Management Qualities in Contemporary Writings," *Academy of Management Review* 22, 1 (1997): 257–282, quoted in Ashleigh Shelby Rosette and Leigh Plunkett Tost, "Agentic Women and Communal Leadership: How Role Prescriptions Confer Advantage to Top Women Leaders," *Journal of Applied Psychology* 95, 2 (2010): 229.

57. Virginia E. Schein, "The Relationship between Sex Role Stereotypes and Requisite Management Characteristics," *Journal of Applied Psychology* 57, 2 (1973): 95–100, DOI:10.1037/h0037128; Virginia E. Schein, "Women in Management: Reflections and Projections," *Women in Management Review* 22, 1 (2007): 6–18, DOI:10.1108/09649420710726193.

58. Madeline E. Heilman, "Description and Prescription: How Gender Stereotypes Prevent Women's Ascent Up the Organizational Ladder," *Journal of Social Issues* 57, 4 (Winter 2001): 657–74.

59. Alice H. Eagly and Steven J. Karau, "Role Congruity Theory of Prejudice Toward Female Leaders," *Psychological Review* 109, 3 (2002): 573–98.

60. John Berger, M. Hamit Fisek, Robert Z. Norman, and Morris Zelditch Jr., *Status Characteristics and Social Interaction* (New York: Elsevier Scientific, 1977); Cecilia L. Ridgeway, "Interaction and the Conservation of Gender Inequality: Considering Employment," *American Sociological Review* 62, 2 (1997): 218–35, DOI:10.2307/2657301; Cecilia L. Ridgeway, "Gender, Status, and Leadership," *Journal of Social Issues* 57, 4 (2001): 637–55, DOI:10.1111/0022-4537.00233.

61. Schein, "The Relationship between Sex Role Stereotypes and Requisite Management Characteristics," 95–100; Schein, "Women in Management: Reflections and Projections," 6–18.

62. Ray Williams, "Why Women May Be Better Leaders Than Men," *Psychology Today*, December 15, 2012, retrieved from http://www.psychologytoday.com/blog/wired-success/201212/why-women-may-be-better-leaders-men.

63. Rosette and Tost, "Agentic Women and Communal Leadership: How Role Prescriptions Confer Advantage to Top Women Leaders," 231.

64. Ibid., 230.

65. J. Augusto Felício, Helena Martins Gonçalves, and Víto Da Conceição Gonçalves, "Social Values and Organizational Performance in Non-Profit Social Organization: Social Entrepreneurship, Leadership, and Socioeconomic Context Effects," *Journal of Business Research* 66, 10 (2013): 2144–45.

66. Ben Gidley and Keith Kahn-Harris, "Contemporary Anglo-Jewish Community Leadership: Coping with Multiculturalism," *The British Journal of Sociology* 63, 1 (2012): 174.

67. Nasiopoulos K. Dimitrios, Damianos P. Sakas, and D. S. Vlachos, "Analysis of Strategic Leadership Simulation Models in Non-Profit Organizations," *Procedia-Social and Behavioral Science* 73 (2003): 276.

68. Lynn Taliento and Lee Silverman, "A Corporate Executive's Short Guide to Leading Non-Profits," *Strategy & Leadership* 33, 2 (2005): 5.

69. Ibid., 6.

70. Ibid., 141–48.

71. Roz D. Lasker and Elisa S. Weiss, "Broadening Participation in Community Problem-Solving: A Multidisciplinary Model to Support Collaborative Practice and Research," *Journal of Urban Health* 80, 1 (2003): 14–60.

72. Chris Ansell and Alison Gash, "Collaborative Governance in Theory and Practice," *Journal of Public Administration Research and Theory* 18, 4 (2007): 554.

73. Karen L. Suyemoto and Mary B. Ballou, "Conducted Monotones to Coacted Harmonies: A Feminist (Re)conceptualization of Leadership Addressing Race, Class, and Gender," in *Women and Leadership: Transforming Visions and Diverse Voices*, ed. Jean Lau Chin, Bernice Lott, Joy K. Rice, and Janis Sanchez-Hucles (Malden, MA: Blackwell, 2007), 41.

74. Ansell and Gash, "Collaborative Governance in Theory and Practice," 543–71.

75. Ibid., 141.

76. Ibid.

77. Burns, *Transforming Leadership*, 171.

78. Ibid., 185.

79. Ibid.

80. Eunjoo Mary Kim, "Preaching as an Art of Shared Leadership," in *Women, Church, and Leadership*, ed. Eunjoo Mary Kim and Deborah Beth Creamer (Eugene, OR: Wipf and Stock, 2012), 69–88.

81. Ibid., 71–72.

82. Eunjoo Mary Kim, *Women Preaching: Theology and Practice Through the Ages* (Eugene, OR: Pickwick, 2009), 159.

83. Ibid., 22–154.

84. Ibid., 156.

85. Kim, "Preaching as an Art of Shared Leadership," 78–79.

86. Eunjoo Mary Kim, *Preaching in an Age of Globalization* (Louisville, KY: Westminster John Knox Press, 2010), 70.

87. Kim, "Preaching as an Art of Shared Leadership," 80.

88. Ibid., 81.

89. Ibid.

90. Ibid., 82.

91. Choi, *A Postcolonial Self*, 144–49.

Selected Bibliography

Adjibolosoo, Senyo B-S. K., ed. *The Human Factor in Shaping the Course of History and Development.* Lanham, MD: University Press of America, 2000.
Akutagawa, Linda. "Breaking Stereotypes: An Asian American's View of Leadership Development." *Asian American Journal of Psychology* 4, 4 (2013): 280. doi:10.1037/a0035390.
Ammerman, Nancy Tatom. *Congregation and Community.* New Brunswick, NJ: Rutgers University Press, 1997.
Andrews, Dale P. *Practical Theology for Black Churches: Bridging Black Theology and African American Folk Religion.* Louisville, KY: Westminster John Knox Press, 2002.
Ansell, Chris, and Alison Gash. "Collaborative Governance in Theory and Practice." *Journal of Public Administration Research and Theory* 18, 4 (2007): 543–71.
Antonakis, John, Anne T. Cianciolo, and Robert J. Sternberg, eds. *The Nature of Leadership.* Thousand Oaks, CA: Sage, 2004.
Ashcroft, Bill, Gareth Griffiths, and Helen Tiffin, eds. *The Postcolonial Studies Reader.* New York: Routledge, 1995.
Asheim, Ivar, and Victor R. Gold, eds. *Episcopacy in the Lutheran Church? Studies in the Development and Definition of the Office of Church Leadership.* Philadelphia: Fortress Press, 1970.
Banaji, Mahzarin R., and Anthony G. Greenwald. *Blindspot: Hidden Biases of Good People.* New York: Delacorte Press, 2013.
Barna Group. "Number of Female Senior Pastors in Protestant Churches Doubles in Past Decade." *Leaders & Pastors.* September 14, 2009. http://www.barna.com/research/number-of-female-senior-pastors-in-protestant-churches-doubles-in-past-decade/#.V8LtDTV1woI.
Bass, Bernard M. *Leadership and Performance beyond Expectations.* New York: Free Press, 1985.
———. *Transformational Leadership: Industry, Military, and Educational Impact.* Mahwah, NJ: Lawrence Erlbaum Associates, 1998.

Behr-Sigel, Elisabeth. *The Ministry of Women in the Church*. Stephen Bigham, trans. Crestwood, NY: St. Vladimir's Seminary Press, 1999.

Bellah, Robert N., Richard Madsen, William M. Sullivan, Ann Swidler, and Steven M. Tipton. *Habits of the Heart: Individualism and Commitment in American Life*. Berkeley: University of California Press, 1985.

Berger, John, M. Hamit Fisek, Robert Z. Norman, and Morris Zelditch Jr. *Status Characteristics and Social Interaction*. New York: Elsevier Scientific, 1977.

Berlinger, Lisa R. "The Behavioral Competency Approach to Effective Ecclesial Leadership." *Journal of Religious Leadership* 2, 2 (Spring 2003): 91–112.

Bhabha, Homi K. *The Location of Culture*. London: Routledge, 1994.

Bowie, Norman E., ed. *The Blackwell Guide to Business Ethics*. Oxford: Blackwell, 2002.

Branson, Mark Lau, and Juan F. Martínez. *Churches, Cultures & Leadership: A Practical Theology of Congregations and Ethnicities*. Downers Grove, IL: InterVarsity Press, 2011.

Brock, Rita Nakashima. *Journeys by Heart: A Christology of Erotic Power*. New York: Crossroad, 1992.

Broverman, Inge K., Donald M. Broverman, Frank E. Clarkson, Paul S. Rosenkrantz, and Susan R. Vogel. "Sex-Role Stereotypes and Clinical Judgements of Mental Health." *Journal of Consulting and Clinical Psychology* 34, 1 (1970): 1–7.

Burke, Daniel. "Survey: Number of Female Senior Pastors Doubles in 10 years." *USA Today*. September 17, 2009. http://usatoday30.usatoday.com/news/religion/2009-09-17-female-pastors_N.htm.

Burns, James MacGregor. *Leadership*. New York: Harper & Row, 1978.

———. *Transforming Leadership: A New Pursuit of Happiness*. New York: Grove Press, 2003.

Burns, Tom, and G.M. Stalker. *The Management of Innovation*. 2nd ed. London: Social Science Paperbacks, 1966.

Butler, Lee H. Jr. *A Loving Home: Caring for African American Marriage and Families*. Cleveland, OH: Pilgrim Press, 2000.

———. *Liberating Our Dignity, Saving Our Souls: A New Theory of African American Identity Formation*. St. Louis, MO: Chalice Press, 2006.

Burris, Kimberly, Roya Ayman, Yi Che, and Hanyi Min. "Asian Americans' and Caucasians' Implicit Leadership Theories: Asian Stereotypes, Transformational, and Authentic Leadership." *Asian American Journal of Psychology* 4, 4 (2013): 258–66.

Callahan, Sharon, ed. *Religious Leadership: A Reference Handbook (1)*. Thousand Oaks, CA: Sage, 2013.

Cameron, Kim S., Jane E. Dutton, and Robert E. Quinn, eds. *Positive Organizational Scholarship*. San Francisco, CA: Barrett-Koehler, 2003.

Carroll, Brigid, and Helen Nicholson. "Resistance and Struggle in Leadership Development." *Human Relations* 67, 11 (2014): 1413–36. doi:10.1177/001872 6714521644.

Chen, Chin-Yi, Chun-Hsi Vivian Chen, and Chun-I Li. "The Influence of Leader's Spiritual Values on Servant Leadership on Employee Motivational Autonomy and Eudaemonic Well-Being." *Journal of Religion and Health* 52, 2 (2013): 418–38.

Chen, Edith Wen-chu, and Glenn Omatsu, eds. *Teaching about Asian Pacific Americans: Effective Activities, Strategies, and Assignments for Classrooms and Communities.* New York: Rowman & Littlefield, 2006.

Cheng, Patrick S. *Radical Love: An Introduction to Queer Theology.* New York: Seabury Books, 2011.

———. *Rainbow Theology: Bridging Race, Sexuality, and Spirit.* New York: Seabury Books, 2013.

Cheung, Chau-kiu, and Andrew Chi-fai Chan. "Benefits of Hong Kong Chinese CEOs' Confucian and Daoist Leadership Styles." *Leadership & Organization Development Journal* 29, 6 (2008): 474–503.

Chin, Jean Lau, Bernice Lott, Joy K. Rice, and Janis Sanchez-Hucles, eds. *Women and Leadership: Transforming Visions and Diverse Voices.* Malden, MA: Blackwell, 2007.

Choi, Hee An. *A Postcolonial Self: Korean Immigrant Theology and Church.* Albany: State University of New York Press, 2015.

Chung, Hyun Kyung. *Struggle to Be the Sun Again: Introducing Asian Women's Theology.* New York: Orbis Books, 1990.

Chung-Herrera, Beth G., and Melenie J. Lankau. "Are We There Yet? An Assessment Fit between Stereotypes of Minority Managers and the Successful-Manager Prototype." *Journal of Applied Social Psychology* 35, 10 (2005): 2029–56. doi:10.1111/j.1559-1816.2005.tb02208.x.

Cohen, Adam B., and Peter C. Hill. "Religion as Culture: Religious Individualism and Collectivism among American Catholics, Jews, and Protestants." *Journal of Personality* 75, 4 (2007): 709–42. doi:10.1111/j.1467-6494.2007.00454.x.

Collins, Jim. *Good to Great: Why Some Companies Make the Leap . . . and Others Don't.* Kindle ed. New York: HarperCollins, 2001.

Collinson, David. "Dialectics of Leadership." *Human Relations* 58, 11 (2005): 1419–42.

———. "Prozac Leadership and the Limits of Positive Thinking." *Leadership* 8, 2 (2012): 78–107.

Cormode, Scott. "Multi-Layered Leadership: The Christian Leader as Builder, Shepherd, and Gardener." *Journey of Religious Leadership* 1, 2 (Fall 2002).

Costa, Paul T., Jr., and Robert R. McCrae. *The NEO Personality Inventory Manual.* Odessa, FL: Psychological Assessment Resources, 1985.

———. *NEO-PI-P-R, Professional Manual.* Odessa, FL: Psychological Assessment Resources, 1992.

Costanza-Chock, Sasha. *Out of the Shadows, into the Streets! Transmedia Organizing and the Immigrant Rights Movement.* Boston: MIT Press, 2014.

Cox, William T.L., and Patricia G. Devine. "Stereotypes Possess Heterogeneous Directionality: A Theoretical and Empirical Exploration of Stereotype Structure and Content." *PLOS ONE* 10, 3 (2015): 1–27, e122292. doi:10.1371/journal.pone.0122292.

Cunningham, Hilary. *God and Caesar at the Rio Grande: Sanctuary and the Politics of Religion.* Minneapolis: University of Minnesota Press, 1995.

Darr, Katheryn Pfisterer. *Far More Precious than Jewels: Perspectives on Biblical Women.* Louisville, KY: Westminster John Knox Press, 1991.

De Bary, William Theodore. *Nobility and Civility: Asian Ideals of Leadership and the Common Good.* Kindle ed. Cambridge, MA: Harvard University Press, 2004.

Derrida, Jacques. *Margins of Philosophy*, trans. Alan Bass. Chicago: The University of Chicago Press, 1982.

———. *Psyche: Inventions of the Other.* Vol. 1, ed. Peggy Kamuf and Elizabeth Rottenberg, Stanford, CA: Stanford University Press, 2007.

Devine, Patricia G., and Andrew. J. Elliot. "Are Racial Stereotypes Really Fading? The Princeton Trilogy Revisited." *Personality and Social Psychology Bulletin* 21, 11 (1995): 1139–50.

Dimitrios, Nasiopoulos K., Damianos P. Sakas, and D.S. Vlachos. "Analysis of Strategic Leadership Simulation Models in Non-Profit Organizations." *Procedia-Social and Behavioral Science* 73 (2003): 276–84.

Dittes, James E. *When the People Say No: Conflict and the Call to Ministry.* New York: Harper & Row, 1979.

Dorsey, Leroy, ed. *The Presidency and Rhetorical Leadership.* College Station, TX: Texas A&M University Press, 2002.

Dulewicz, Victor, and Malcolm Higgs. "Leadership at the Top: The Need for Emotional Intelligence in Organizations." *International Journal of Organizational Analysis* 11, 3 (1993): 193–210.

Dumont, Frank. *A History of Personality Psychology: Theory, Science and Research from Hellenism to the Twenty-First Century.* Cambridge: Cambridge University Press, 2010.

Eagly, Alice H., and Jean Lau Chin. "Diversity and Leadership in a Changing World." *American Psychologist* 65, 3 (2010): 217.

———, and Steven J. Karau. "Role Congruity Theory of Prejudice toward Female Leaders." *Psychological Review* 109, 3 (2002): 573–98.

Ebaugh, Helen Rose, and Janet Saltzman Chafetz. *Religion and the New Immigrants: Continuities and Adaptations in Immigrant Congregations.* New York: AltaMira, 2000.

Edwards, Ruth. *The Case of Women's Ordination*. London: SPCK, 1989.
Ehrenreich, Barbara. *Bright-Sided: How the Relentless Promotion of Positive Thinking Has Undermined America*. New York: Metropolitan Books, 2009.
Felder, Deborah G. *The 100 Most Influential Women of All Time*. New York: Citadel, 2001.
Felício, J. Augusto, Helena Martins Gonçalves, and Víto Da Conceição Gonçalves. "Social Values and Organizational Performance in Non-Profit Social Organizations: Social Entrepreneurship, Leadership, and Socioeconomic Context Effects." *Journal of Business Research* 66, 10 (2013): 2139–46.
Fineman, Stephen. "On Being Positive." *Academy of Management Review* 31, 2 (2006): 270–91.
Fleming, Peter, and Andre Spicer. "Beyond Power and Resistance: New Approaches to Organizational Politics." *Management Communication Quarterly* 21, 3 (2008): 301–9.
Fluker, Walter Earl. *Ethical Leadership: The Quest for Character, Civility, and Community*. Minneapolis: Fortress Press, 2009.
———, ed. *The Stones That the Builders Rejected: The Development of Ethical Leadership from the Black Church Tradition*. Harrisburg, PA: Trinity Press International, 1998.
Foley, Michael W., and Dean R. Hoge. *Religion and the New Immigrants: How Faith Communities Form Our Newest Citizens*. New York: Oxford University Press, 2007.
Fondas, Nanette. "Femininization Unveiled: Management Qualities in Contemporary Writings." *Academy of Management Review* 22, 1 (1997): 257–82.
Foucault, Michel. *Discipline and Punish: The Birth of the Prison*. 2nd ed. London: Penguin Books, 1977.
Frank, David A. "Obama's Rhetorical Signature: Cosmopolitan Civil Religion in the Presidential Inaugural Address January 20, 2009." *Rhetoric and Public Affairs* 14, 4 (2011): 605–30.
Frankfurter, Oscar. "Buddhist Nirvāna, and the Noble Eightfold Path." *The Journal of the Royal Asiatic Society of Great Britain and Ireland* New Series 12, 4 (1880): 548–74. http://www.jstor.org.ezproxy.bu.edu/stable/25196863.
Freeland, Gregory. "Negotiating Place, Space, and Borders: The New Sanctuary Movement." *Latino Studies* 8, 4 (2011): 485–508.
Freire, Paulo. *Pedagogy of the Oppressed*. 30th anniversary ed. New York: Continuum, 2009.
Fry, Louis W. "Toward a Theory of Spiritual Leadership." *The Leadership Quarterly* 14, 6 (2003): 693–727.
Gaffey, Adam J. "Obama's Change: Republicanism, Remembrance, and Rhetorical Leadership in the 2007 Presidential Announcement Speech." *Southern Communication Journal* 79, 5 (2014): 407–26.

Gardner, John W. *On Leadership.* New York: Free Press, 1990.

George, Bill. *Authentic Leadership: Rediscovering the Secrets to Creating Lasting Value.* San Francisco: Jossey-Bass, 2003.

Gidley, Ben, and Keith Kahn-Harris. "Contemporary Anglo-Jewish Community Leadership: Coping with Multiculturalism." *The British Journal of Sociology* 63, 1 (2012): 168–87.

Gilbert, G.M. "Stereotype Persistence and Change among College Students." *Journal of Abnormal and Social Psychology* 46, 2 (1951): 245–54.

Gray, Barbara. *Collaborating: Finding Common Ground for Multi-Party Problems.* San Francisco, CA: Jossey-Bass, 1989.

Greenleaf, Robert K. *Servant Leadership: A Journey into the Nature of Legitimate Power & Greatness.* New York: Paulist Press, 1997.

Gupta, Monisha Das. *Unruly Immigrants: Rights, Activism, and Transnational South Asian Politics in the United States.* Durham, NC: Duke University Press, 2006.

Hart, Paul 't. *Understanding Public Leadership.* New York: Palgrave Macmillan, 2014.

Haslett, Beth J., Florence L. Geis, and Mae R. Carter. *The Organizational Woman: Power and Paradox.* Norwood, NJ: Ablex, 1992.

Heifetz, Ron, and Donald Laurie. "The Work of Leadership." *Harvard Business Review* 79, 11 (2001): 131–40.

Heilman, Madeline E. "Description and Prescription: How Gender Stereotypes Prevent Women's Ascent Up the Organizational Ladder." *Journal of Social Issues* 57, 4 (Winter 2001): 657–74.

———, and Alice H. Eagly. "Gender Stereotypes Are Alive, Well, and Busy Producing Workplace Discrimination." *Industrial and Organizational Psychology* 1, 4 (2008): 393–98.

———, Caryn J. Block, Richard F. Martell, and Michael C. Simon. "Has Anything Changed? Current Characteristics of Men, Women, and Managers." *Journal of Applied Psychology* 74, 6 (1989): 935–42.

Hiltner, Seward. *Preface to Pastoral Theology: The Ministry and Theory of Shepherding.* Nashville, TN: Abingdon Press, 1958.

Hollenbeck, George P., and Douglas T. Hall. "Self-Confidence and Leader Performance." *Organizational Dynamics* 33, 3 (2004): 254–69.

Hosoda, Megumi. "The Effects of Foreign Accents on Employment-Related Decisions." *Journal of Managerial Psychology* 25, 2 (2010): 113–32. doi:10.1108/02683941011019339.

House, Robert J., Paul. J. Hanges, Mansour Javidan, Peter W. Dorfman, and Vipin Gupta, eds. *Culture, Leadership and Organizations: The GLOBE Study of 62 Societies.* Thousand Oaks, CA: Sage, 2004.

Hunsburger, George, and Craig Van Gelder, eds. *The Church between Gospel and Culture.* Grand Rapids, MN: Wm. B. Eerdmans, 1996.

Hunt, J.G., and L.L. Larson, eds. *Leadership: The Cutting Edge.* Carbondale: Southern Illinois University, 1977.

Hunter, Rhashell. "PC(USA) Celebrates 60 years of Women Clergy: Remembering Six Decades of Pioneering Pastors." May 24, 2016. http://www.pcusa.org/news/2016/5/24/pcusa-celebrates-60-years-womens-ordination/.

Isaacman, Allen F., and Barbara Isaacman. *The Tradition of Resistance in Mozambique: Anti-Colonial Activity in the Zambesi Valley, 1850–1921.* London: Heinemann, 1976.

Jensen, Joan M., and Sue Davidson, eds. *A Needle, a Bobbin, a Strike.* Philadelphia, PA: Temple University Press, 1984.

Joh, Wonhee Anne. *Heart of the Cross: A Postcolonial Christology.* Louisville, KY: Westminster John Knox Press, 2006.

Johnson, Stefanie K., and Thomas Sy. "Why Aren't There More Asian Americans in Leadership Positions?" *Harvard Business Review.* December 19, 2016. https://hbr.org/2016/12/why-arent-there-more-asian-americans-in-leadership-positions?

Jones, Ian, Janet Wootton, and Kirsty Thorpe, eds. *Women and Ordination in the Christian Churches: International Perspectives.* New York: T&T Clark International, 2008.

Kang, Namsoon. *Cosmopolitan Theology: Reconstituting Planetary Hospitality, Neighbor-Love, and Solidarity in an Uneven World.* Kindle ed. Atlanta, GA: Chalice Press, 2013.

Kanter, Rosabeth Moss. *Men and Women of the Corporation.* New York: Basic Books, 1977.

Karlins, Marvin, Thomas L. Coffman, and Gary Walters. "On the Fading of Social Stereotypes: Studies in Three Generations of College Students." *Journal of Personality and Social Psychology* 13, 1 (1969): 1–16.

Katz, Daniel, and Kenneth Braly. "Racial Stereotypes in One Hundred College Students." *Journal of Abnormal and Social Psychology* 28, 3 (1933): 280–90.

Keller, Timothy. *Center Church: Doing Balanced Gospel-Centered Ministry in Your City.* Grand Rapids, MI: Zondervan, 2012.

Kim, Dong Min, Jang Wan Ko, and Seon-Joo Kim. "Exploring the Ethical Aspects of Leadership: From a Korean Perspective." *Asian Philosophy* 25, 2 (2015): 113–31. doi:10.1080/09552367.2015.1013732.

Kim, Eunjoo Mary. *Women Preaching: Theology and Practice through the Ages.* Eugene, OR: Pickwick, 2009.

———. *Preaching in an Age of Globalization.* Louisville, KY: Westminster John Knox Press, 2010.

———, and Deborah Beth Creamer, eds. *Women, Church, and Leadership.* Eugene, OR: Wipf and Stock, 2012.

Kim, Grace Ji-Sun. *The Grace of Sophia: A Korean North American Women's Christology.* Cleveland: The Pilgrim Press, 2002.

King, Toni C., and S. Alease Ferguson, eds. *Black Womanist Leadership: Tracing the Motherline.* Albany: State University of New York Press, 2011.

King, Martin Luther Jr. "The Dimensions of a Complete Life." In *Tongues of Angels, Tongues of Men*, ed. John F. Thornton and Katharine Washburn. New York: Doubleday, 1999.

———. *Strength to Love*. 1st ed. Philadelphia: Fortress Press, 1981.

———. *Why We Can't Wait*. New York: Harper & Row, 1963.

Kitano, Harry H.L., and Roger Daniels. *Asian Americans: Emerging Minorities*. 3rd ed. Upper Saddle River, NJ: Prentice Hall, 2001.

Koenig, Anne M., Alice H. Eagly, Abigail A. Mitchell, and Tiina Ristikari. "Are Leader Stereotypes Masculine? A Meta-Analysis of Three Research Paradigms." *Psychological Bulletin* 137, 4 (2011): 616–42.

Koyama, Kosuke. *Water Buffalo Theology*. New York: Orbis Books, 1999.

———. *No Handle on the Cross: An Asian Meditation on the Crucified Mind*. New York: Orbis Books, 1977.

Kwok, Pui-lan. *Chinese Women and Christianity 1860–1927*. Atlanta, GA: Scholars Press, 1992.

———. *Introducing Asian Feminist Theology*. Sheffield, England: Sheffield Academic Press, 2000.

———. *Postcolonial Imagination and Feminist Theology*. Louisville, KY: Westminster John Knox Press, 2005.

Kwon, Ho-Youn, Kwang Chung Kim, and R. Stephen Warner, eds. *Korean Americans and Their Religions: Pilgrims and Missionaries from a Different Shore*. University Park, PA: The Pennsylvania State University Press, 2001.

Lang, LingLing, Beverly J. Irby, and Genevieve Brown. "An Emergent Leadership Model Based on Confucian Virtues and East Asian Leadership Practices." *International Journal of Education Leadership Preparation* 7, 2 (Summer 2012): 1–14.

Lao-Tzu. *Te-Tao Ching: A New Translation Based on the Recently Discovered Ma-wang-tui Texts*. Trans. Robert G. Henricks, with an introduction and commentary. New York: Ballantine Books, 1989.

Larson, Arthur. *The President Nobody Knew*. New York: Popular Library, 1968.

Lasker, Roz D., and Elisa S. Weiss. "Broadening Participation in Community Problem-Solving: A Multidisciplinary Model to Support Collaborative Practice and Research." *Journal of Urban Health* 80, 1 (2003): 14–60.

Lazzari, Marceline M., Lisa Colarossi, and Kathryn S. Collins. "Feminists in Social Work: Where Have All the Leaders Gone?" *Journal of Women and Social Work* 24, 4 (2009): 348–59.

Lee, Boyung. *Transforming Congregations through Community: Faith Formation from the Seminary to the Church*. Louisville, KY: Westminster John Knox Press, 2013.

Lee, Helen. "Silent Exodus: Can the East Asian Church in America Reverse the Flight of Its Next Generation?" *Christianity Today*. August 12, 1996.

Lee, Jung Young. *Marginality: The Key to Multicultural Theology.* Minneapolis, MN: Fortress Press, 1995.
Lippi-Green, Rosina. *English with an Accent: Language, Ideology and Discrimination in the United States.* 2nd ed. Kindle ed. New York: Routledge, 2012.
Maccoby, Michael. *The Leaders We Need and What Makes Us Follow.* Boston, MA: Harvard Business School Press, 2007.
Marques, Joan, Satinder Dhiman, and Jerry Biberman. "Moral Crossroads: Contemplating Formal and Informal Economy through the Noble Eightfold Path." *Journal of Applied Business and Economics* 14, 1 (2013): 99–109.
Martin, James. *Jesus: A Pilgrimage.* New York: HarperOne, 1989.
Matsuoka, Fumitaka, and Eleazar S. Fernandez, eds. *Realizing the America of Our Hearts: Theological Voices of Asian Americans.* St. Louis, MI: Chalice Press, 2003.
Matthews, Gerald, Moshe Zeidner, and Richard D. Roberts, eds. *The Science of Emotional Intelligence: Knowns and Unknowns.* Oxford Scholarship Online, 2012. doi:10.1093/acprof:oso/9780195181890.003.0009.
Melina, Lois Ruskai, Gloria J. Burgess, Lena Lid Falkman, and Antonio Marturano, eds. *The Embodiment of Leadership.* San Francisco, CA: Jossey-Bass, 2013.
Memmi, Albert. *The Colonizer and the Colonized.* Expanded ed. Boston: Beacon Press, 1991.
Milkman, Ruth, and Veronica Terriquez. "'We Are the Ones Who Are Out in Front': Women's Leadership in the Immigrant Rights Movement." *Feminist Studies* 38, 3 (Fall 2012): 723–52.
Miller-McLemore, Bonnie J., ed. *The Wiley Blackwell Companion to Practical Theology.* Malden, MA: Wiley-Blackwell, 2014.
Min, Anselm Kyongsuk. "The Political Economy of Marginality: Comments on Jung Young Lee, Marginality: The Key to Multicultural Theology." *Journal of Asian and Asian American Theology* 1 (1996): 82–94.
———. *The Solidarity of Others in a Divided World: A Postmodern Theology after Postmodernism.* New York: T & T Clark International, 2004.
Min, Pyong Gap, ed. *Asian Americans: Contemporary Trends and Issues.* 2nd ed. Thousand Oaks, CA: Pine Forge Press, 2006.
———, and Jung Ha Kim, eds. *Religions in Asian America: Building Faith Communities.* Walnut Creek, CA: AltaMira Press, 2002.
Moghaddam, Fathali M. *The Psychology of Dictatorship.* Washington, DC: American Psychological Association, 2013.
Nesbitt, Muriel N., and Nolan E. Penn. "Gender Stereotypes after Thirty Years: A Replication of Rosenkrantz, et al. (1968)." *Psychological Reports* 87, 2 (2000): 493–511.
Nhat Hanh, Thich. *The Heart of the Buddha's Teaching: Transforming Suffering into Peace, Joy, and Liberation: The Four Noble Truths, the Noble Eightfold Path, and Other Basic Buddhist Teachings.* Kindle ed. New York: Harmony Books, 2015.

Niemann, Yolanda, Leilani Jennings, Richard Rozelle, James Baxter, and Elroy Sullivan."Use of Free Responses and Cluster Analysis to Determine Stereotypes of Eight Groups." *Personality and Social Psychology Bulletin* 24, 4 (1994): 379–90.

Ng, David, ed. *People on the Way: Asian North Americans Discovering Christ, Culture, and Community*. Valley Forge, PA: Judson Press, 1996.

Northouse, Peter G. *Leadership: Theory and Practice*. 6th ed. Thousand Oaks, CA: Sage, 2013.

Noxolo, Pat. "Postcolonial Leadership: A Discursive Analysis of the Conservative Green Paper 'A Conservative Agenda for International Development.'" *Area* 43, 4 (2011): 509–11.

Omatsu, Glenn. "Mobilizing Students to Respond to Community Needs: Organizing a Class around a Community Project." In *Teaching about Asian Pacific Americans: Effective Activities, Strategies, and Assignments for Classrooms and Communities*, eds. Edith Wenchu Chen and Glenn Omatsu. New York: Rowman & Littlefield, 2006.

Omi, Michael, and Howard Winant. *Racial Formation in the United States: From the 1960 to the 1990s*. 2nd ed. New York: Routledge, 1994.

Paris, Peter J. *Black Religious Leaders: Conflict in Unity*. Louisville, KY: Westminster John Knox Press, 1991.

Park, Andrew Sung. *The Wounded Heart of God: The Asian Concept of Han and the Christian Doctrine of Sin*. Nashville, TN: Abingdon Press, 1993.

———, and Susan L. Nelson, eds. *The Other Side of Sin: Woundedness from the Perspective of the Sinned-Against*. Albany: State University of New York Press, 2001.

Parker, Patricia S. "Gender, Culture, and Leadership: Toward a Culturally Distinct Model of African-American Women Executives' Leadership Strategies." *The Leadership Quarterly* 7, 2 (1996): 189–214.

Pastor, Manuel, and John Mollenkopf, eds. *Unsettled Americans: Metropolitan Context and Civic Leadership for Immigrant Integration*. Ithaca, NY: Cornell University Press, 2016.

Peale, Norman Vincent. *The Power of Positive Thinking*. New York: Prentice-Hall, 1952.

Pearce, Craig L., and Jay A. Conger, eds. *Shared Leadership: Reframing the Hows and Whys of Leadership*. Thousand Oaks, CA: Sage, 2003.

Pearce, Susan C., Elizabeth J. Clifford, and Reena Tandon. *Immigration and Women: Understanding the American Experience: Finding Agency, Negotiating, and Bridging Cultures*. New York: New York University Press, 2011.

Peter C. Phan. *Being Religious Interreligiously: Asian Perspectives on Interfaith Dialogue*. New York: Orbis Books, 2004.

———. *Christianity with an Asian Face: Asian American Theology in the Making*. New York: Orbis Books, 2003.

———, ed. *Christianities in Asia*. Malden, MA: Wiley-Blackwell, 2011.
———, ed. *The Gift of the Church: A Textbook on Ecclesiology in Honor of Patrick Granfield, O. S. B.* Collegeville, MN: The Liturgical Press, 2000.
Phipps, Kelly A., and Mark E. Burbach. "Strategic Leadership in the Non-Profit Sector Opportunities for Research." *Journal of Behavioral and Applied Management* 11, 2 (2010): 137–54.
Powell, Mark Allan. *Jesus as a Figure in History: How Modern Historians View the Man from Galilee*. Louisville, KY: Westminster John Knox Press, 1998.
Quinn, Robert E., and Richard H. Hall. *Organizational Theory and Public Policy*. Thousand Oaks, CA: Sage, 1983.
Ramakrishnan, Karthick, and Celia Viramontes. *Civil Inequalities: Immigrant Volunteerism and Community Organizations in California*. San Francisco: Public Policy Institutes of California, 2006.
Ridgeway, Cecilia L. "Gender, Status, and Leadership" *Journal of Social Issues* 57, 4 (2001): 637–55. doi:10.1111/0022-4537.00233.
———. "Interaction and the Conservation of Gender Inequality: Considering Employment." *American Sociological Review* 62, 2 (1997).
Riggs, Marcia Y. *Awake, Arise and Act: A Womanist Call for Liberation*. Cleveland: Pilgrim Press, 1994.
Rosener, Judy B. "Ways Women Lead." *Harvard Business Review* 68, 6 (November/December 1990): 119–25.
Rosenkrantz, Paul, Susan Vogel, Helen Bee, Inge Broverman, and Donald M. Broverman. "Sex-Role Stereotypes and Self-Concepts in College Students." *Journal of Consulting and Clinical Psychology* 32, 3 (1968): 287–95.
Rosette, Ashleigh Shelby, and Leigh Plunkett Tost. "Agentic Women and Communal Leadership: How Role Prescriptions Confer Advantage to Top Women Leaders." *Journal of Applied Psychology* 95, 2 (2010): 221–35.
Rost, Joseph C. *Leadership for the Twenty-First Century*. New York: Praeger, 1991.
Rudman, Laurie A. "Self-Promotion as a Risk Factor for Women: The Cost and Benefits of Counterstereotypical Impression Management." *Journal of Personality and Social Psychology* 74, 3 (1998): 629–45.
Russell, Letty M., and J. Shannon Clarkson, eds. *Dictionary of Feminist Theologies*. Louisville, KY: Westminster John Knox Press, 1996.
Schein, Virginia E. "The Relationship between Sex Role Stereotypes and Requisite Management Characteristics." *Journal of Applied Psychology* 57, 2 (1973): 95–100. doi:10.1037/h0037128.
———. "Women in Management: Reflections and Projections." *Women in Management Review* 22, 1 (2007): 6–18. doi:10.1108/09649420710726193.
Schüssler Fiorenza, Elisabeth. *In Memory of Her: A Feminist Theological Reconstruction of Christian Origins*. New York: Crossroad, 1998.
Shaw, Randy. *Beyond the Fields: Cesar Chavez, the UFW, and the Struggle for Justice in the 21st Century*. Berkeley: University of California Press, 2008.

Shirin, Andrey V. "Is Servant Leadership Inherently Christian?" *Religion and Business Ethnics* 3, 1 (2015): 1–27.

Shriberg, Arthur, David Shriberg, and Carol Lloyd, eds. *Practicing Leadership: Principles and Applications*. 2nd ed. New York: John Wiley & Sons, 2002.

Slote, Walter H., and George A. DeVos, eds. *Confucianism and the Family*. Albany: State University of New York Press, 1998.

Song, C.S. *The Compassionate God: An Exercise in the Theology of Transposition*. New York: Orbis Books, 1982.

———. *Jesus & the Reign of God*. Minneapolis, MN: Augsburg Fortress, 1993.

———. *Jesus, the Crucified People*. Minneapolis, MN: Fortress Press, 1996.

Spears, Larry C., ed. *Insights on Leadership: Service, Stewardship, Spirit, and Servant-Leadership*. New York: John Wiley, 1998.

———, and Michele Lawrence, eds. *Focus on Leadership: Servant-Leadership for the 21st Century*. New York: John Wiley & Sons, 2002.

Spivak, Gayatri Chakravorty. *Nationalism and the Imagination*. New York: Seagul Books, 2015.

Sternberg, Robert J., ed. *Handbook of Intelligence*. Cambridge: Cambridge University Press, 2000.

Stewart, John W. *Envisioning the Congregation Practicing the Gospel: A Guide for Pastors and Lay Leaders*. Grand Rapids, MI: Wm. B. Eerdmans, 2015.

Stogdill, Ralph M. *Handbook of Leadership: A Survey of Theory and Research*. New York: The Free Press, 1974.

Stone, A. Gregory, Robert F. Russell, and Kathleen Patterson. "Transformational versus Servant Leadership: A Difference in Leader Focus." *Leadership & Organization Development Journal* 25, 3/4 (2004): 349–61.

Stortz, Martha Ellen. *PastorPower*. Nashville, TN: Abingdon Press, 1993.

Sugirtharajah, R.S., ed. *Asian Faces of Jesus*. New York: Orbis Books, 1993.

Sun, Peter Y.T., and Marc H. Anderson. "The Importance of Attributional Complexity for Transformational Leadership Studies." *Journal of Management Studies* 49, 6 (September 2012): 1001–22.

Susskind, Lawrence, and Jeffrey Cruikshank. *Breaking the Impasse: Consensual Approaches to Resolving Public Disputes*. New York: Basic Books, 1987.

Sy, Thomas, Lynn M. Shore, Judy Strauss, Ted H. Shore, Susanna Tram, Paul Whiteley, Kristine Ikeda-Muromachi. "Leadership Perceptions on a Function of Race-Occupation Fit: The Case of Asian Americans." *Journal of Applied Psychology* 95, 5 (2010): 902–19. doi:10.1037/a0019501.

Taliento, Lynn, and Lee Silverman. "A Corporate Executive's Short Guide to Leading Non-Profits." *Strategy & Leadership* 33, 2 (2005): 5–11.

Terry, Robert W. *Authentic Leadership: Courage in Action*. San Francisco: Jossey-Bass, 1993.

Thandeka. *Learning to Be White: Money, Race, and God in America*. New York: Continuum, 2001.

Thangaraj, M. Thomas. *The Crucified Guru: An Experiment in Cross-Cultural Christology*. Nashville, TN: Abingdon Press, 1994.

Thomas, Robyn, and Annette Davies. "Theorizing the Micro-Politics of Resistance: New Public Management and Managerial Identities in the UK Public Services." *Organization Studies* 26, 5 (2005): 683–706.

Torjesen, Karen Jo. *When Women Were Priests: Women's Leadership in the Early Church and the Scandal of Their Subordination in the Rise of Christianity*. San Francisco, CA: HarperCollins, 1993.

Truman, Harry S. *Memoirs*. New York: Doubleday, 1958.

Tseng, Timothy, et al. "Asian Religious Leadership Today: A Preliminary Inquiry." *Pulpit & Pew Research on Pastoral Leadership*. Durham, NC: Duke Divinity School, 2005. Eds.

Kim Voss and Irene Bloemraad. *Rallying for Immigrant Rights*. Berkeley: University of California Press, 2011.

Widiger, Thomas A., and Shirley A. Settle. "Broverman et al. Revisited: An Artifactual Sex Bias." *Journal of Personality and Social Psychology* 53, 3 (1987): 463–69.

Wild, Kara L. "The New Sanctuary Movement: When Moral Mission Means Breaking the Law, and the Consequences for Churches and Illegal Immigrants." *Santa Clara Law Review* 50, 3 (2010): 981–1015.

Willhauck, Susan, and Jacqulyn Thorpe. *The Web of Women's Leadership: Recasting Congregation Ministry*. Nashville, TN: Abingdon Press, 2001.

Williams, Delores S. *Sisters in the Wilderness: The Challenges of Womanist God-Talk*. New York: Orbis Books, 1993.

Williams, Paul. *Mahāyāna Buddhism: The Doctrinal Foundations*. New York: Routledge, 1989.

Williams, Ray. "Why Women May Be Better Leaders than Men." *Psychology Today*. December 15, 2012. http://www.psychologytoday.com/blog/wired-success/201212/why-women-may-be-better-leaders-men.

Williamson, Thad. "The Good Society and the Good Soul: Plato's *Republic* on Leadership." *The Leadership Quarterly* 19, 4 (2008): 397–408.

Willimon, William H. *Pastor: The Theology and Practice of Ordained Ministry*. Nashville, TN: Abingdon Press, 2002.

Witt, Michael A., and Günter K. Stahl. "Foundations of Responsible Leadership: Asian versus Western Executive Responsibility Orientations toward Key Stakeholders." *Journal of Business Ethics* 136, 3 (2016): 623–38. doi:10.1007/s10551-014-2534-8.

Wuthnow, Robert, and John Evans, eds. *The Quiet Hand of God: Faith-Based Activism and the Public Role of Mainline Protestants*. Berkeley: University of California Press, 2002.

Wycislo, William E. "Narcissism and Tyranny." *The Classical Bulletin* 76, 1 (2000): 71–80.

Xin, Katherine R. "Asian American Managers: An Impression Gap? An Investigation of Impression Management and Supervisor-Subordinate Relationships." *Journal of Applied Behavior Science* 40, 2 (2004): 168–91. doi:10.1177/0021886304263853.

Young, Robert J.C. *Postcolonialism: An Historical Introduction.* Malden, MA: Blackwell, 2001.

Yukich, Grace. "Constructing the Model Immigrants: Movement Strategy and Immigrant Deservingness in the New Sanctuary Movement." *Social Problems* 60, 3 (2013): 302–20.

———. *One Family under God: Immigration Politics and Progressive Religion in America.* New York: Oxford University Press, 2013.

Yukl, Gary A., and David D. Van Fleet. "Cross-Situational, Multimethod Research on Military Leader Effectiveness." *Organizational Behavior and Human Performance* 30 (1982): 87–108.

Zaleznik, Abraham. "The Leadership Gap," *Washington Quarterly* 6, 1 (1983): 32–39.

Zhang, Haina, André M. Everett, Graham Elkin, and Malcolm H. Cone. "Authentic Leadership Theory Development: Theorizing on Chinese Philosophy." *Asian Pacific Business Review* 18, 4 (2012): 587–605.

Index

Aaron, 25–26
African American
  Black Power movement, 83
  congregations, 49
  leadership. *See* leadership
African American women executives
  (AAWEs), 69–70
Agranoff, Robert, 21
Akutagawa, Linda, 134
Allport, Gordon, 6
Ammerman, Nancy, 157, 167
Anderson, Evangeline, 25–26
Andrews, Dale P., 79
Ansell, Chris, 21
Anselm, 29
Antonakis, John, 4
Aquinas, Thomas, 29, 76
Archer, David, 21
Aristotle, 29, 74
Asia, 96, 108, 110–11, 117, 139, 149,
  160, 170, 173, 181, 185, 187,
  210, 214–15
Asian
  female, 70, 143–46, 148, 161–65
  male, 70–71, 143
Augustine, 29
authenticity, 35, 113, 189, 191,
  199–205, 213, 215
Avolio, Bruce J., 11, 13

Baker, Ella, 75, 83
Ballou, Mary B., 19
Banaji, Mahzarin R., 62
Baptist churches, 40
Bass, Bernard M., 11–14, 16
Baxter, James, 68
Bee, Helen, 63
behavior theories in leadership. *See*
  leadership theories
Behr-Sigel, Elisabeth, 44–46
Being Religious Interreligiously: Asian
  Perspectives on Interfaith Dialogue,
  150
Benefiel, Margaret, 35
Bennis, Warren, 10
Bethune, Mary McLeod, 75, 83
Bhabha, Homi K., 191–92
Biberman, Jerry, 35
Blake, Robert, 10
Blomgren-Bingham, Lisa, 21
Braly, Kenneth, 67–68
Branson, Mark Lau, 40
Brock, Rita Nakashima, 46, 144–45
Broverman, Donald M., 63
Brown, Antoinette, 47
Brown, Genevieve, 111, 117
Buddhism, 108, 113, 115, 119
Burns, James MacGregor, 11–12, 14,
  119, 140, 212

Burroughs, Nannie Helen, 75
Butler, Lee H., 80–81

Cain, Herman, 88–89
Caleb, 25–26
Cameron, Alex, 21
capitalism, 39–40, 54, 60, 73, 86, 91, 109–10, 120, 124, 130, 173, 183, 185
Carnegie, Andrew, 15, 56
Carroll, Brigid, 196–97
Carter, Mae R., 19
Cattell, Raymond B., 6–7
Chan, Andrew Chi-fai, 116
charismatic leadership model. *See* leadership theories
Chávez, César, 93
Chen, Chin-Yi, 35
Chen, Chun-Hsi Vivian, 35
Cheng, Patrick S., 153
Cheung, Chau-kiu, 116
Chin, Jean Lau, 3, 19, 22, 72, 134–35
China, 88, 96, 108, 145–46, 152
Chisholm, Shirley, 84
Chrislip, David D., 20–21
Christ, Carol P., 46
Christal, Raymond, 7
Christian
  Early Church, 28, 30, 44–47, 214
  history, 5, 31, 41, 46–47, 140
  leadership. *See* leadership
Christianity, 25, 27–29, 119, 139, 141, 144–46, 150–51, 153, 159, 161–62, 176, 182, 190, 203–4
Chung, Hyun Kyung, 143–44
Chung-Herrera, Beth G., 121, 124
Cianciolo, Anne T., 4
Ciulla, Joanne B., 4
civil rights movement, 14, 62, 73, 76–78, 83–84, 93, 95
Clarkson, Frank E., 63
classism, 40, 80, 84, 187, 203

Clement, 29
Clergy and Laity United for Economic Justice (CLUE), 102
Clifford, Elizabeth J., 98
Coalition for Humane Immigrant Rights of Los Angeles (CHIRLA), 94
Coffman, Thomas, 67–68
Colarossi, Lisa, 19, 22
collaborative leadership theory. *See* leadership theories
Collins, Jim, 56–58
  Level 5 hierarchy, 56–58
Collins, Kathryn S., 19, 22
Collins, Patricia Hill, 82
colonialism, 40, 90–92, 176, 181, 183, 186–88
communicator, 150–51, 157
Confucianism, 108, 111, 119
Congregation and Community, 167
Congregational Church, 40, 47, 49
consumerism, 35, 39–40
contingency theory. *See* leadership theories
Cormode, Scott, 158
Costa, Paul, 7–8
Cox, William T. L., 66, 68
Creamer, Deborah Beth, 49
Cruikshank, Jeffrey, 21

Daly, Mary, 46
Darr, Katheryn Pfisterer, 47
Davies, Annette, 196
Davis, Angela, 83
Declaration on the Question of Admission of Women to the Ministerial Priesthood, 41
Deferred Action for Childhood Arrivals (DACA), 104–5
Devine, Patricia G., 66, 68
Digman, John M., 7
discipleship, 47, 169

Dittes, James E., 156
Dowd, Jerome, 5
Dream Act legislation, 104–5
Dulewicz, Victor, 4

Eagly, Alice H., 64–65, 72
Edelman, Marian Wright, 75
Edwards, Ruth, 44–45
egalitarianism, 20, 22, 44–45, 108
Eggers, William D., 21
Eisenhower, Dwight D., 16
Elliot, Andrew J., 68
emotional intelligence (EI), 4, 9–10
empowerment, 17, 23, 86, 212
Enlightenment, 32, 113
Episcopal Church, 30–31, 40, 48–49, 84, 175
Esther, 25–27, 47
ethical leadership. *See* leadership theories
expectancy theories. *See* leadership theories
Eysenck, Hans J., 7

feminism, 200
   agenda, 23
   feminist leadership theory. *See* leadership theories
   policy, 23
Ferebee, Dorothy, 83
Ferguson, S. Alease, 86
Fiorenza, Elisabeth Schüssler, 47
Fiske, Donald, 7
Fluker, Walter Earl, 75–76
Foley, Michael W., 166, 168
Franklin, Martha, 84
Fry, Louis W., 35

Galton, Sir Francis, 5
Gardner, John, 9–10
Garrett-Akinsanya, BraVada, 82–84
Gash, Alison, 21

Geis, Florence L., 19
gender roles, 18–19, 49, 64–66, 144
Giacalone, Robert A., 35
Gilbert, G. M., 67–68, 70–71
Global Leadership and Organizational Behavior Effectiveness (GLOBE), 108, 205
globalization, 41, 120
Goldberg, Lewis, 7
Goldsmith, Stephen, 21
Good to Great, 56
Grant, Jacquelyn, 46
Gray, Barbara, 21
Greenleaf, Robert K., 33–34
Greenwald, Anthony G., 62
Gregory of Nazianzus, 45
Guy-Sheftall, Beverly, 82

Hagar, 47
Hall, Douglas T., 122–23
Hall, Richard H., 16
Hall, Ruth L., 82–84
Hamer, Fannie Lou, 75, 83
Hanold, Maylon, 66
Harris, Patricia Roberts, 84
Hart, Paul 't, 21
Haslett, Beth J., 19
Heifetz, Ron, 123
Hesse, Hermann, 33
hierarchy, 5, 18–19, 23, 31–32, 54–56, 112, 135, 145, 158, 179, 195, 197, 202, 205, 207–8
   in leadership. *See* leadership
Higgs, Malcolm, 4
Hiltner, Seward, 156
Hinduism, 113, 119, 175
Hoge, Dean R., 166, 168
Holiday, Billie, 83
Holiness Church, 40, 48
Hollenbeck, George P., 122–23
hooks, bell, 82, 86

House, Robert J., 15, 108–10
Howell, Jane M., 11, 13
Hucles, Michael, 82–84
Huerta, Dolores, 93
hybridity, 145–47, 191–95, 197, 199–201, 203–5, 213, 215
  definition of, 191

Ignatius, 30
Ikeda-Muromachi, Kristine, 135
images of Jesus, 30, 43, 140–51, 153–55
  as Asian Jesus, 141–43, 145, 147, 149–51
  as co-sufferer, 142, 155
  as Crucified Guru, 150
  as egalitarian, 44
  as female, 143–45, 147
  as high priest, 45
  as male, 43, 46, 141, 143–45, 147, 154
  as Rainbow Christ, 154
  as Servant, 37–38, 143, 151
  as Shepherd, 30, 33, 55
  as Teacher, 37, 154
  white images of, 141–43, 147, 149, 154
immigration, 40, 70, 146, 169, 172–73
  laws, 88–89, 92, 95, 101
  rights, 96
individualism, 109, 170
  American, 79–80, 86, 148, 174–79, 194, 199, 202
  religious, 79
injustice, 38, 69, 75, 78, 99, 102, 142, 191
interfaith, 101–2, 150
Interfaith Workers Justice (IWJ), 102
Introducing Asian Feminist Theology, 146

introversion, 7
Irby, Beverly J., 111, 117
Islam, 113, 119, 151
Israel, 26, 151

Jennings, Leilani, 68
Jesus
  images of. *See* images of Jesus
Jethro, 26
Joh, Wonhee Anne, 148, 192
Johnson, Elizabeth A., 46
Johnson, Stefanie K., 121
Jones, Mary Harris, 96
Joseph, 27
Joshua, 25–26
Journey to the East, 33
Jue, A. L., 35
Jurkiewicz, Carole L., 35
justice, 28, 44, 62, 75–76, 80, 85–87, 90, 99–101, 112, 116, 118, 141, 152–53, 169, 176, 188, 193, 195, 203, 218

Kang, Namsoon, 204
Karau, Steven J., 64
Karlins, Marvin, 67–68
Katz, Daniel, 67–68
Keller, Timothy, 157, 169
Kennedy, John F., 14, 84
Kim, Dong Min, 127
Kim, Eunjoo Mary, 49–50, 214
Kim, Grace Ji-Sun, 147, 170
Kim, Seon-Joo, 127
King, Toni C., 86
King, Martin Luther, Jr., 14, 62, 73–76
Ko, Jang Wan, 127
Koenig, Anne M., 65
Kouzes, James M., 10
Koyama, Kosuke, 150–51
Kwok, Pui-lan, 145–47, 192

Lang, LingLing, 111, 117
Lankau, Melanie J., 121, 124
Larson, Carl E., 20–21
Lasker, Roz D., 20
Latina, 65, 99
theology, 46
Latinx, 71–72, 88–89, 92–93, 95–96, 107, 142, 154
leadership. *See* leadership
Laurie, Donald, 123
Lazzari, Marceline M., 19, 22
Lead Women Pastors Project, 49
leadership
  African American leaders and leadership, 47, 68–70, 73–76, 79–72, 82–87, 107, 122
  Asian immigrant leadership, 110–11, 120, 122, 135, 146, 148, 188, 194–95, 205, 215
  Asian religious leadership, 111, 118–19, 121, 154, 169, 173, 215
  Asian self-awareness in an Asian context, 127–34, 136, 203
  Asian self-confidence in an Asian context, 127, 129–34
  barriers in leadership, 65, 67, 69, 72, 84, 98, 100, 124, 130, 132, 154, 161–62
  black leadership, 62, 86
  Christian model of, 25, 27, 29, 33, 40–41, 140–41, 154
  collaborative communal, 190, 207–8, 210, 213–15, 218–19
  communal, 145, 190, 205–8, 210–15
  definition of, 140–41
  Early Church model of, 28
  feminist, 5, 18–20, 22–24, 82–84, 86, 97, 130
  good-to-great, 56–57
  Greek and Roman cultural influence of, 28
  hierarchy in, 5, 18–19, 23, 31–32, 54–56, 112, 135, 145, 158, 205, 207–8
  in the New Sanctuary Movement, 101–5
  Jesus' leadership model, 25, 29, 33, 37, 140–41, 144, 147
  Latinx, 72, 87, 88, 93, 96, 100, 107
  LGBTQIA, 66–67, 105
  nonprofit, 117, 161, 208–9
  postcolonialism, 40, 92, 181, 188–89, 196
  prejudice against female leaders, 43, 63–65
  prejudice against racial ethnic groups, 67, 104
  resistant and resilient, 195–96, 198–99, 218
  secular context, 3, 24, 53–55, 105
  servant, 4, 33–37, 39, 43, 143
  styles, 10, 20, 22–23, 29, 35, 58, 62, 69–70, 107, 110–11, 117, 136, 170, 174, 205
  traits in 1904–1947, 8–9
  traits in 1948–1970, 8–9
  US culture, 53
  web, 50
  white leadership, 60–62, 66, 73, 141
  women, 4, 18–19, 22–24, 41, 43–45, 47, 50, 64–67, 69–70, 82–86, 98, 100, 144–45, 148, 159, 161–65, 168, 179, 190, 198, 206–7, 210, 215
Leadership Education for Asian Pacifics, Inc., 134
leadership theories, 4–5, 11, 18–19, 34, 71
  behavior theories, 10–11
  charismatic leadership model, 11, 13, 15, 25, 27, 98

leadership theories *(continued)*
  collaborative leadership theory, 18–23, 25–26, 39, 49–50, 109, 189, 210
  contingency theory, 4, 11
  democratic leadership, 22, 69, 160
  ethical leadership, 73, 75, 84
  expectancy theories, 11
  feminist leadership theory, 5, 18–20, 22–24, 82–83, 97, 130
  Five-Factor Model theory (the Big Five), 6–7
  Life Cycle model theory, 11
  participatory leadership, 22, 110
  path-goal theory, 4, 10–11
  relational-cultural theory, 22
  shared leadership, 22, 25, 50, 214
  situational theories, 4, 9–11
  trait leadership theory, 5, 19, 143
  transactional leadership theory, 11–13, 17–18, 183, 189
  transformational leadership theory, 4–5, 11–17, 22, 34–35, 74, 117–18, 212
Letter to the Bishops of the Catholic Church on the Collaboration of Men and Women in the Church and in the World, 42
Lewis, Hal M., 7, 25
LGBTQIA members, 66–67, 103, 105, 153
  leadership. *See* leadership
Li, Chun-l, 35
Likert, Rensis, 10
Lincoln, Abraham, 14, 45
Linden, Russell M., 21
Luther, Martin, 31–32

Maccoby, Michael, 56, 58–59
Madden, Margaret E., 19
Malcolm X, 74, 79

Malik, Alexander J., 150
Martin, James, 38
Mary, 27, 45–46
Mayer-Salovey-Caruso Emotional Intelligence Test (MSCEIT), 10
McCrae, Robert, 7–8
McFague, Sallie, 46
McKenzie, Vasthi, 75
Min, Anselm Kyongsuk, 152, 210
Miriam, 25–27
Mitchell, Abigail A., 65
Moghaddam, Fathali M., 183
Mohammed, Overy N., 150
Mordecai, 27
Moses, 25–27
  leadership model, 25–26
Mouton, Jane, 10
Mulieris Dignitatem, 42
multiculturalism, multicultural, 40–41, 134, 150, 179
  challenges, 39
Murray, Pauli, 75, 84

National Association of Colored Graduate Nurses (NACGN), 84
National Association of Colored Women (NACW), 83–84
Nesbitt, Muriel N., 63
Nicholson, Helen, 196–97
Niemann, Yolanda, 68, 70–71
Northouse, Peter G., 4, 200

Obama, Barack, 59, 62, 88, 104
Oberlin College, 47
O'Leary, Rosemary, 21
Omi, Michael, 91
On Leadership, 9
  leadership attributes, 9

Page, Don, 35–36
Pak, Su Yon, 161–62

Paris, Peter J., 74–76
Park, Andrew Sung, 142–43
Park, HiRho, 49
Parks, Rosa Louise McCauley, 62, 83, 86
patriarchy, 24, 46, 96–97, 147, 163
Paul, 25, 27, 30
Pearce, Susan C., 98
Penn, Nolan E., 63
Pentecost, 42
Peter, 25, 27, 29, 42
Phan, Peter C., 139, 149–50
Pieris, Aloysius, 150
Plato, 28–29
Posner, Barry Z., 10
Postcolonial Imagination and Feminist Theology, 146
postmodernism, 19, 40
power
  in leadership, 196
  patriarchal, 18, 24, 190
  sharing, 22–24, 50, 110
  women's equal power, 44
Presbyterian Church (USA), 40, 48–49, 161–62
Protestant
  churches, 32, 36, 41, 43, 48–49, 155–56, 158–62, 164–66, 175–77
  clergy, 32–33
  context, 29

Quinn, Robert E., 16

racism, 40, 62, 67–69, 79–81, 84, 87–90, 92, 153, 162, 174, 177, 181, 185–88, 200, 203
Rainey, Ma, 83
Reformation, 31–32, 175
Republic, 28
Riggs, Marcia Y., 84–85
Ristikari, Tiina, 65

Roman Catholic Church, 29, 31–32, 36, 40–43, 97, 102, 150, 156, 158–59, 166, 175
  clergy, 33, 155
Roosevelt, Franklin D., 14
Rosener, Judy B., 23
Rosenkrantz, Paul S., 63
Rost, Joseph C., 3–4
Rozelle, Richard, 68
Ruether, Rosemary Radford, 46
Ruth, 47

Sarah, 47
Servant Leadership, 33
servant leadership. *See* leadership
service
  as the Church's responsibility, 39
  foot washing as, 37–39
  in action, 39
Settle, Shirley, 63
sexism, 40, 69, 80, 84, 87, 90, 100, 164–65, 174, 181, 187, 203
Shore, Lynn M., 135
Shore, Ted H., 135
situational theories. *See* leadership theories
Smith, Bessie, 83
Smith, Minnie, 83
Socrates, 28
Song, Choan-Seng, 149–50
Spears, Larry C., 34
Sternberg, Robert J., 4
Stewart, John W., 38
Stewart, Maria, 83
Stogdill, Ralph M., 8
Stone, Merlin, 46
Stortz, Martha Ellen, 158
Strauss, Judy, 135
Sullivan, Elroy, 68
Susskind, Lawrence, 21

Suyemoto, Karen L., 19
Sy, Thomas, 121, 135

Tandon, Reena, 98
Tanouye, Ellen, 171
Taoism, 108, 114, 119
Teresa of Avila, 41
Terrell, Mary Church, 75, 83
Terry, Robert W., 201–2
Thangaraj, M. Thomas, 150
theology
   feminist, 44, 46, 50, 147
   rainbow, 154
   sacramental, 156
   white, 143
   womanist, 46
Thistlethwaite, Susan, 46
Thomas, Robyn, 196
Thorpe, Jacqulyn, 50
Thurman, Howard, 62, 75
Torjesen, Karen Jo, 44
trait leadership theory. *See* leadership theories
Tram, Susanna, 135
transactional leadership theory. *See* leadership theories
transformational leadership theory. *See* leadership theories
Trible, Phyllis, 47
Truman, Harry, 16
Trump, Donald, 88–89
Truth, Sojourner, 83, 86
Tubman, Harriet, 83, 86
Tupes, Ernest, 7

United Church of Christ, 40, 102
United Farm Workers of American (UFW), 93, 97
United Methodist Church, 40, 48–49, 161–62

Van Fleet, David D., 15
Vietnam War, 101
vision, visioning, 34–36, 99–100, 150, 189, 196
   creating the, 13, 15, 22–24, 57, 82, 204
Vogel, Susan R., 63

Walker, Alice, 82, 86
Walker, C. J., 83
Walters, Gary, 67–68
Watson, Thomas J., 14
Weiss, Elisa S., 20
Wells, Ida B., 75, 83, 86
Western
   Christian, 140, 159, 161
   context, 43, 142
   culture, 113, 123, 133, 145
   history, 31
   images of Jesus, 150
   patriarchy, 49
   religion, 139
Whiteley, Paul, 135
Widiger, Thomas A., 63
Wiggam, Albert Edward, 5
Willhauck, Susan, 49–50
Williams, Delores S., 47, 86
Willimon, William H., 157
Winant, Howard, 91
Winfrey, Oprah, 59, 62
Wolak, Arthur J., 25
women
   call to ministry, 42–44
   in leadership. *See* leadership
   motherhood, 42
   ordination, 41, 43–48
   rejection of women's ordination, 41–43
   roles, 18, 43
   service, 43
   single, 42

support of women's ordination, 39, 41, 44–48
women's work, 18, 42, 144
Women, Church, and Leadership: New Paradigms, 49
Wong, Paul T. P., 35–36
Woods, Frederick Adams, 5
World War II, 183

Xin, Katharine R., 121

Yagi, Seiichi, 150
Yuen, Peter, 172
Yukich, Grace, 103–4
Yukl, Gary A., 15

Zhang, Haina, 202

www.ingramcontent.com/pod-product-compliance
Lightning Source LLC
Chambersburg PA
CBHW070755230426
43665CB00017B/2363